LOVE'S
LABOUR'S LOST

The RSC Shakespeare

Edited by Jonathan Bate and Eric Rasmussen

Chief Associate Editor: Héloïse Sénéchal

Associate Editors: Trey Jansen, Eleanor Lowe, Lucy Munro, Dee Anna Phares, Jan Sewell

Love's Labour's Lost

Textual editing: Eric Rasmussen

Introduction and Shakespeare's Career in the Theatre: Jonathan Bate

Commentary: Eleanor Lowe and Héloïse Sénéchal

Scene-by-Scene Analysis: Esme Miskimmin

In Performance: Karin Brown (RSC stagings) and
Jan Sewell (overview)

The Director's Cut (interviews by Jonathan Bate and Kevin Wright):
Terry Hands and Liz Shipman

Reflections: Gregory Doran

Editorial Advisory Board

The RSC Shakespeare

WILLIAM SHAKESPEARE

LOVE'S
LABOUR'S LOST

Edited by
Jonathan Bate and Eric Rasmussen

Introduced by Jonathan Bate

© The Royal Shakespeare Company 2008

Published by arrangement with Modern Library, an imprint of The Random House Publishing Group, a division of Random House, Inc.

All rights reserved. No reproduction, copy or transmission of this publication may be made without written permission.

No paragraph of this publication may be reproduced, copied or transmitted save with written permission or in accordance with the provisions of the Copyright, Designs and Patents Act 1988, or under the terms of any licence permitting limited copying issued by the Copyright Licensing Agency, 90 Tottenham Court Road, London W1T 4LP.

Any person who does any unauthorised act in relation to this publication may be liable to criminal prosecution and civil claims for damages.

'Royal Shakespeare Company', 'RSC' and the RSC logo are trade marks or registered trade marks of The Royal Shakespeare Company.

The right of The Royal Shakespeare Company to be identified as the author of the editorial apparatus to this work by William Shakespeare has been asserted by The Royal Shakespeare Company in accordance with the Copyright, Designs and Patents Act 1988.

Published 2008 by
MACMILLAN PUBLISHERS LTD
Houndmills, Basingstoke, Hampshire RG21 6XS
Companies and representatives throughout the world

ISBN-13   978-0-230-21790-4 hardback
ISBN-13   978-0-230-21791-1 paperback

This book is printed on paper suitable for recycling and made from fully managed and sustained forest sources.

A catalogue record for this book is available from the British Library.

10   9   8   7   6   5   4   3   2   1
17 16 15 14 13 12 11 10 09 08

Printed in China

CONTENTS

INTRODUCTION

A GREAT FEAST OF LANGUAGES

Love's Labour's Lost is a play for Shakespeare connoisseurs. It is a great feast of linguistic sophistication on the theme of the inadequacy of linguistic sophistication. It is full of poetry – and mockery of poetry. Its preposterous academic posturing is either hilarious or incomprehensible, according to the disposition of the listener. Some of its jokes and puns are now so obscure that a modern audience frequently finds itself in the position of Dull, listening in bemusement as the others plan their play: '*Via*, Goodman Dull!' says Holofernes, 'Thou hast spoken no word all this while.' To which the simple constable replies, 'Nor understood none neither, sir.'

The play was a favourite for the elite audience at court – Queen Elizabeth herself would without question have greatly enjoyed the authority, wit and hunting skills of the princess. But she would also have taken pleasure in the 'sweet smoke of rhetoric' that pervades the elaborate speechifying of the male courtiers. And she had the education to appreciate the comedy in the wordy academic humour of Holofernes and Don Armado. The reaction of some members of the general theatre-going public – 'the base vulgar', as the play itself calls them – might have been more like that of Dull. It comes as no surprise that in the eighteenth and nineteenth centuries this was Shakespeare's least-performed play.

Its minimal plot, intellectual rigour and architectural symmetry make *Love's Labour's Lost* seem to belong to some genre far from the popular theatre – Enlightenment *opera buffa*, perhaps. There are, indeed, remarkable thematic and structural resemblances to Mozart and Da Ponte's *Così fan tutte*. A Paris production of 1863 actually merged the two works, combining Mozart's music with a text based on Shakespeare. In the following century, W. H. Auden and his lover collaborated with Vladimir Nabokov's cousin on an operatic version of the play, perhaps inspired by the fictional composer Leverkühn in Thomas Mann's novel *Doctor Faustus*, whose only opera is a setting of *Love's Labour's* 'in a spirit of the most artificial mockery and parody of the artificial: something highly playful and highly precious'.

Dr Samuel Johnson thought that *Love's Labour's* was one of the most Shakespearean of Shakespeare's plays. Like the characters of Berowne and Boyet (who dislike each other because they are so like each other), Shakespeare himself was famous for his verbal facility, for being 'honey-tongued'. In no other play does he so fully indulge his gift for 'Taffeta phrases, silken terms precise, / Three-piled hyperboles'. At the same time, in no other play does he so mercilessly expose that gift as a fly-blown form of 'maggot ostentation', ripe for renunciation in favour of those 'honest plain words' that 'best pierce the ear of grief'.

What is so Shakespearean is this capacity to have it both ways. 'Taffeta phrases' are ostentatiously rejected and yet the simple rustic language that supposedly replaces them is equally thick with allusion – or, as Dull has it, 'collusion' and 'pollution'. Berowne's 'russet yeas and honest kersey noes' puns on 'eyes' and 'nose', so reintroducing the figure of Ovid, surnamed Naso (Latin for 'nose'), who is not only Holofernes' but also Shakespeare's master in the art of verbal pyrotechnics. For 'the elegancy, facility, and golden cadence of poesy', 'Ovidius Naso was the man: and why indeed "Naso", but for smelling out the odoriferous flowers of fancy, the jerks of invention?'

Ovid taught Shakespeare how to write love poetry but also how to parody love poetry. If ladies are conventionally praised for being blonde and pale-skinned, Ovid and Shakespeare know how to offer paradoxical praise of blackness. Where lesser poets catalogue the body parts of the beloved in smoothly predictable blazons (blue eyes, creamy breasts), Ovid and Shakespeare turn the convention on its head: 'two pitch-balls stuck in her face for eyes' and a piercing glare not at the bosom but at the dark place between the legs. Though

Dr Johnson was too polite to say so, one of the reasons why *Love's Labour's* is Shakespeare at his most Shakespearean is that it is simultaneously one of his most elegant plays (rivalled only by *As You Like It*) and his most filthy (rivalled only by *Troilus and Cressida*). The exchange in the fourth act concerning prickets, shooting, sores, ells and sorrels is on the surface about deer-hunting, but beneath the veneer it alludes unmistakably to inflamed genitalia and sexually transmitted disease.

At the climax of the play, the mood changes with the entrance of Marcadé, ambassador of death. Immediately before his entrance, the play-within-the-play has dissolved into a brawl between a clown and a braggart knight on the subject of a pregnant dairymaid who is named after the Elizabethan term for a toilet. The knight is accused of wearing a 'dishclout' of the maid's as a favour next to his heart. A stinking dishcloth is enough to prick the bubble of chivalric romance, but the word also seems to have been a slang term for a rag strapped on to soak up menstrual blood. To hold that image in conjunction with the *memento mori* figure of Marcadé is to understand something of Shakespeare's taste for extremity and paradox.

THE PARK AND THE WORTHIES

In contrast to those Shakespearean comedies that turn on a movement between a court and a green world, *Love's Labour's Lost* is confined within the single location of a court that has turned itself into a green world. The action all takes place within the King of Navarre's park, in a very short timeframe and with only a few (sometimes not so short) scenes. The set-up could hardly be simpler. The king and his courtiers have forsworn love in the name of academic study, but the arrival of the Princess of France and her charming attendant ladies proves something of an inconvenience for this plan.

Green is the colour associated with retreat to a garden for the purposes of intellectual contemplation. In his lyric 'The Garden', the mid-seventeenth-century poet Andrew Marvell imagined

'Annihilating all that's made / To a green thought in a green shade.' But, as Don Armado comes to realize when prompted by Moth, his clever page, green is also 'the colour of lovers'. The play is a demonstration of the triumph of love over intellectual labour. True wisdom belongs not to the intellectuals but to the clown Costard, who is of the view that it 'is the simplicity of man to hearken after the flesh'. Neither academic aspiration nor poetic elaboration will save man from this elementary truth.

Being sophisticated, Navarre and his three fellows only learn the truth by being embarrassed. In the play's most theatrically effective scene, plotted like the best of farces, each of the four men is caught with his metaphoric trousers down – not just falling in love, but writing abysmal love poetry. George Bernard Shaw summarized the dramatic effect neatly: 'No.1 being inaudible to 2, 3 and 4; No.2 audible to No.1, but not to 3 and 4; No.3 audible to 1 and 2, but not to No.4; and No.4 audible to all the rest, but himself temporarily stone deaf.' There is further delight when the men, now working in unison, disguise themselves as Russians in order to woo the ladies, but the ladies run rings round them because the disguise is so easily seen through. At this point we anticipate an unmasking, universal forgiveness, the forgetting of foolishness, multiple marriages and everyone living happily ever after. First, however, the lower-ranked characters must perform a celebratory entertainment for the court.

Just as 'The most lamentable comedy and most cruel death of Pyramus and Thisbe' echoes the main plot of *A Midsummer Night's Dream*, so the pageant of 'the Nine Worthies' offers a commentary on that of *Love's Labour's Lost*. Navarre begins the main action with the premise that he and his courtiers will achieve immortal fame by means of their academic prowess, but, in a striking analogy to the opening sequence of Shakespeare's Sonnets, the unfolding of the plot suggests that falling in love and reproducing oneself sexually is the only real means of guaranteeing survival after death. It is 'women's eyes', not books and academes, that 'contain and nourish all the world'.

Shakespeare turns the raw material for his play-within-the-play so that it fits with this theme. The Nine Worthies were traditionally three figures from each of the three traditions that constituted Shakespeare's cultural inheritance: the Bible (Joshua, David, Judas Maccabaeus), classical antiquity (Hector of Troy, Alexander the Great, Julius Caesar) and the romances of the Middle Ages (Arthur, Charlemagne, Godfrey of Bouillon). All nine had achieved immortality by means of heroic military action. This in itself is a rebuke to the court for its presumption that 'fame that all hunt after in their lives' could come from something so passive as academic study.

At the same time, Shakespeare changes the traditional cast: Julius Caesar is replaced by Costard the clown playing the part of Pompey the Great and, more significantly, Moth as Hercules stands in for one of the biblical or medieval figures. This is partly a joke about size: Hercules is the archetypal big man, whereas Moth is compared to an insect or a dust particle. In addition, the introduction of Hercules highlights the motif of heroic endeavour brought low by desire. He was famous not only for his *labours* such as stealing golden apples from the garden of the Hesperides (alluded to in Berowne's long speech on love near the end of the fourth act), but also for the losses caused by his *loves*. Hercules was humiliated and unmanned by his love for Omphale, then driven mad and murderous by his desire for Deianira. 'What great men have been in love?' Armado asks Moth. 'Hercules, master' comes the reply. The biblical Samson and his catastrophic love for Delilah is invoked at the same point. One suspects that if the pageant of Worthies had run to its conclusion, he too would have muscled his way into the cast.

As in 'Pyramus and Thisbe', the noble audience are unnecessarily rude to the ignoble players. They subvert the illusion on which theatre depends: 'I Pompey am –', 'You lie, you are not he.' And they make rude jokes at the expense of the actors: 'For the ass to the Jude? Give it him: Jud-as, away!' Holofernes engages our hearts when he offers the dignified response: 'This is not generous, not gentle, not humble.' The lords must undergo a further humbling before they prove their gentility and gain their reward: after all the linguistic labour, their loves are not won. Berowne is set the task of moving wild laughter in the throat of death and, in contrast to the traditional comic ending where Jack shall have Jill and naught shall go ill, here 'Jack hath not Jill'. There is a kind of suspended animation, intended to last for a year, heralded by the closing song of spring and winter.

With its rhymes and dances, its four pairs of lovers and curious-knotted garden, the play has a symmetrical structure that seems to demand harmonious resolution, and yet it ends with interruption – the unfinished pageant, the unfinished courtship, and finally another unfinished performance. Armado announces that Holofernes and Nathaniel will stage an epilogue in the form of an academic dialogue, but we never get to hear it. The haunting simplicity of the song intended to introduce their debate brings Armado, the embodiment of verbosity, to one final rejection of language-feasting: he calls a halt to the show and dismisses the audiences onstage and off with the conclusion that more words would be harsh after such music.

THE FRENCH CONNECTION

At the beginning of a long book called *The French Academy, wherein is discoursed the institution of manners, and whatsoever else concerneth the good and happy life of all estates and callings, by precepts of doctrine, and examples of the lives of ancient Sages and famous men*, by Peter de la Primaudaye, published in French in 1577 and translated into English by one T. B. C. in 1586, the reader is introduced to four (fictional) young gentlemen of Anjou. Their encounter is set at the time of the religious civil war that tore France apart in the second half of the sixteenth century. The young men withdraw from the stress of war and sectarian dissension, retreating to the country house of an elderly nobleman who puts them under the educational care of a learned man. 'He propounded for the chief part and portion of their studies the moral philosophy of ancient Sages and wise men, together with the understanding, and searching out of histories, which are the light of life.' La Primaudaye's long book purports to be a record of the young gentlemen's discussions concerning the nature

A proper knotte to be cast in the quarter of a Garden, or other wise, as there is sufficient roomth.

1. Design for a knot-garden: there is an elegant analogy between the symmetrical formality of Elizabethan garden design and the patterns of repetition and variation in rhetorically ornamented speech, so it is fitting that a 'curious-knotted garden' (see Armado's letter, as quoted by the king at 1.1.247) is a key location in this most verbally elaborate and garden-centred of Shakespeare's comedies.

of 'the good and happy life'. Each chapter begins with a dialogue between the four and then turns into a little essay on moral philosophy. There is much talk of the necessity of controlling the emotions and cultivating a Stoical detachment of mind. At the end of 'the first day's work' in their little 'academy', the student called Aser, who embodies happiness or 'felicity', comes up with the proposition that 'philosophy', by which he means the Stoic philosophy of self-restraint in particular, 'purgeth pride, presumption, ambition, choler, revenge, covetousness, injustice'. Philosophy also teaches us 'not to be carried away by lust'.

The cultivation of temperance, with a particular emphasis on sexual restraint, becomes a major theme of subsequent discussion, with the invocation of numerous positive and negative examples, mostly out of classical history and literature. The emphasis on sexual sin is an indication that la Primaudaye is propounding a typically sixteenth-century combination of classical Stoicism and Christian, specifically Pauline, theology. He was a product of what intellectual historians call the 'neo-Stoic revival' of the period.

La Primaudaye's compendium of commonplace philosophical and moral thought was widely read in France and, following its translation, in England. But there was a flaw in its premise. The device for dispensing large doses of neo-Stoic exhortations to prudence, temperance, fortitude and justice was to sequester the young men in the academy of the title. But, as is pointed out in the preface to the English translation of 1586, true virtue must be practised '*in life*'. As Aristotle had reminded the ancient Greeks, '*bare knowledge and contemplation thereof in* [*the*] *brain*' is insufficient. The theory was that, having studied history and philosophy and contemplated the nature of virtue in the academy for, say, three years, one would emerge into the world ready to practise what one had learned. Yet the inevitable consequence of the structural device was to create an image of leisured ease, in which the good life could be cultivated without any awkward intrusions from the day-to-day realities of politics, social inequality, religious contention – or women.

Whether or not Shakespeare specifically knew la Primaudaye's book, his starting point for *Love's Labour's Lost* was the same: a French academy set up as a retreat from historical, political and sexual engagement. The names of Shakespeare's four young men were all well known from the French wars. The play seems to have been written not long after the King of Navarre converted to Catholicism and took the French throne. 'Paris is worth a mass', he was reputed to have said. Biron, or Berowne, was the name of Navarre's marshal, who had fought in the siege of Rouen alongside the Earl of Essex and a contingent of English troops. Longaville was a supporter of Navarre, and the Duke de Mayenne (Dumaine) a former opponent who became an ally following a truce in 1595.

Shakespeare imagines a group of courtly men of Navarre who share these names. He removes them from the world of politics and religious faction, and places them in a 'little academe'. The king's first speech is peppered with military language – 'brave conquerors', 'war', 'huge army' – as if to say 'Now that we have won the war, let us win the peace by devoting ourselves to learning and Stoic detachment.' The premise of the exercise is that there is no place for love in intellectual life. Shakespeare, who did not of course spend three years in the all-male environment of an Oxford or Cambridge college, clearly thought that this was nonsense and set about mocking the idea. Love, he proposes instead, is at the centre of intellectual life. The really interesting task is not to reject it, but to find the appropriate language to express it.

LOVE'S PHILOSOPHY

Dumaine is happy to sign up to the King of Navarre's contract: he will mortify the flesh and be dead 'to love, to wealth, to pomp', and live only 'in philosophy'. But Berowne immediately expresses a reservation: he agrees to sign up to the three years' programme of academic study, but has grave doubts about the additional 'strict observances': to fast, to sleep but three hours a night and 'not to see a woman' for the entire three-year term. For Berowne, these are 'barren tasks', devoid of life. The essence of Berowne's criticism of the king's project is that the needs of the body – for food, for sleep, for sexual fulfilment – should not be denied. By his account, the pursuit of learning and fame are all very well, but not at the expense of natural instincts, 'For every man with his affects is born, / Not by might mastered but by special grace.' The Stoic ambition of keeping the passions fully under control is an illusion. Only the 'special grace' of divine intervention can prevent us from being the embodied, desiring human that we are. Divine intervention does not occur in the real world: as Shakespeare put it in another of his most thought-filled comedies, *All's Well that Ends Well*, 'miracles are past'.

In the absence of miracles, the 'affects', the passions, intrude into the academe. The unfolding action proves Berowne right. Wisdom, as so often in Shakespeare, comes from the mouth of a fool: the clownish Costard's irrefutable statement that 'it is the manner of a man to speak to a woman' comes to the core of the play. The presence of Jaquenetta the dairymaid is a reminder of the inescapable human body. The question of her pregnancy dominates the sub-plot and her very name – a female version of 'Jaques', which was pronounced 'jakes' – conjures up a bodily function that is alluded to in the pageant of the Nine Worthies: Alexander the Great is imagined sitting not on a royal throne but on a 'close-stool'. Ingesting and expelling are among the actions that make us human, whatever the Stoic philosopher may say about the primacy of 'reason'.

Love's Labour's Lost is a play packed with wit, elegance, philosophical reflection and filthy jokes. For Shakespeare, love meant immersing oneself in each of these four dimensions. The king turns his court into a little academe in the hope of finding philosophical wisdom. It comes in the very form that he has renounced: women, who prove themselves a great deal more intelligent and sensible than the men. The philosophical lesson that has to be learned is that 'women's eyes' have it in them to be 'the books, the arts, the academes, / That show, contain and nourish all the world'. But the male courtly lovers make a double mistake. Having foolishly renounced love, they then foolishly embrace a false idea of love: they begin praising their ladies' eyes (and other parts) in the affected language of the courtly poetic tradition that goes back to Petrarch in high Renaissance Italy. They write formulaic sonnets and love songs, they dance a ridiculous masque. The ladies have to teach them their further lesson, namely that those 'Taffeta phrases, silken terms precise, / Three-piled hyperboles, spruce affectation, / Figures pedantical' may also be an impediment to love. They have to learn a plainer language that can cope with the harsh realities of life, including death. The men are accordingly not granted the customary ending of comedy: instead of the play concluding with multiple marriages, the courtiers are sentences to a year's community service, after which the ladies will assess the situation. That assessment presumably occurred in the lost sequel, *Love's Labour's Won*.

Berowne is the wittiest character in the play, but the princess is the wisest. 'I hear your grace hath sworn out house-keeping', she says to her opposite number, the king. 'House-keeping' simulta-neously means domestic business (Latin *res familiares*, 'familiar things', everyday worldly affairs) and 'hospitality'. The renunciation of the former in the name of higher philosophical contemplation is not only unrealistic, since bodily needs are not to be denied, but it is also an abnegation of that duty to be hospitable which is a strong moral and social obligation in both classical and Christian thought. The princess concludes that, while it would be a sin for the men to break their solemn oath, it would accordingly be a more 'deadly sin' to keep it.

Insight of a similar kind comes from one of the play's several fools. 'Society', proclaims Nathaniel, citing a piece of proverbial wisdom, 'is the happiness of life'. Whereas the play begins with a neo-Stoical aspiration to philosophical detachment, this suggests a movement towards the values of a different ancient philosopher, Epicurus, who called his school the 'garden' and who argued that friendship – embodied here in the image of the 'society' of a hospitable table – is the most important of all human virtues. Nathaniel's is a fitting motto for that most communal of cultural events, the theatrical performance.

ABOUT THE TEXT

Shakespeare endures through history. He illuminates later times as well as his own. He helps us to understand the human condition. But he cannot do this without a good text of the plays. Without editions there would be no Shakespeare. That is why every twenty years or so throughout the last three centuries there has been a major new edition of his complete works. One aspect of editing is the process of keeping the texts up to date – modernizing the spelling, punctuation and typography (though not, of course, the actual words), providing explanatory notes in the light of changing educational practices (a generation ago, most of Shakespeare's classical and biblical allusions could be assumed to be generally understood, but now they can't).

But because Shakespeare did not personally oversee the publication of his plays, editors also have to make decisions about the relative authority of the early printed editions. Half of the sum of his plays only appeared posthumously, in the elaborately produced First Folio text of 1623, the original 'Complete Works' prepared for the press by Shakespeare's fellow-actors, the people who knew the plays better than anyone else. The other half had appeared in print in his lifetime, in the more compact and cheaper form of 'Quarto' editions, some of which reproduced good quality texts, others of which were to a greater or lesser degree garbled and error-strewn.

Generations of editors have adopted a 'pick and mix' approach, moving between Quarto and Folio readings, making choices on either aesthetic or bibliographic grounds, sometimes creating a composite text that Shakespeare never actually wrote. Not until the 1980s did editors follow the logic of what ought to have been obvious to anyone who works in the theatre: that the Quarto and Folio texts often represent discrete moments in the life of a script, that plays change in the course of rehearsal, production and revival, and that many of the major variants between the early printed versions almost certainly reflect this process.

If you look at printers' handbooks from the age of Shakespeare, you quickly discover that one of the first rules was that, whenever possible, compositors were recommended to set their type from existing printed books rather than manuscripts. This was the age before mechanical typesetting, where each individual letter had to be picked out by hand from the compositor's case and placed on a stick (upside down and back to front) before being laid on the press. It was an age of murky rush-light and of manuscripts written in a secretary hand that had dozens of different, hard-to-decipher forms. Printers' lives were a lot easier when they were reprinting existing books rather than struggling with handwritten copy. Easily the quickest way to have created the First Folio would have been simply to reprint those eighteen plays that had already appeared in Quarto and only work from manuscript on the other eighteen.

But that is not what happened. Whenever Quartos were used, as in the case of *Love's Labour's Lost*, playhouse 'promptbooks' were also consulted and stage directions copied in from them. This means that Folio *Love's Labour's Lost* is superior to Quarto in some of its exit direction and speech headings, though Quarto is superior to Folio in some of its individual readings of words and phrases.

With several major plays where a well-printed Quarto was available, the Folio printers were instructed to work from an alternative, playhouse-derived manuscript. This meant that the whole process of producing the first complete Shakespeare took months, even years, longer than it might have done. But for the men overseeing the project, John Hemings and Henry Condell, friends and fellow-actors who had been remembered in Shakespeare's will, the additional labour and cost were worth the effort for the sake of producing an edition that was close to the practice of the theatre. They wanted all the plays in print so that people could, as they wrote in their prefatory address to the reader, 'read him and again and again', but they also wanted 'the great variety of readers' to work from texts that were close to the theatre-life for which Shakespeare originally intended them. For this reason, the *RSC Shakespeare*, in both *Complete Works* and individual volumes, uses the Folio as base text wherever possible. Significant Quarto variants are, however, noted in the Textual Notes.

The following notes highlight various aspects of the editorial process and indicate conventions used in the text of this edition:

Lists of Parts are supplied in the First Folio for only six plays, not including *Love's Labour's Lost*, so the list here is editorially supplied. Capitals indicate that part of the name which is used for speech headings in the script (thus 'Don Adriano de ARMADO').

Locations are provided by the Folio for only two plays, of which *Love's Labour's Lost* is not one. Eighteenth-century editors, working in an age of elaborately realistic stage sets, were the first to provide detailed locations ('another part of the park'). Given that Shakespeare wrote for a bare stage and often an imprecise sense of place, we have relegated locations to the explanatory notes at the foot of the page, where they are given at the beginning of each scene where the imaginary location is different from the one before. In the case of *Love's Labour's Lost*, the entire action is set in the king's park.

Act and Scene Divisions were provided in the Folio in a much more thoroughgoing way than in the Quartos. Sometimes, however, they were erroneous or omitted; corrections and additions supplied by editorial tradition are indicated by square brackets. Five-act division is based on a classical model, and act breaks provided the opportunity to replace the candles in the indoor Blackfriars playhouse which the King's Men used after 1608, but Shakespeare did not necessarily think in terms of a five-part structure of dramatic composition. The Folio convention is that a scene ends when the stage is empty. Nowadays, partly under the influence of film, we tend to consider a scene to be a dramatic unit that ends with either a change of imaginary location or a significant passage of time within the narrative. Shakespeare's fluidity of composition accords well with this convention, so in addition to act and scene numbers we provide a *running scene* count in the right margin at the beginning of each new scene, in the typeface used for editorial directions. Where there is a scene break caused by a momentary bare stage, but the location does not change and extra time does not pass, we use the convention *running scene continues*. There is inevitably a degree of editorial judgement in making such calls, but the system is very valuable in suggesting the pace of the plays.

Speakers' Names are often inconsistent in Folio. We have regularized speech headings, but retained an element of deliberate inconsistency in entry directions, in order to give the flavour of Folio. Thus ARMADO is always so-called in his speech headings, but is sometimes 'Braggart' in entry directions.

Verse is indicated by lines that do not run to the right margin and by capitalization of each line. The Folio printers sometimes set verse as prose, and vice versa (either out of misunderstanding or for reasons of space). We have silently corrected in such cases, although in some instances there is ambiguity, in which case we have leaned towards the preservation of Folio layout. Folio sometimes uses contraction ('turnd' rather than 'turned') to indicate whether or not the final '-ed' of a past participle is sounded, an area where there is variation for the sake of the five-beat iambic pentameter rhythm. We use the convention of a grave accent to indicate sounding (thus 'turnèd' would be two syllables), but would urge actors not to overstress. In cases where one speaker ends with a verse half-line and the next begins with the other half of the pentameter, editors since the late eighteenth century have indented the second line. We have abandoned this convention, since the Folio does not use it, and nor did actors' cues in the Shakespearean theatre. An exception is made when the second speaker actively interrupts or completes the first speaker's sentence.

Spelling is modernized, but older forms are very occasionally maintained where necessary for rhythm or aural effect.

Punctuation in Shakespeare's time was as much rhetorical as grammatical. 'Colon' was originally a term for a unit of thought in an argument. The semi-colon was a new unit of punctuation (some of the Quartos lack them altogether). We have modernized punctuation throughout, but have given more weight to Folio punctuation than many editors, since, though not Shakespearean, it reflects the usage of his period. In particular, we have used the colon far more than many editors: it is exceptionally useful as a way of indicating how many Shakespearean speeches unfold clause by clause in a developing argument that gives the illusion of enacting the process of thinking in the moment. We have also kept in mind the origin of punctuation in classical times as a way of assisting the actor and orator: the comma suggests the briefest of pauses for breath, the colon a middling one and a full stop or period a longer pause. Semi-colons, by contrast, belong to an era of punctuation that was only just coming in during Shakespeare's time and that is coming to an end now: we have accordingly only used them where they occur in our copy-texts (and not always then). Dashes are sometimes used for parenthetical interjections where the Folio has brackets. They are also used for interruptions and changes in train of thought. Where a change of addressee occurs within a speech, we have used a dash preceded by a full stop (or occasionally another form of punctuation). Often the identity of the respective addressees is obvious from the context. When it is not, this has been indicated in a marginal stage direction.

Entrances and Exits are fairly thorough in Folio, which has accordingly been followed as faithfully as possible. Where characters are omitted or corrections are necessary, this is indicated by square brackets (e.g. '[*and Attendants*]'). *Exit* is sometimes silently normalized to *Exeunt* and *Manet* anglicized to 'remains'. We trust Folio positioning of entrances and exits to a greater degree than most editors.

Editorial Stage Directions such as stage business, asides, indications of addressee and of characters' position on the gallery stage are only used sparingly in Folio. Other editions mingle directions of this kind with original Folio and Quarto directions, sometimes marking them by means of square brackets. We have sought to distinguish what could be described as *directorial* interventions of this kind from Folio-style directions (either original or supplied) by placing them in the right margin in a different typeface. There is a degree of subjectivity about which directions are of which kind, but the procedure is intended as a reminder to the reader and the actor that Shakespearean stage directions are often dependent upon editorial inference alone and are not set in stone. We also depart from editorial tradition in sometimes admitting uncertainty and thus printing permissive stage directions, such as an *Aside?* (often a line may be equally effective as an aside or a direct address – it is for each production or reading to make its own decision) or a *may exit* or a piece of business placed between arrows to indicate that it may occur at various different moments within a scene.

Line Numbers in the left margin are editorial, for reference and to key the explanatory and textual notes.

Explanatory Notes at the foot of each page explain allusions and gloss obsolete and difficult words, confusing phraseology, occasional major textual cruces, and so on. Particular attention is given to non-standard usage, bawdy innuendo and technical terms (e.g. legal and military language). Where more than one sense is given, commas indicate shades of related meaning, slashes alternative or double meanings.

Textual Notes at the end of the play indicate major departures from the Folio. They take the following form: the reading of our text is given in bold and its source given after an equals sign, with 'Q' indicating a Quarto reading, 'F2' a reading that derives from the Second Folio of 1632 and 'Ed' one that derives from the subsequent editorial tradition. The rejected Folio ('F') reading is then given. Thus for Act 1 scene 1 line 62: '**62 feast** = Ed. F = fast' means that the Folio compositor repeated the Quarto printer's erroneous 'fast' and that we have followed editorial tradition in changing the line to read 'feast'.

KEY FACTS

MAJOR PARTS: (*with percentage of lines/number of speeches/scenes on stage*) Berowne (22%/159/5), King (11%/117/4), Princess (10%/102/3), Don Armado (10%/102/4), Boyet (8%/80/3), Costard (7%/83/7), Rosaline (7%/75/3), Holofernes (6%/54/3), Moth (5%/78/3), Dumaine (3%/54/4), Longaville (2%/40/4), Maria (2%/25/3), Katherine (2%/22/3), Nathaniel (2%/19/3), Dull (1%/15/4), Jaquenetta (1%/13/3).

LINGUISTIC MEDIUM: 65% verse, 35% prose. High proportion of rhyme and interwoven poetry, including sonnets.

DATE: Before 1598. Edition of that year refers to the play being 'presented before her Highness [Queen Elizabeth] this last Christmas'. A poem by Robert Tofte, also published in 1598, apparently refers to a performance seen in the public theatre. Stylistic similarity to *A Midsummer Night's Dream* and other lyrical plays, together with possible references to an Inns of Court Christmas entertainment of 1594–95, lead most scholars to date composition to 1595–96.

SOURCES: One of Shakespeare's few genuinely sourceless plays, though draws on many aspects of the literary culture of the early 1590s (e.g. the vogue for love sonnets and the elaborate 'euphuistic' writing style pioneered by John Lyly); the idea of four courtiers retreating from political engagement in order to engage in academic reflection and philosophical discussion may have been inspired by Pierre de la Primaudaye's *The French Academy* (English translation 1586, reprinted 1589 and 1594). Though not a contemporary political allegory, some of the names in the play apparently allude to historical figures in contemporary France and Navarre (of great interest at the time, since in March 1594 King Henri of Navarre – a discrete kingdom between France and Spain – converted to Catholicism and became King of France).

TEXT: Quarto edition of 1598, 'newly corrected and augmented by W. Shakespere' – this may imply that there was an earlier Quarto, now lost. The Folio was printed from the Quarto, making some corrections and introducing some errors. There are some severe textual tangles, particularly over characters' names, where Shakespeare sometimes seems to have become muddled. Some passages, including Berowne's crucial long speech about love at the end of the fourth act, contain repetition that strongly suggests that the printed text retains elements of Shakespeare's first draft as well as the final version: we indicate such 'first thoughts' with marginal marks (//).

LOVE'S LABOUR'S LOST

Ferdinand **KING** of Navarre

BEROWNE ⎫
LONGAVILLE ⎬ lords attending on the king
DUMAINE ⎭

Don Adriano de **ARMADO**, a Spanish braggart

MOTH, a boy, his page

COSTARD, a clown

JAQUENETTA, a dairymaid

Anthony **DULL**, a constable

Sir **NATHANIEL**, a curate

HOLOFERNES, a pedantic schoolmaster

The **PRINCESS** of France

ROSALINE ⎫
MARIA ⎬ ladies attending on the princess
KATHERINE ⎭

BOYET, a lord attending on the princess

Monsieur **MARCADÉ**, a messenger from the King of France

A **FORESTER**

Lords, Ladies, Attendants

List of parts BEROWNE in Act 4 scene 3 rhymes with 'moon' **MOTH** probably pronounced 'mott'; some editors modernize to 'Mote' **JAQUENETTA** perhaps pronounced 'Jake-netta', suggestive of 'jakes' (privy, toilet)

Act 1 [Scene 1]   *running scene 1*

*Enter Ferdinand King of Navarre, Berowne, Longaville and
Dumaine*

KING Let fame, that all hunt after in their lives,
    Live registered upon our brazen tombs,
    And then grace us in the disgrace of death
    When, spite of cormorant devouring time,
5   Th'endeavour of this present breath may buy
    That honour which shall bate his scythe's keen edge
    And make us heirs of all eternity.
    Therefore, brave conquerors — for so you are,
    That war against your own affections
10   And the huge army of the world's desires —
    Our late edict shall strongly stand in force.
    Navarre shall be the wonder of the world,
    Our court shall be a little academe,
    Still and contemplative in living art.
15   You three, Berowne, Dumaine and Longaville,
    Have sworn for three years' term to live with me,
    My fellow-scholars, and to keep those statutes
    That are recorded in this schedule here.   *Shows a paper*
    Your oaths are passed, and now subscribe your names,
20   That his own hand may strike his honour down
    That violates the smallest branch herein.
    If you are armed to do as sworn to do,
    Subscribe to your deep oaths, and keep it too.
    LONGAVILLE I am resolved: 'tis but a three years' fast.
25   The mind shall banquet though the body pine.   *Signs*
    Fat paunches have lean pates, and dainty bits
    Make rich the ribs, but bankrupt quite the wits.

1.1 *Location: Navarre, in the king's park. This is the location for the entire play*   **Ferdinand** in fact, the King of Navarre at the time of the play's composition was Henri   **Berowne, Longaville** the Duc de Berowne and the Duc de Longueville both fought for King Henri   **Dumaine** perhaps based on Charles de Lorraine, Duc de Mayenne and initially King Henri's opponent   **1 fame** renown   **2 registered** recorded   **brazen** brass-plated, enduring (plays on sense of 'shameless')   **3 grace** honour   **disgrace** disfigurement/shame   **4 spite** in spite   **cormorant** i.e. ravenous (literally, a greedy seabird)   **5 breath** i.e. life/speech   **6 bate** abate, blunt   **his** i.e. time's   **keen** sharp/eager   **9 affections** passions   **11 late** recent   **stand in force** i.e. be binding   **12 Navarre** the place/the king   **13 academe** institution of learning (originally Plato's academy near Athens)   **14 Still ... in** calmly, constantly studying   **contemplative in** meditating on   **living art** the art of living/vitality within scholarship   **16 term** period of time   **17 keep** observe   **18 schedule** document/list   **19 passed** pledged   **subscribe** sign   **20 hand** sword/handwriting   **21 branch** clause   **22 armed** prepared (plays on sense of 'carrying weapons')   **23 deep** solemn   **it** subscription (to the oath)   **25 pine** starve, languish   **26 pates** heads (i.e. wits)   **dainty bits** choice morsels of food

DUMAINE My loving lord, Dumaine is mortified.
    The grosser manner of these world's delights
30   He throws upon the gross world's baser slaves.   *Signs*
    To love, to wealth, to pomp, I pine and die,
    With all these living in philosophy.
BEROWNE I can but say their protestation over.
    So much, dear liege, I have already sworn,
35   That is, to live and study here three years.
    But there are other strict observances,
    As not to see a woman in that term,
    Which I hope well is not enrollèd there.
    And one day in a week to touch no food,
40   And but one meal on every day beside,
    The which I hope is not enrollèd there.
    And then to sleep but three hours in the night,
    And not be seen to wink of all the day —
    When I was wont to think no harm all night
45   And make a dark night too of half the day —
    Which I hope well is not enrollèd there.
    O, these are barren tasks, too hard to keep:
    Not to see ladies, study, fast, not sleep.
KING Your oath is passed to pass away from these.
50 **BEROWNE** Let me say no, my liege, an if you please.
    I only swore to study with your grace
    And stay here in your court for three years' space.
LONGAVILLE You swore to that, Berowne, and to the rest.
BEROWNE By yea and nay, sir, then I swore in jest.
55   What is the end of study, let me know?
KING Why, that to know which else we should not know.
BEROWNE Things hid and barred, you mean, from
        common sense?
KING Ay, that is study's godlike recompense.
BEROWNE Come on then, I will swear to study so,
60   To know the thing I am forbid to know:
    As thus, to study where I well may dine,
    When I to feast expressly am forbid.
    Or study where to meet some mistress fine,
    When mistresses from common sense are hid.

---

28 mortified dead to worldly pleasures   **29 grosser** coarser, earthier   **30 gross** whole/coarse   **baser slaves** those subject to inferior pleasures   **32 in** according to the tenets of/by the study of   **33 say ... over** repeat their vows   **36 observances** requirements   **37 As** such as   **38 enrollèd** written   **43 wink** close one's eyes/sleep   **44 wont** accustomed   **think no harm** i.e. sleep   **49 pass away from** renounce   **50 an if** if   **52 space** duration   **54 By ... nay** a common oath   **55 end** aim   **57 common sense** ordinary understanding   **58 recompense** reward   **59 Come on** quibbles on **common**

65   Or, having sworn too hard-a-keeping oath,
        Study to break it and not break my troth.
        If study's gain be thus and this be so,
        Study knows that which yet it doth not know.
        Swear me to this, and I will ne'er say no.
70   **KING** These be the stops that hinder study quite
        And train our intellects to vain delight.
        BEROWNE Why, all delights are vain, and that most vain,
        Which with pain purchased doth inherit pain:
        As painfully to pore upon a book
75   To seek the light of truth, while truth the while
        Doth falsely blind the eyesight of his look.
        Light seeking light doth light of light beguile:
        So, ere you find where light in darkness lies,
        Your light grows dark by losing of your eyes.
80   Study me how to please the eye indeed
        By fixing it upon a fairer eye,
        Who dazzling so, that eye shall be his heed
        And give him light that it was blinded by.
        Study is like the heaven's glorious sun
85   That will not be deep-searched with saucy looks:
        Small have continual plodders ever won
        Save base authority from others' books.
        These earthly godfathers of heaven's lights,
        That give a name to every fixèd star,
90   Have no more profit of their shining nights
        Than those that walk and wot not what they are.
        Too much to know is to know nought but fame,
        And every godfather can give a name.
        KING How well he's read, to reason against reading.
95   **DUMAINE** Proceeded well, to stop all good proceeding.

---

65 too hard-a-keeping oath an oath too hard to keep   **66 troth** faith   **70 stops** impediments   **quite** completely   **71 train** entice   **vain** foolish, trifling, self-gratifying   **73 pain** effort, suffering, labour   **purchased** acquired   **inherit** bring about more   **74 As** for example   **75 the while** in the meantime   **76 falsely** treacherously   **his look** its sight   **77 Light** i.e. eyes, thought to produce the beams of light by which they saw   **light** intellectual enlightenment   **light … beguile** the eyes are cheated out of enlightenment (by excessive study)   **78 ere** before   **darkness** intellectual obscurity   **80 Study me** let me learn   **81 fairer** more beautiful (plays on sense of 'lighter')   **82 dazzling** blinding (my eyes)   **that eye** i.e. of the fairer woman   **heed** focus of attention/guardian   **85 saucy** insolent   **86 Small** little   **87 Save** except   **base** lowly, second-hand   **88 godfathers … lights** astronomers who name the stars, as godparents name children at baptism   **90 profit of** benefit from   **shining** i.e. starlit   **91 wot** know   **they** the stars/the walkers   **92 Too … fame** an excess of knowledge brings only a vainglorious reputation   **93 every godfather** i.e. any ordinary person   **95 Proceeded** argued (plays on sense of 'taking a university degree')   **proceeding** intellectual advancement

LONGAVILLE He weeds the corn, and still lets grow the
    weeding.
BEROWNE The spring is near when green geese are
    a-breeding.
DUMAINE How follows that?
BEROWNE Fit in his place and time.
100 **DUMAINE** In reason nothing.
BEROWNE Something then in rhyme.
KING Berowne is like an envious sneaping frost
    That bites the first-born infants of the spring.
BEROWNE Well, say I am. Why should proud summer
    boast
105   Before the birds have any cause to sing?
    Why should I joy in any abortive birth?
    At Christmas I no more desire a rose
    Than wish a snow in May's new-fangled shows,
    But like of each thing that in season grows.
110   So you, to study now it is too late,
    That were to climb o'er the house to unlock the gate.
KING Well, sit you out. Go home, Berowne, adieu.
BEROWNE No, my good lord, I have sworn to stay with
    you.
    And though I have for barbarism spoke more
115   Than for that angel knowledge you can say,
    Yet confident I'll keep what I have sworn
    And bide the penance of each three years' day.
    Give me the paper, let me read the same,
    And to the strict'st decrees I'll write my name.   *Takes the paper*
120 **KING** How well this yielding rescues thee from shame.
BEROWNE '*Item*, That no woman shall come within a   *Reads*
    mile of my court.' Hath this been proclaimed?
LONGAVILLE Four days ago.
BEROWNE Let's see the penalty: 'On pain of losing her
125   tongue.' Who devised this penalty?
LONGAVILLE Marry, that did I.
BEROWNE Sweet lord, and why?

---

96 weeds pulls up   **lets . . . weeding** allows the weeds to flourish   **97 green geese** innocent simpletons/
geese fed on grass   **99 Fit in his** in a manner appropriate to its   **100 In reason nothing** i.e. it doesn't follow
logically   **101 rhyme** i.e. the opposite of **reason**   **102 envious** malicious   **sneaping** biting/nipping
(**rhyme** puns on 'rime' – i.e. frost)   **103 first-born infants** youngest plants   **104 proud** glorious/arrogant
106 abortive premature, unnatural   **108 new-fangled shows** newly created, elaborate displays (of
flowers)   **109 like of** I delight in   **in season** i.e. at its proper time   **110 too late** i.e. in life   **111 climb . . .
gate** i.e. pointless   **112 sit you out** don't take part   **114 barbarism** uncivilized ignorance   **117 bide**
endure   **three years' day** day of three years   **126 Marry** by the Virgin Mary

LONGAVILLE To fright them hence with that dread
    penalty.

BEROWNE A dangerous law against gentility!

130 '*Item*, If any man be seen to talk with a woman within   *Reads*
the term of three years, he shall endure such public
shame as the rest of the court shall possibly devise.'
This article, my liege, yourself must break,
For well you know here comes in embassy

135 The French king's daughter with yourself to speak —
A maid of grace and complete majesty —
About surrender up of Aquitaine
To her decrepit, sick and bedrid father:
Therefore this article is made in vain,

140 Or vainly comes th'admirèd princess hither.

KING What say you, lords? Why, this was quite forgot.

BEROWNE So study evermore is overshot.
While it doth study to have what it would,
It doth forget to do the thing it should:

145 And when it hath the thing it hunteth most,
'Tis won as towns with fire, so won, so lost.

KING We must of force dispense with this decree.
She must lie here on mere necessity.

BEROWNE Necessity will make us all forsworn

150 Three thousand times within this three years' space,
For every man with his affects is born,
Not by might mastered but by special grace.
If I break faith, this word shall speak for me:
I am forsworn 'on mere necessity'.

155 So to the laws at large I write my name,   *Signs*
And he that breaks them in the least degree
Stands in attainder of eternal shame.
Suggestions are to others as to me:
But I believe, although I seem so loath,

160 I am the last that will last keep his oath.
But is there no quick recreation granted?

---

128 **hence** away from here   **dread** dreadful/frightening   **129 gentility** civilized behaviour   **133 article** clause   **134 in embassy** as an ambassador   **136 complete** perfect   **137 Aquitaine** area of south-west France   **140 vainly** pointlessly   **142 overshot** wide of the mark (i.e. mistaken)   **143 would** wants
146 **towns ... lost** i.e. a town that is burnt down as part of a military campaign is no gain at all   **147 force** necessity   **148 lie** lodge   **on mere** out of absolute   **149 forsworn** perjured, oath-breakers   **151 affects** passions, desires   **152 might** personal strength   **grace** divine favour   **153 word** phrase   **155 at large** as a whole   **157 in attainder** accused/convicted   **158 Suggestions ... me** I am as susceptible to temptation as any man   **160 the ... oath** the last one to swear, but the one who will keep his word the longest/the least likely to keep my oath the longest   **161 quick** lively

KING Ay, that there is. Our court, you know, is haunted
　　　With a refinèd traveller of Spain,
　　　A man in all the world's new fashion planted,
165　　That hath a mint of phrases in his brain,
　　　One who the music of his own vain tongue
　　　Doth ravish like enchanting harmony,
　　　A man of compliments, whom right and wrong
　　　Have chose as umpire of their mutiny.
170　　This child of fancy, that Armado hight,
　　　For interim to our studies shall relate
　　　In high-born words the worth of many a knight
　　　From tawny Spain lost in the world's debate.
　　　How you delight, my lords, I know not, I,
175　　But I protest I love to hear him lie,
　　　And I will use him for my minstrelsy.

BEROWNE Armado is a most illustrious wight,
　　　A man of fire-new words, fashion's own knight.

LONGAVILLE Costard the swain and he shall be our sport,
180　　And so to study three years is but short.

Enter a constable [Dull] with a letter, with Costard

DULL Which is the duke's own person?

BEROWNE This, fellow. What wouldst?

DULL I myself reprehend his own person, for I am his
　　　grace's tharborough. But I would see his own person in
185　　flesh and blood.

BEROWNE This is he.

DULL Signior Arme ... Arme ... commends you. There's
　　　villainy abroad. This letter will tell you more.　　*Shows a letter*

COSTARD Sir, the contempts thereof are as touching me.

190　KING A letter from the magnificent Armado.

BEROWNE How low soever the matter, I hope in God for
　　　high words.

LONGAVILLE A high hope for a low heaven. God grant us
　　　patience.

162 **haunted With** frequented by　164 **in ... planted** involved in whatever is fashionable　165 **mint** creative source/wealth (literally, place where money is coined)　168 **compliments** accomplishments, courtesy　169 **mutiny** discord　170 **child of fancy** flamboyant, fanciful creature　**hight** is called　171 **For interim** as an interval　172 **high-born** noble/lofty　173 **tawny** browned (by sun)　**debate** strife　174 **delight** take pleasure　176 **for my minstrelsy** as my minstrel (i.e. musician, entertainer)　177 **wight** person　179 **Costard** literally 'large apple'; slang for 'head'　**swain** low-ranking man/rustic　**he** i.e. Armado　**sport** entertainment　181 **duke's** i.e. king's　183 **reprehend** malapropism for 'represent'　184 **tharborough** thirdborough (i.e. parish constable)　187 **commends you** commends himself to you (i.e. greets you respectfully)　188 **abroad** at large　189 **contempts** malapropism for 'contents'　**touching** concerning　190 **magnificent** ostentatious/splendid (joking allusion to the 1588 Spanish Armada, often referred to as 'magnificent')　191 **How ... matter** however debased the content　192 **high** lofty　193 **high hope** great expectation　**low heaven** i.e. small blessing

195   **BEROWNE** To hear, or forbear hearing?

LONGAVILLE To hear meekly, sir, and to laugh moderately, or to forbear both.

BEROWNE Well, sir, be it as the style shall give us cause to climb in the merriness.

200   **COSTARD** The matter is to me, sir, as concerning Jaquenetta. The manner of it is, I was taken with the manner.

BEROWNE In what manner?

COSTARD In manner and form following, sir, all those
205   three. I was seen with her in the manor-house, sitting with her upon the form, and taken following her into the park, which, put together, is 'in manner and form following'. Now, sir, for the manner: it is the manner of a man to speak to a woman. For the form: in some
210   form.

BEROWNE For the 'following', sir?

COSTARD As it shall follow in my correction, and God defend the right!

KING Will you hear this letter with attention?

215   **BEROWNE** As we would hear an oracle.

COSTARD Such is the simplicity of man to hearken after the flesh.

KING 'Great deputy, the welkin's vicegerent and sole   *Reads*
dominator of Navarre, my soul's earth's god, and
220   body's fostering patron'—

COSTARD Not a word of Costard yet.

KING 'So it is'—   *Reads*

COSTARD It may be so: but if he say it is so, he is, in telling true, but so.

225   **KING** Peace!

COSTARD Be to me and every man that dares not fight.

KING No words!

COSTARD Of other men's secrets, I beseech you.

---

195 forbear refrain from   **198 be it** let it be   **style** puns on 'stile'   **to climb** **200 to** about   **201 manner** nature, way it is expressed   **taken … manner** caught in the act/with the stolen goods   **204 In … following** a commonly used legal phrase   **those three** i.e. words (**manner, form, following**; punned on in the ensuing explanation)   **206 form** bench   **207 park** enclosed land used for hunting   **208 manner** custom, nature   **212 correction** punishment   **God … right** a formal prayer said before trial by combat   **216 simplicity** stupidity/simple nature   **218 welkin's** heavens'   **vicegerent** deputy   **219 dominator** ruler   **220 fostering** supporting   **224 but so** merely so-so, not saying much   **226 Be** i.e. **peace** be extended   **228 Of … secrets** Costard again extends the meaning of the king's words

KING 'So it is, besieged with sable-coloured melancholy, I   *Reads*
230   did commend the black oppressing humour to the most
wholesome physic of thy health-giving air, and, as I
am a gentleman, betook myself to walk. The time,
when? About the sixth hour, when beasts most graze,
birds best peck, and men sit down to that nourishment
235   which is called supper: so much for the time when.
Now for the ground, which? Which, I mean, I walked
upon. It is ycleped thy park. Then for the place, where?
Where, I mean, I did encounter that obscene and most
preposterous event that draweth from my snow-white
240   pen the ebon-coloured ink, which here thou viewest,
beholdest, surveyest, or seest. But to the place, where?
It standeth north-north-east and by east from the west
corner of thy curious-knotted garden; there did I see
that low-spirited swain, that base minnow of thy
245   mirth'—

COSTARD Me?

KING 'That unlettered small-knowing soul'—   *Reads*

COSTARD Me?

KING 'That shallow vassal'—   *Reads*

250   COSTARD Still me?

KING 'Which, as I remember, hight Costard'—   *Reads*

COSTARD O, me!

KING 'Sorted and consorted, contrary to thy established   *Reads*
proclaimed edict and continent canon, which with —
255   O, with — but with this I passion to say wherewith'—

COSTARD With a wench.

KING 'With a child of our grandmother Eve, a female, or,   *Reads*
for thy more sweet understanding, a woman. Him I
(as my ever-esteemed duty pricks me on) have sent to
260   thee, to receive the meed of punishment, by thy
sweet grace's officer, Anthony Dull, a man of good
repute, carriage, bearing, and estimation.'

DULL Me, an't shall please you. I am Anthony Dull.

---

229 **sable-coloured** black   230 **commend** commit   **black oppressing humour** i.e. melancholy
humour mood (one of the four bodily 'humours' that governed the disposition)   231 **physic** medicine   **as I
am** on my word as   237 **ycleped** called   238 **obscene** repulsive   239 **preposterous** improper, perverse
snow-white pen i.e. goose quill   240 **ebon-coloured** black   243 **curious-knotted** with intricately
designed flower-beds   244 **low-spirited** base   **minnow** ... **mirth** laughable, insignificant object
247 **unlettered** illiterate   249 **vassal** wretch   253 **Sorted** associated   **consorted** accompanied
254 **continent canon** law enforcing (especially sexual) restraint   255 **passion** grieve   **wherewith** with
what   259 **pricks** spurs (may pun on sense of 'penis')   260 **meed** reward   262 **carriage** behaviour
estimation reputation   263 **an't** if it

KING 'For Jaquenetta — so is the weaker vessel called   *Reads*
265   which I apprehended with the aforesaid swain — I
        keep her as a vessel of the law's fury, and shall, at the
        least of thy sweet notice, bring her to trial. Thine, in
        all compliments of devoted and heart-burning heat of
        duty. Don Adriano de Armado.'

270 BEROWNE This is not so well as I looked for, but the best
        that ever I heard.

    KING Ay, the best for the worst. But, sirrah, what say
        you to this?

    COSTARD Sir, I confess the wench.

275 KING Did you hear the proclamation?

    COSTARD I do confess much of the hearing it but little of
        the marking of it.

    KING It was proclaimed a year's imprisonment to be
        taken with a wench.

280 COSTARD I was taken with none, sir: I was taken with a
        damsel.

    KING Well, it was proclaimed damsel.

    COSTARD This was no damsel, neither, sir: she was a
        virgin.

285 KING It is so varied too, for it was proclaimed virgin.

    COSTARD If it were, I deny her virginity: I was taken
        with a maid.

    KING This maid will not serve your turn, sir.

    COSTARD This maid will serve my turn, sir.

290 KING Sir, I will pronounce your sentence: you shall fast a
        week with bran and water.

    COSTARD I had rather pray a month with mutton and
        porridge.

    KING And Don Armado shall be your keeper.

295   My Lord Berowne, see him delivered o'er:
        And go we, lords, to put in practice that
        Which each to other hath so strongly sworn.
                        [*Exeunt King, Longaville and Dumaine*]

---

264 **weaker vessel** i.e. woman 266 **keep** retain (may play on sense of 'keep as a mistress') 267 **least ...
notice** slightest notification **trial** probably plays on sense of 'sexual test' 270 **looked for** expected
272 **for** i.e. example of **sirrah** sir (used to an inferior) 274 **confess** admit to having been involved
with 277 **marking of** paying attention to 285 **so varied** expressed equivocally 288 **maid** i.e. use of the
word **maid** **serve your turn** get you out of trouble (Costard plays on the sense of 'gratify me sexually')
292 **pray** plays on sense of 'have sex' **mutton and porridge** mutton soup (**mutton** plays on the sense of
'prostitute' and **porridge** on the sense of 'sex/genitalia') 295 **delivered o'er** handed over

BEROWNE I'll lay my head to any goodman's hat,
These oaths and laws will prove an idle scorn.

300   Sirrah, come on.

COSTARD I suffer for the truth, sir, for true it is, I was
taken with Jaquenetta, and Jaquenetta is a true girl.
And therefore welcome the sour cup of prosperity!
Affliction may one day smile again, and until then, sit

305   down, sorrow!   *Exeunt*

[Act 1 Scene 2]   *running scene 1 continues*

Enter Armado and Moth, his page

ARMADO Boy, what sign is it when a man of great spirit
grows melancholy?

MOTH A great sign, sir, that he will look sad.

ARMADO Why, sadness is one and the self-same thing,

5   dear imp.

MOTH No, no, O lord, sir, no.

ARMADO How canst thou part sadness and melancholy,
my tender juvenal?

MOTH By a familiar demonstration of the working, my

10   tough señor.

ARMADO Why tough señor? Why tough señor?

MOTH Why tender juvenal? Why tender juvenal?

ARMADO I spoke it, tender juvenal, as a congruent
epitheton appertaining to thy young days, which we

15   may nominate tender.

MOTH And I, tough senior, as an appertinent title to your
old time, which we may name tough.

ARMADO Pretty and apt.

MOTH How mean you, sir? I pretty, and my saying apt?

20   Or I apt, and my saying pretty?

ARMADO Thou pretty, because little.

MOTH Little pretty, because little. Wherefore apt?

ARMADO And therefore apt, because quick.

---

298 lay wager   **goodman** title for someone below the rank of gentleman   **299 idle** worthless (matter for)
302 true honest, chaste, good   **303 prosperity** malapropism for 'adversity'   **304 Affliction** Costard means
'prosperity'   **sit down** i.e. be patient   **1.2**   *Moth* winged insect (puns on the similarly pronounced 'mote' –
i.e. dust speck; possible pun on *mot*, the French for 'word')   **1 sign is it** is it a sign of   **5 imp** sapling/
child   **7 part** distinguish between   **8 tender** youthful, inexperienced   **juvenal** youth (plays on the name of
the Roman satirist, Juvenal)   **9 familiar** easily comprehended   **working** operation (of the emotions)
13 congruent epitheton fitting epithet   **14 appertaining** relating   **15 nominate** name   **16 appertinent**
appropriate   **18 Pretty** neat, ingenious, fine-looking   **21 pretty, because little** proverbial   **23 quick**
quick-witted

MOTH Speak you this in my praise, master?

25   ARMADO In thy condign praise.

MOTH I will praise an eel with the same praise.

ARMADO What, that an eel is ingenious?

MOTH That an eel is quick.

ARMADO I do say thou art quick in answers. Thou heat'st
30   my blood.

MOTH I am answered, sir.

ARMADO I love not to be crossed.

MOTH He speaks the mere contrary: crosses love not him.   *Aside*

ARMADO I have promised to study three years with the
35   duke.

MOTH You may do it in an hour, sir.

ARMADO Impossible.

MOTH How many is one thrice told?

ARMADO I am ill at reckoning. It fits the spirit of a tapster.

40   MOTH You are a gentleman and a gamester, sir.

ARMADO I confess both: they are both the varnish of a
complete man.

MOTH Then I am sure you know how much the
gross sum of deuce-ace amounts to.

45   ARMADO It doth amount to one more than two.

MOTH Which the base vulgar call three.

ARMADO True.

MOTH Why, sir, is this such a piece of study? Now here's
three studied ere you'll thrice wink. And how easy it
50   is to put 'years' to the word 'three', and study three
years in two words, the dancing horse will tell you.

ARMADO A most fine figure!

MOTH To prove you a cipher.   *Aside*

ARMADO I will hereupon confess I am in love. And as it is
55   base for a soldier to love, so am I in love with a base
wench. If drawing my sword against the humour of
affection would deliver me from the reprobate thought
of it, I would take desire prisoner, and ransom him to
any French courtier for a new-devised curtsy. I think

---

25 condign well-deserved   **28 quick** speedy   **29 heat'st my blood** make me angry   **32 crossed**
contradicted   **33 mere** absolute   **crosses** coins (sometimes stamped with a cross)   **35 duke** i.e. the king
38 told counted   **39 ill** not good   **reckoning** calculation   **tapster** barman, tavern-keeper   **40 gamester**
gambler/merry person/lewd person   **42 complete** accomplished   **44 deuce-ace** a (poor) throw of two
and one in dice   **46 vulgar** common people   **48 piece** masterpiece/example   **51 dancing horse** probably
refers to Morocco, a trained horse performing in 1590s London that could beat out numbers with its hoof
52 figure figure of speech/numeral   **53 cipher** zero   **55 base** unbefitting (sense then shifts to 'low-born')
56 humour of affection disposition to love   **57 reprobate** corrupt   **59 new-devised curtsy** newly
invented (fashionable) bow   **think scorn** disdain

60 scorn to sigh: methinks I should outswear Cupid.
    Comfort me, boy. What great men have been in love?
    MOTH Hercules, master.
    ARMADO Most sweet Hercules! More authority, dear
    boy, name more; and, sweet my child, let them be
65 men of good repute and carriage.
    MOTH Samson, master. He was a man of good carriage,
    great carriage, for he carried the town-gates on his
    back like a porter, and he was in love.
    ARMADO O well-knit Samson, strong-jointed Samson! I
70 do excel thee in my rapier as much as thou didst me
    in carrying gates. I am in love too. Who was
    Samson's love, my dear Moth?
    MOTH A woman, master.
    ARMADO Of what complexion?
75 **MOTH** Of all the four, or the three, or the two, or one of
    the four.
    ARMADO Tell me precisely of what complexion.
    MOTH Of the sea-water green, sir.
    ARMADO Is that one of the four complexions?
80 **MOTH** As I have read, sir, and the best of them too.
    ARMADO Green indeed is the colour of lovers, but to have
    a love of that colour, methinks Samson had small
    reason for it. He surely affected her for her wit.
    MOTH It was so, sir, for she had a green wit.
85 **ARMADO** My love is most immaculate white and red.
    MOTH Most maculate thoughts, master, are masked
    under such colours.
    ARMADO Define, define, well-educated infant.
    MOTH My father's wit and my mother's tongue assist me!
90 **ARMADO** Sweet invocation of a child, most pretty and
    pathetical!
    MOTH If she be made of white and red,
        Her faults will ne'er be known,

---

60 **outswear** overcome by swearing/swear to do without   **Cupid** Roman god of love   **62 Hercules**
mythological Greek hero   **65 carriage** demeanour/bearing   **66 Samson** famously strong biblical character
carriage plays on the sense of 'carrying ability'   **67 he … porter** Samson carried off the gates of Gaza
(Judges 16:3)   **69 well-knit** well-constructed   **70 rapier** long, thin sword   **74 complexion** disposition/
skin colour   **75 Of … four** refers to the four humours (blood, phlegm, choler and melancholy) thought to
determine temperament   **78 sea-water green** refers to green-sickness, an anaemic condition affecting
young women   **81 Green** i.e. because associated with spring and youthfulness   **83 affected** loved   **wit**
intelligence   **84 green** immature   **86 maculate** spotted, polluted   **87 colours** plays on sense of 'pretexts'
88 Define explain   **91 pathetical** moving   **92 she … of** her complexion is (**made** puns on 'maid' as well
as possibly suggesting cosmetic artifice)

For blushing cheeks by faults are bred
95 And fears by pale white shown.
Then if she fear, or be to blame,
By this you shall not know,
For still her cheeks possess the same
Which native she doth owe.

100 A dangerous rhyme, master, against the reason of
white and red.

ARMADO Is there not a ballad, boy, of the King and the
Beggar?

MOTH The world was very guilty of such a ballad some
105 three ages since, but I think now 'tis not to be found, or,
if it were, it would neither serve for the writing nor
the tune.

ARMADO I will have that subject newly writ o'er, that I
may example my digression by some mighty precedent.
110 Boy, I do love that country girl that I took in the park
with the rational hind Costard. She deserves well.

MOTH To be whipped: and yet a better love than my   *Aside*
master.

ARMADO Sing, boy. My spirit grows heavy in love.

115 MOTH And that's great marvel, loving a light wench.   *Aside*

ARMADO I say sing.

MOTH Forbear till this company be past.

Enter [Costard, the] Clown, [Dull, the] Constable and
[Jaquenetta, a] wench

DULL Sir, the duke's pleasure is that you keep Costard
safe: and you must let him take no delight nor no
120 penance, but he must fast three days a week. For
this damsel, I must keep her at the park: she is
allowed for the dey-woman. Fare you well.   *Exit*

ARMADO I do betray myself with blushing.— Maid!   *Aside*

JAQUENETTA Man?

125 ARMADO I will visit thee at the lodge.

JAQUENETTA That's hereby.

ARMADO I know where it is situate.

JAQUENETTA Lord, how wise you are!

---

97 this i.e. her complexion   98 still always   99 native naturally   owe own   100 A … red i.e. a warning against real or cosmetic red and white complexions; plays on the familiar opposition between rhyme and reason   102 ballad … Beggar probably that relating the tale of King Cophetua who fell in love with a beggar maid   105 ages since generations ago   106 serve be acceptable   109 example justify/provide an example of   digression transgression   111 rational hind rustic capable of reason   112 whipped a punishment for prostitutes   yet yet she deserves   114 heavy sad   115 light not heavy/promiscuous   *Clown* rustic120 penance malapropism for 'pleasure'   For as for   122 for the dey-woman to serve the dairy woman   125 lodge hunting lodge/gamekeeper's cottage   126 hereby nearby

ARMADO I will tell thee wonders.

130 JAQUENETTA With that face?

ARMADO I love thee.

JAQUENETTA So I heard you say.

ARMADO And so farewell.

JAQUENETTA Fair weather after you.

135 COSTARD Come, Jaquenetta, away.   *Exit [Jaquenetta]*

ARMADO Villain, thou shalt fast for thy offences ere thou
be pardoned.

COSTARD Well, sir, I hope, when I do it, I shall do it on a
full stomach.

140 ARMADO Thou shalt be heavily punished.

COSTARD I am more bound to you than your fellows,
for they are but lightly rewarded.

ARMADO Take away this villain. Shut him up.   *To Moth*

MOTH Come, you transgressing slave, away!

145 COSTARD Let me not be pent up, sir, I will fast being loose.

MOTH No, sir, that were fast and loose. Thou shalt to
prison.

COSTARD Well, if ever I do see the merry days of
desolation that I have seen, some shall see—

150 MOTH What shall some see?

COSTARD Nay, nothing, Master Moth, but what they
look upon. It is not for prisoners to be too silent in
their words and therefore I will say nothing. I thank
God I have as little patience as another man and

155 therefore I can be quiet.

[Exeunt Moth and Costard]

ARMADO I do affect the very ground, which is base, where
her shoe, which is baser, guided by her foot, which is
basest, doth tread. I shall be forsworn, which is a great
argument of falsehood, if I love. And how can that be

160 true love which is falsely attempted? Love is a familiar,
love is a devil. There is no evil angel but love. Yet
Samson was so tempted, and he had an excellent
strength. Yet was Solomon so seduced, and he had a
very good wit. Cupid's butt-shaft is too hard for

130 **With that face?** i.e. Really?/You don't say? (**tell** may pun on the sense of 'count', so that the **face** would be that of a clock)   136 **Villain** rascal/peasant/servant   138 **on … stomach** full of food/courageously   141 **bound** obliged   **fellows** servants   142 **but lightly** little (plays on opposite of **heavily**)   145 **pent up** imprisoned/constipated   **loose** free/loose in the bowels   146 **fast and loose** cheating   **shalt to** shall go to   149 **desolation** malapropism, perhaps for 'consolation'   152 **silent** perhaps an error for 'free'   154 **little** error for 'much' (or **patience** is an error for its opposite)   156 **affect** love   158 **be forsworn** break my oath   159 **argument** proof   160 **familiar** attendant evil spirit   163 **Solomon** biblical king known for his wisdom and love of women   164 **butt-shaft** unbarbed arrow used for target practice

165 Hercules' club, and therefore too much odds for a
Spaniard's rapier. The first and second cause will not
serve my turn. The *passado* he respects not, the *duello*
he regards not. His disgrace is to be called boy, but his
glory is to subdue men. Adieu, valour: rust, rapier: be
170 still, drum, for your manager is in love; yea, he loveth.
Assist me, some extemporal god of rhyme, for I am sure
I shall turn sonnet. Devise, wit: write, pen, for I am for
whole volumes in folio.   *Exit*

Act 2 [Scene 1]   *running scene 2*

Enter the Princess of France with three attending Ladies
[Rosaline, Maria and Katherine] and three Lords [Boyet and
two others]

BOYET Now, madam, summon up your dearest spirits.
Consider who the king your father sends,
To whom he sends, and what's his embassy:
Yourself, held precious in the world's esteem,
5 To parley with the sole inheritor
Of all perfections that a man may owe,
Matchless Navarre, the plea of no less weight
Than Aquitaine, a dowry for a queen.
Be now as prodigal of all dear grace
10 As Nature was in making graces dear
When she did starve the general world beside
And prodigally gave them all to you.
PRINCESS Good Lord Boyet, my beauty, though but mean,
Needs not the painted flourish of your praise.
15 Beauty is bought by judgement of the eye,
Not uttered by base sale of chapmen's tongues:
I am less proud to hear you tell my worth
Than you much willing to be counted wise
In spending your wit in the praise of mine.

165 **too much odds** at too great an advantage   166 **first … cause** refers to the codes of duelling
practice   167 **turn** purpose   *passado* forward thrust with one foot advanced   *duello* established duelling
code   170 **manager** master/user   171 **extemporal … rhyme** god of improvised poetry   172 **turn sonnet**
become a sonneteer   **for** for producing   173 **folio** large-format book   2.1 *Princess of France* possible
parallel in Marguerite de Valois, who married Henri of Navarre   1 **dearest** most valuable/strongest
spirits energies/thoughts   3 **embassy** message   5 **parley** speak/negotiate   **inheritor** owner   6 **owe**
own   7 **Matchless** unrivalled (may pun on the king's unmarried status)   **plea** claim   9 **prodigal of** lavish
with   **dear** precious, beloved   10 **dear** costly   11 **starve** i.e. deprive of   **graces**   **beside** i.e. apart from
yourself   13 **mean** meagre/moderate   16 **uttered** offered for sale/spoken   **chapmen's** merchants'/
pedlars'   17 **tell** speak of/reckon up   18 **much** greatly   **counted** accounted   19 **spending** wasting/
paying out

20   But now to task the tasker. Good Boyet,
        You are not ignorant all-telling fame
        Doth noise abroad Navarre hath made a vow,
        Till painful study shall outwear three years,
        No woman may approach his silent court:
25   Therefore to's seemeth it a needful course,
        Before we enter his forbidden gates,
        To know his pleasure, and in that behalf,
        Bold of your worthiness, we single you
        As our best-moving fair solicitor.
30   Tell him the daughter of the King of France,
        On serious business craving quick dispatch,
        Importunes personal conference with his grace.
        Haste, signify so much, while we attend,
        Like humble-visaged suitors, his high will.
35 **BOYET** Proud of employment, willingly I go.   *Exit*
    PRINCESS All pride is willing pride, and yours is so.
        Who are the votaries, my loving lords,
        That are vow-fellows with this virtuous duke?
    A LORD Longaville is one.
40 **PRINCESS** Know you the man?
    MARIA I know him, madam: at a marriage-feast
        Between Lord Perigort and the beauteous heir
        Of Jaques Falconbridge, solemnized
        In Normandy, saw I this Longaville.
45   A man of sovereign parts he is esteemed,
        Well fitted in arts, glorious in arms.
        Nothing becomes him ill that he would well.
        The only soil of his fair virtue's gloss,
        If virtue's gloss will stain with any soil,
50   Is a sharp wit matched with too blunt a will,
        Whose edge hath power to cut, whose will still wills
        It should none spare that come within his power.
    PRINCESS Some merry mocking lord, belike: is't so?
    MARIA They say so most that most his humours know.

20 **task** set a task for/take to task   **tasker** he who sets a task   21 **ignorant** unaware that   **fame**
rumour   22 **noise abroad** broadcast   23 **painful** laborious/diligent   25 **to's seemeth it** it seems to us
needful necessary   27 **pleasure** wishes   **that behalf** regard to that   28 **Bold** confident   **single** select
29 **best-moving** most persuasive   **fair** just/plausible/flattering   **solicitor** advocate   32 **Importunes** begs
for   **conference** conversation   33 **attend** wait   35 **Proud of** honoured by   **willingly** puns on will in the
previous line   36 **pride** the princess shifts the sense to 'arrogance, vanity'   37 **votaries** those bound by a
vow   42 **Perigort** Perigord is a district in south-west France   **heir** heiress   44 **Normandy** region of
northern France   45 **sovereign parts** excellent qualities   46 **fitted** equipped   **arts** scholarship   **arms**
warfare   47 **Nothing … well** whatever he wants to do well he does well, and it suits him   48 **soil**
blemish   **gloss** lustre   50 **blunt a will** i.e. unfeeling readiness to use his wit   51 **still** continually   52 **his**
its   53 **belike** most likely   54 **humours** moods

55   PRINCESS Such short-lived wits do wither as they grow.
        Who are the rest?
     KATHERINE The young Dumaine, a well-accomplished
           youth,
        Of all that virtue love for virtue loved:
        Most power to do most harm, least knowing ill,
60   For he hath wit to make an ill shape good,
        And shape to win grace though he had no wit.
        I saw him at the Duke Alençon's once,
        And much too little of that good I saw
        Is my report to his great worthiness.
65   ROSALINE Another of these students at that time
        Was there with him, if I have heard a truth.
        Berowne they call him, but a merrier man,
        Within the limit of becoming mirth,
        I never spent an hour's talk withal.
70   His eye begets occasion for his wit,
        For every object that the one doth catch,
        The other turns to a mirth-moving jest,
        Which his fair tongue, conceit's expositor,
        Delivers in such apt and gracious words
75   That agèd ears play truant at his tales
        And younger hearings are quite ravishèd,
        So sweet and voluble is his discourse.
     PRINCESS God bless my ladies! Are they all in love,
        That every one her own hath garnishèd
80   With such bedecking ornaments of praise?
     MARIA Here comes Boyet.
     Enter Boyet
     PRINCESS Now, what admittance, lord?
     BOYET Navarre had notice of your fair approach,
        And he and his competitors in oath
85   Were all addressed to meet you, gentle lady,
        Before I came. Marry, thus much I have learned:
        He rather means to lodge you in the field,
        Like one that comes here to besiege his court,

---

58 Of by   **for virtue** for his virtue   **59 least knowing ill** though he is ignorant of evil   **60 wit ... good** such intelligence that he could make something bad seem good   **61 shape** the appearance   **though** even if   **62 Duke Alençon** King Henri III of France's younger brother, who unsuccessfully courted Queen Elizabeth around 1580   **63 much ... worthiness** my report of him is inadequate compared to the worth I saw in him   **68 becoming** appropriate   **69 withal** with   **70 begets** creates   **occasion** opportunities   **71 catch** i.e. see   **72 mirth-moving** laughter-provoking   **73 conceit's expositor** the expounder of witty ideas   **75 play truant at** abandon their duties in order to listen to   **77 voluble** fluent   **80 bedecking** adorning   **82 admittance** reception   **84 competitors** partners/rivals   **85 addressed** prepared   **87 lodge** entertain/encamp   **field** open land/battleground

Than seek a dispensation for his oath
90   To let you enter his unpeopled house.
Here comes Navarre.

Enter [the King of] Navarre, Longaville, Dumaine, Berowne
[and Attendants]

KING Fair princess, welcome to the court of Navarre.
PRINCESS 'Fair' I give you back again, and 'welcome' I
    have not yet: the roof of this court is too high to be
95   yours, and welcome to the wide fields too base to be
    mine.
KING You shall be welcome, madam, to my court.
PRINCESS I will be welcome, then. Conduct me thither.
KING Hear me, dear lady: I have sworn an oath.
100   **PRINCESS** Our Lady help my lord! He'll be forsworn.
KING Not for the world, fair madam, by my will.
PRINCESS Why, will shall break it: will, and nothing else.
KING Your ladyship is ignorant what it is.
PRINCESS Were my lord so, his ignorance were wise,
105   Where now his knowledge must prove ignorance.
    I hear your grace hath sworn out house-keeping.
    'Tis deadly sin to keep that oath, my lord,
    And sin to break it.
    But pardon me. I am too sudden-bold:
110   To teach a teacher ill beseemeth me.
    Vouchsafe to read the purpose of my coming,   *Gives a paper*
    And suddenly resolve me in my suit.
KING Madam, I will, if suddenly I may.   *Reads*
PRINCESS You will the sooner that I were away,
115   For you'll prove perjured if you make me stay.
BEROWNE Did not I dance with you in Brabant once?   *To Rosaline*
ROSALINE Did not I dance with you in Brabant once?
BEROWNE I know you did.
ROSALINE How needless was it then to ask the question!
120   **BEROWNE** You must not be so quick.
ROSALINE 'Tis long of you that spur me with such
        questions.
BEROWNE Your wit's too hot, it speeds too fast, 'twill tire.
ROSALINE Not till it leave the rider in the mire.
BEROWNE What time o'day?

---

90 **unpeopled** inadequately staffed   94 **roof . . . court** i.e. the sky   101 **by my will** willingly   102 **will** desire   105 **Where** whereas   106 **sworn out house-keeping** renounced hospitality   110 **beseemeth** suits   111 **Vouchsafe** agree   112 **suddenly** immediately   **resolve . . . suit** answer my request   114 **that . . . away** in order to make me leave   116 **Brabant** in the Low Countries   120 **quick** impatient, sharp   121 **long** on account   122 **hot** eager, hasty   123 **mire** bog   124 **time o'day** time is it

125 ROSALINE The hour that fools should ask.
BEROWNE Now fair befall your mask.
ROSALINE Fair fall the face it covers.
BEROWNE And send you many lovers.
ROSALINE Amen, so you be none.
130 BEROWNE Nay, then will I be gone.   *Walks away*
KING Madam, your father here doth intimate   *To the Princess*
    The payment of a hundred thousand crowns,
    Being but th'one half of an entire sum
    Disbursèd by my father in his wars.
135   But say that he or we, as neither have,
    Received that sum, yet there remains unpaid
    A hundred thousand more, in surety of the which,
    One part of Aquitaine is bound to us,
    Although not valued to the money's worth.
140   If then the king your father will restore
    But that one half which is unsatisfied,
    We will give up our right in Aquitaine
    And hold fair friendship with his majesty.
    But that, it seems, he little purposeth,
145   For here he doth demand to have repaid
    An hundred thousand crowns, and not demands,
    On payment of a hundred thousand crowns,
    To have his title live in Aquitaine,
    Which we much rather had depart withal,
150   And have the money by our father lent,
    Than Aquitaine, so gelded as it is.
    Dear princess, were not his requests so far
    From reason's yielding, your fair self should make
    A yielding gainst some reason in my breast
155   And go well satisfied to France again.
PRINCESS You do the king my father too much wrong
    And wrong the reputation of your name,
    In so unseeming to confess receipt
    Of that which hath so faithfully been paid.

---

126 **mask** worn by ladies to protect the complexion from the sun 127 **fall** befall 129 **so** provided that
131 **intimate** refer to/imply 134 **Disbursèd** paid out **his** i.e. the King of France's 135 **he** Navarre's
father **as neither have** which neither of us has 137 **in surety** as guarantee 138 **bound** contracted
139 **valued to** of the same value as 140 **restore** repay 141 **unsatisfied** unpaid 144 **little purposeth**
scarcely intends 145 **demand ... repaid** legally claims back/insists he has already paid 146 **not ...
crowns** does not even request, on payment of the rest of the money 148 **have ... in** regain his entitlement
to 149 **depart withal** part with 151 **gelded** weakened (literally, castrated) 154 **A ... reason** me
compromise even against reason 158 **unseeming** not seeming

160 **KING** I do protest I never heard of it.
    And if you prove it, I'll repay it back
    Or yield up Aquitaine.

PRINCESS We arrest your word.
    Boyet, you can produce acquittances

165 For such a sum from special officers
    Of Charles, his father.

KING Satisfy me so.

BOYET So please your grace, the packet is not come
    Where that and other specialties are bound.

170 Tomorrow you shall have a sight of them.

KING It shall suffice me; at which interview,
    All liberal reason would I yield unto.
    Meantime receive such welcome at my hand
    As honour without breach of honour may

175 Make tender of to thy true worthiness.
    You may not come, fair princess, in my gates,
    But here without you shall be so received
    As you shall deem yourself lodged in my heart,
    Though so denied fair harbour in my house.

180 Your own good thoughts excuse me, and farewell:
    Tomorrow we shall visit you again.

PRINCESS Sweet health and fair desires consort your
        grace.

KING Thy own wish wish I thee in every place!
            Exit [the King, with Longaville and Dumaine]

BEROWNE Lady, I will commend you to my own heart.

185 **ROSALINE** Pray you, do my commendations, I would be
        glad to see it.

BEROWNE I would you heard it groan.

ROSALINE Is the fool sick?

BEROWNE Sick at the heart.

190 **ROSALINE** Alack, let it blood.

BEROWNE Would that do it good?

ROSALINE My physic says 'ay'.

BEROWNE Will you prick't with your eye?

ROSALINE *Non point*, with my knife.

195 **BEROWNE** Now, God save thy life!

---

163 arrest take you at   **word** utterance/promise   **164 acquittances** documents confirming payment of a debt   **166 his** i.e. the King of Navarre's   **167 Satisfy me so** provide me with this   **169 specialties** sealed contracts   **172 liberal reason** reasonable terms   **174 breach of honour** i.e. breaking the oath **175 Make tender of** offer   **177 without** outside   **178 As** that   **180 Your** may your   **182 consort** attend **183 Thy ... place!** I wish you the same wherever you may be!   **185 do my commendations** give it my greetings   **188 fool** poor thing   **190 let it blood** bleed it   **192 physic** medical knowledge   **193 eye** gaze (puns on **ay**)   **194 *Non point*** 'not at all' (French), perhaps also suggesting 'no penis' (picking up on **prick**)

ROSALINE And yours from long living!

BEROWNE I cannot stay thanksgiving.   *Exit*

Enter Dumaine

DUMAINE Sir, I pray you a word: what lady is that same?   *To Boyet*

BOYET The heir of Alençon, Katherine her name.

200 **DUMAINE** A gallant lady. Monsieur, fare you well. [*Exit*]

[*Enter Longaville*]

LONGAVILLE I beseech you a word: what is she in the   *To Boyet*
    white?

BOYET A woman sometimes, if you saw her in the light.

LONGAVILLE Perchance light in the light. I desire her

205   name.

BOYET She hath but one for herself, to desire that were a
    shame.

LONGAVILLE Pray you, sir, whose daughter?

BOYET Her mother's, I have heard.

210 **LONGAVILLE** God's blessing o'your beard!

BOYET Good sir, be not offended.
    She is an heir of Falconbridge.

LONGAVILLE Nay, my choler is ended.
    She is a most sweet lady.   *Exit Longaville*

215 **BOYET** Not unlike, sir, that may be.

Enter Berowne

BEROWNE What's her name in the cap?

BOYET Rosaline, by good hap.

BEROWNE Is she wedded or no?

BOYET To her will, sir, or so.

220 **BEROWNE** You are welcome, sir. Adieu.

BOYET Farewell to me, sir, and welcome to you.

                                Exit [Berowne]

MARIA That last is Berowne, the merry madcap lord.
    Not a word with him but a jest.

BOYET And every jest but a word.

225 **PRINCESS** It was well done of you to take him at his word.

BOYET I was as willing to grapple as he was to board.

MARIA Two hot sheeps, marry.

---

197 **stay thanksgiving** remain to express thanks   199 **Katherine** Shakespeare confused the names and
wrote 'Rosaline' here: editors and directors must emend for clarity of coupling   200 **gallant** fine-looking
204 **light ... light** wanton when her behaviour is known   206 **desire** want to have   213 **choler** anger
215 **unlike** unlikely   217 **Rosaline** Shakespeare confused the names and wrote 'Katherine' here: editors
and directors must emend for clarity of coupling   **hap** chance, fortune   219 **so** something like that
221 **welcome to you** you are welcome to go   225 **take ... word** accept what he says/take him on at his
own word-games   226 **grapple** contend with, seize (literally, attach one's ship to another vessel)   **board**
accost (literally, climb aboard another ship)   227 **hot** fiery, ardent   **sheeps** puns on **ships**

BOYET And wherefore not 'ships'?
No sheep, sweet lamb, unless we feed on your lips.
230 MARIA You sheep, and I pasture. Shall that finish the jest?
BOYET So you grant pasture for me.   *Tries to kiss her*
MARIA Not so, gentle beast.
My lips are no common, though several they be.
BOYET Belonging to whom?
235 MARIA To my fortunes and me.
PRINCESS Good wits will be jangling; but, gentles, agree.
This civil war of wits were much better used
On Navarre and his bookmen, for here 'tis abused.
BOYET If my observation — which very seldom lies
240 By the heart's still rhetoric disclosèd with eyes —
Deceive me not now, Navarre is infected.
PRINCESS With what?
BOYET With that which we lovers entitle affected.
PRINCESS Your reason?
245 BOYET Why, all his behaviours did make their retire
To the court of his eye, peeping thorough desire.
His heart, like an agate, with your print impressed,
Proud with his form, in his eye pride expressed.
His tongue, all impatient to speak and not see,
250 Did stumble with haste in his eyesight to be.
All senses to that sense did make their repair,
To feel only looking on fairest of fair.
Methought all his senses were locked in his eye,
As jewels in crystal for some prince to buy,
255 Who, tend'ring their own worth from whence they
were glassed,
Did point out to buy them along as you passed.
His face's own margin did quote such amazes
That all eyes saw his eyes enchanted with gazes.
I'll give you Aquitaine, and all that is his,
260 An you give him for my sake but one loving kiss.

---

230 **pasture** puns on 'pastor' (i.e. shepherd)   231 **So** as long as   233 **common** common ground (available to all sheep/men)   **several** private land/more than one/parted   236 **jangling** squabbling   **gentles** gentlefolk   237 **civil** domestic/polite   238 **bookmen** scholars   **abused** misapplied   240 **By** about   **still** silent   243 **affected** being in love   245 **did . . . retire** retreated   246 **court** royal dwelling (puns on sense of 'courtship')   **thorough** through   247 **agate** precious stone often carved with tiny figures   **print** image **impressed** stamped/affected   248 **Proud** made proud/swollen   **his form** i.e. the princess' image   249 **all . . . see** frustrated at only being able to speak rather than gaze   251 **that sense** i.e. eyesight   **make their repair** go   254 **crystal** under crystal glass   255 **Who, tend'ring** which, offering   **glassed** encased in glass   256 **point** direct, invite   257 **margin** i.e. like that of a page, which often carried additional notes   **quote** display   260 **An** if

PRINCESS Come to our pavilion. Boyet is disposed.

BOYET But to speak that in words which his eye hath
disposed.

I only have made a mouth of his eye,

By adding a tongue which I know will not lie.

265 **ROSALINE** Thou art an old love-monger and speakest
skilfully.

MARIA He is Cupid's grandfather and learns news of him.

KATHERINE Then was Venus like her mother, for her
father is but grim.

270 **BOYET** Do you hear, my mad wenches?

MARIA No.

BOYET What then, do you see?

KATHERINE Ay, our way to be gone.

BOYET You are too hard for me.   *Exeunt*

Act 3 [Scene 1]   *running scene 3*

Enter Braggart [Armado] and [his] Boy [Moth, singing a] song

ARMADO Warble, child, make passionate my sense of
hearing.

MOTH Concolinel.   *Sings*

ARMADO Sweet air! Go, tenderness of years, take this key,

5   give enlargement to the swain, bring him festinately
hither. I must employ him in a letter to my love.

MOTH Master, will you win your love with a French brawl?

ARMADO How meanest thou? Brawling in French?

MOTH No, my complete master: but to jig off a tune at the

10   tongue's end, canary to it with your feet, humour it
with turning up your eyelids, sigh a note and sing a
note, sometime through the throat, if you swallowed
love with singing love, sometime through the nose as if
you snuffed up love by smelling love, with your hat

15   penthouse-like o'er the shop of your eyes, with your
arms crossed on your thin-belly doublet like a rabbit on
a spit, or your hands in your pocket like a man after

---

261 pavilion ceremonial tent   **disposed** inclined (to be merry)   **262 But** only   **268 Venus** goddess of
love, mother of Cupid   **father** i.e. Boyet, as **Cupid's grandfather**   **269 grim** ugly   **270 mad** excitable
274 hard tough (to outwit)   **3.1   3 Concolinel** presumably the title of Moth's song, perhaps of Irish or
French origin   **4 air** tune   **5 enlargement** freedom   **festinately** speedily   **7 brawl** French dance
8 Brawling quarrelling   **9 jig . . . tune** sing the tune of a jig   **10 canary** i.e. dance (name of a lively dance)
humour adapt (yourself) to/indulge   **15 penthouse-like** like a roof projecting over a **shop**   **16 thin-belly
doublet** unpadded lower part of a close-fitting jacket   **17 after** in the style of

the old painting, and keep not too long in one tune, but
a snip and away. These are compliments, these are
20   humours, these betray nice wenches that would be
betrayed without these and make them men of note —
do you note, men? — that most are affected to these.

ARMADO How hast thou purchased this experience?

MOTH By my penny of observation.

25   **ARMADO** But O, but O—

MOTH 'The hobby-horse is forgot.'

ARMADO Callest thou my love 'hobby-horse'?

MOTH No, master. The hobby-horse is but a colt, and your
love perhaps, a hackney. But have you forgot your
30   love?

ARMADO Almost I had.

MOTH Negligent student! Learn her by heart.

ARMADO By heart and in heart, boy.

MOTH And out of heart, master: all those three I will prove.

35   **ARMADO** What wilt thou prove?

MOTH A man, if I live, and this, 'by', 'in', and 'without',
upon the instant: 'by' heart you love her, because your
heart cannot come by her. 'In' heart you love her,
because your heart is in love with her. And 'out' of
40   heart you love her, being out of heart that you cannot
enjoy her.

ARMADO I am all these three.

MOTH And three times as much more, and yet nothing at
all.

45   **ARMADO** Fetch hither the swain. He must carry me a
letter.

MOTH A message well sympathized: a horse to be
ambassador for an ass.

ARMADO Ha, ha, what sayest thou?

50   **MOTH** Marry, sir, you must send the ass upon the horse,
for he is very slow-gaited. But I go.

ARMADO The way is but short. Away!

MOTH As swift as lead, sir.

---

19 snip and away snatch before moving on to the next   **compliments** gentlemanly accomplishments
20 humours whims   **betray** seduce/mislead   **nice** coy/capricious/lecherous   **21 note** reputation (plays
on the sense of 'musical note')   **22 note** pay attention   **men** possibly addressed to the men in the
audience   **affected** inclined   **23 purchased** acquired   **26 'The ... forgot'** probably lines from a popular
song, now lost   **hobby-horse** false or toy horse/prostitute   **28 colt** young horse/lascivious person
29 hackney horse for hire/whore   **34 prove** demonstrate (sense then shifts to 'turn out to be')   **38 come
by** possess   **40 out of heart** discouraged   **45 me** for me   **47 sympathized** suited   **51 slow-gaited** slow-
moving

ARMADO Thy meaning, pretty ingenious? Is not lead a
55   metal heavy, dull and slow?

MOTH *Minime*, honest master, or rather, master, no.

ARMADO I say lead is slow.

MOTH You are too swift, sir, to say so.
        Is that lead slow which is fired from a gun?

60 **ARMADO** Sweet smoke of rhetoric!
        He reputes me a cannon; and the bullet, that's he.
        I shoot thee at the swain.

MOTH Thump then, and I flee.   [*Exit*]

ARMADO A most acute juvenal, voluble and free of grace!
65   By thy favour, sweet welkin, I must sigh in thy face.
        Most rude melancholy, valour gives thee place.
        My herald is returned.

Enter Page [*Moth*] *and Clown* [*Costard*]

MOTH A wonder, master! Here's a costard broken in a
        shin.

70 **ARMADO** Some enigma, some riddle: come, thy l'envoy,
        begin.

COSTARD No egma, no riddle, no l'envoy, no salve in the
        mail, sir. O, sir, plantain, a plain plantain! No l'envoy,
        no l'envoy, no salve, sir, but a plantain!

75 **ARMADO** By virtue, thou enforcest laughter: thy silly
        thought, my spleen. The heaving of my lungs
        provokes me to ridiculous smiling. O, pardon me,
        my stars! Doth the inconsiderate take *salve* for
        l'envoy, and the word 'l'envoy' for a salve?

80 **MOTH** Do the wise think them other? Is not l'envoy a
        salve?

ARMADO No, page: it is an epilogue or discourse, to make
        plain
        Some obscure precedence that hath tofore been sain.
        Now will I begin your moral, and do you follow with
        my l'envoy:

85   The fox, the ape, and the humble-bee
        Were still at odds, being but three.

---

54 ingenious clever one   **56** *Minime* 'by no means' (Latin)   **63 Thump** i.e. noise of a **cannon** going
off   **64 acute** clever   **free of grace** liberal with charm   **65 welkin** sky, heaven   **66 gives thee place**
yields its place to you   **68 costard** apple/head   **70 l'envoy** postscript (i.e. explanation)   **72 egma**
Costard's mistake for 'enigma' (which he seems to think, along with **riddle** and **l'envoy**, means some type of
remedy)   **salve** healing ointment   **73 mail** (medicine) bag   **plantain** medicinal herb   **75 By virtue** mild
oath   **silly** foolish   **76 spleen** laughter   **77 ridiculous** derisive   **78 inconsiderate** thoughtless, idiotic
person   *salve* Latin for 'hail, greetings' (the opposite of **l'envoy**)   **83 precedence** something said before
tofore earlier   **sain** said   **85 humble-bee** bumble-bee   **86 still** always   **at odds** quarrelling/of an
uneven number

Until the goose came out of door,
Staying the odds by adding four.

MOTH A good l'envoy, ending in the goose. Would you
90   desire more?

COSTARD The boy hath sold him a bargain, a goose, that's
flat.

Sir, your pennyworth is good, an your goose be fat.
To sell a bargain well is as cunning as fast and loose.
Let me see: a fat l'envoy — ay, that's a fat goose.

95   **ARMADO** Come hither, come hither. How did this
argument begin?

MOTH By saying that a costard was broken in a shin.
Then called you for the l'envoy.

COSTARD True, and I for a plantain: thus came your
argument in.

100   Then the boy's fat l'envoy, the goose that you bought,
And he ended the market.

ARMADO But tell me, how was there a costard broken in
a shin?

MOTH I will tell you sensibly.

105   **COSTARD** Thou hast no feeling of it, Moth. I will speak that
l'envoy:

I Costard, running out, that was safely within,
Fell over the threshold and broke my shin.

ARMADO We will talk no more of this matter.

COSTARD Till there be more matter in the shin.

110   **ARMADO** Sirrah Costard, I will enfranchise thee.

COSTARD O, marry me to one Frances: I smell some
l'envoy, some goose in this.

ARMADO By my sweet soul, I mean setting thee at liberty,
enfreedoming thy person. Thou wert immured,
115   restrained, captivated, bound.

COSTARD True, true, and now you will be my purgation
and let me loose.

ARMADO I give thee thy liberty, set thee from durance, and
in lieu thereof impose on thee nothing but this: bear   *Gives a*
120   this significant to the country maid Jaquenetta.   *letter*

---

88 Staying the odds ending the quarrel/making the number even   **adding four** making up the fourth
89 l'envoy ... goose *oie* is French for 'goose' and the final sound of **envoy**   **91 sold ... bargain** i.e. made a
fool of him (proverbial)   **flat** obvious   **92 good** i.e. well-spent   **an** if   **93 fast and loose** cheating
96 argument discussion   **101 ended the market** refers to 'Three women and a goose make a market'
(proverbial)   **104 sensibly** with common sense/feelingly   **105 feeling** sense of the pain   **107 threshold**
doorway   **109 matter** pus   **110 enfranchise** liberate (Costard hears as 'en-Frances' – i.e. 'give you a
Frances')   **111 Frances** typical name for a prostitute   **112 goose** prostitute (slang)   **114 immured**
confined   **116 purgation** purger of guilt/laxative   **117 let me loose** free me/loosen my bowels   **118 from
durance** free from imprisonment   **119 lieu** exchange   **120 significant** sign

There is remuneration, for the best ward of mine   *Gives*
honours is rewarding my dependants. Moth, follow.   *money*

[*Exit*]

MOTH Like the sequel, I. Signior Costard, adieu.   *Exit*

COSTARD My sweet ounce of man's flesh, my incony Jew!

125   Now will I look to his remuneration. 'Remuneration'
— O, that's the Latin word for three farthings. Three
farthings — remuneration. 'What's the price of this
inkle?' 'One penny.' 'No, I'll give you a remuneration.'
Why, it carries it. 'Remuneration.' Why, it is a fairer

130   name than French crown. I will never buy and sell out
of this word.

Enter Berowne

BEROWNE O, my good knave Costard, exceedingly well
met.

COSTARD Pray you, sir, how much carnation ribbon

135   may a man buy for a remuneration?

BEROWNE What is a remuneration?

COSTARD Marry, sir, halfpenny farthing.

BEROWNE O, why then three farthings worth of silk.

COSTARD I thank your worship. God be wi'you!   *Starts to leave*

140   **BEROWNE** O, stay, slave, I must employ thee:
As thou wilt win my favour, good my knave,
Do one thing for me that I shall entreat.

COSTARD When would you have it done, sir?

BEROWNE O, this afternoon.

145   **COSTARD** Well, I will do it, sir. Fare you well.

BEROWNE O, thou knowest not what it is.

COSTARD I shall know, sir, when I have done it.

BEROWNE Why, villain, thou must know first.

COSTARD I will come to your worship tomorrow morning.

150   **BEROWNE** It must be done this afternoon.
Hark, slave, it is but this:
The princess comes to hunt here in the park,
And in her train there is a gentle lady,
When tongues speak sweetly, then they name her
name,

---

121 remuneration payment **ward** protection **122 dependants** servants **123 sequel** that which
follows (recalls the **l'envoy** joke) **124 incony** fine **Jew** affectionate term; possible pun on **juvenal** or
diminutive of 'jewel' **126 farthings** coins worth quarter of a penny **128 inkle** kind of linen tape
129 carries it wins the day **130 French crown** coin/bald head caused by syphilis, the 'French disease'
out of without using **134 carnation** flesh-coloured **137 halfpenny farthing** i.e. three farthings, three
quarters of a penny **140 slave** rascal/fellow **141 good my knave** my good fellow **148 villain** rascal/
fellow **153 train** entourage

155 And Rosaline they call her. Ask for her
    And to her white hand see thou do commend   *Gives a letter*
    This sealed-up counsel. There's thy guerdon: go.   *and money*
    COSTARD Gardon, O sweet gardon! Better than remuner-
    ation, a'leven-pence-farthing better. Most sweet gardon!
160 I will do it, sir, in print. Gardon! Remuneration!

                                                         Exit

    BEROWNE O and I, forsooth, in love! I, that have been
        love's whip,
    A very beadle to a humorous sigh,
    A critic, nay, a night-watch constable,
    A domineering pedant o'er the boy,
165 Than whom no mortal so magnificent!
    This wimpled, whining, purblind, wayward boy,
    This Signior Junior, giant-dwarf, Don Cupid,
    Regent of love-rhymes, lord of folded arms,
    Th'anointed sovereign of sighs and groans,
170 Liege of all loiterers and malcontents,
    Dread prince of plackets, king of codpieces,
    Sole imperator and great general
    Of trotting paritors — O my little heart! —
    And I to be a corporal of his field
175 And wear his colours like a tumbler's hoop.
    What? I love, I sue, I seek a wife?
    A woman that is like a German clock,
    Still a-repairing, ever out of frame,
    And never going aright, being a watch,
180 But being watched that it may still go right!
    Nay, to be perjured, which is worst of all,
    And, among three, to love the worst of all;
    A whitely wanton with a velvet brow,
    With two pitch-balls stuck in her face for eyes.
185 Ay, and by heaven, one that will do the deed
    Though Argus were her eunuch and her guard.

---

156 commend entrust   **157 counsel** private communication   **guerdon** reward   **158 Gardon** anglicized version of **guerdon**   **159 better** i.e. the shilling (twelvepence) is eleven and a quarter pence better than his previous reward   **160 in print** to the letter   **162 beadle** parish officer responsible for whipping minor offenders   **humorous** moody   **164 pedant** schoolmaster   **165 Than** compared with   **magnificent** proud   **166 wimpled** blindfolded   **purblind** completely blind   **168 Regent** ruler   **171 Dread** revered   **172 imperator** emperor   **173 paritors** those who summoned offenders to ecclesiastical courts   **174 corporal … field** Cupid's field officer   **175 colours** insignia   **tumbler's hoop** acrobat's ribboned hoop   **176 sue** pay court   **177 German clock** i.e. elaborate, likely to go wrong   **178 Still a-repairing** always in need of repair   **frame** order   **179 going aright** keeping time/behaving well   **180 But being** unless it is   **183 whitely** pale   **wanton** wilful one   **brow** forehead   **184 pitch-balls** balls as black as pitch (tar-like substance)   **185 deed** i.e. sex   **186 Though** even if   **Argus** monster with a hundred eyes   **eunuch** castrated male (i.e. **guard**)

And I to sigh for her, to watch for her,
To pray for her! Go to, it is a plague
That Cupid will impose for my neglect
190   Of his almighty dreadful little might.
Well, I will love, write, sigh, pray, sue and groan.
Some men must love my lady, and some Joan. [*Exit*]

Act 4 [Scene 1]   *running scene 4*

*Enter the Princess, a Forester [with a bow], her Ladies
[Rosaline, Maria and Katherine] and her Lords [Boyet and
others]*

PRINCESS Was that the king that spurred his horse so
          hard
    Against the steep uprising of the hill?
BOYET I know not, but I think it was not he.
PRINCESS Whoe'er a was, a showed a mounting mind.
5   Well, lords, today we shall have our dispatch:
    On Saturday we will return to France.
    Then, forester, my friend, where is the bush
    That we must stand and play the murderer in?
FORESTER Hereby, upon the edge of yonder coppice,
10   A stand where you may make the fairest shoot.
PRINCESS I thank my beauty, I am fair that shoot,
    And thereupon thou speak'st the fairest shoot.
FORESTER Pardon me, madam, for I meant not so.
PRINCESS What, what? First praise me and again say no?
15   O short-lived pride! Not fair? Alack for woe!
FORESTER Yes, madam, fair.
PRINCESS Nay, never paint me now.
    Where fair is not, praise cannot mend the brow.
    Here, good my glass, take this for telling true: *Gives money*
20   Fair payment for foul words is more than due.
FORESTER Nothing but fair is that which you inherit.
PRINCESS See see, my beauty will be saved by merit.
    O heresy in fair, fit for these days!
    A giving hand, though foul, shall have fair praise.

---

187 **watch** be unable to sleep   188 **Go to** expression of impatient dismissal   189 **neglect** disregard
192 **my ... Joan** i.e. a worthy versus a lowly woman   **4.1   4 a was, a** he was, he   **mounting** climbing/
aspiring   5 **dispatch** dismissal   9 **coppice** thicket   10 **stand** hunter's position   12 **fairest** most
favourable/beautiful   14 **again** in response   17 **paint** flatter   18 **fair** beauty   **brow** appearance
19 **good my glass** my good mirror   21 **inherit** possess   22 **merit** its intrinsic worth/reward/good deeds
23 **in fair** regarding beauty   24 **giving ... praise** proverbial: 'the giving hand is fair'

25   But come, the bow. Now mercy goes to kill,   *Takes a bow*
      And shooting well is then accounted ill.
      Thus will I save my credit in the shoot:
      Not wounding, pity would not let me do't.
      If wounding, then it was to show my skill,
30   That more for praise than purpose meant to kill.
      And out of question so it is sometimes,
      Glory grows guilty of detested crimes,
      When for fame's sake, for praise, an outward part,
      We bend to that the working of the heart.
35   As I for praise alone now seek to spill
      The poor deer's blood that my heart means no ill.
BOYET Do not curst wives hold that self-sovereignty
      Only for praise' sake, when they strive to be
      Lords o'er their lords?
40 **PRINCESS** Only for praise, and praise we may afford
      To any lady that subdues a lord.
Enter Clown [Costard, with a letter]
BOYET Here comes a member of the commonwealth.
COSTARD God dig-you-den all! Pray you which is the
      head lady?
45 **PRINCESS** Thou shalt know her, fellow, by the rest that
      have no heads.
COSTARD Which is the greatest lady, the highest?
PRINCESS The thickest and the tallest.
COSTARD The thickest and the tallest. It is so, truth is
      truth.
50   An you waist, mistress, were as slender as my wit,
      One o'these maids' girdles for your waist should be fit.
      Are not you the chief woman? You are the thickest
      here.
PRINCESS What's your will, sir? What's your will?
COSTARD I have a letter from Monsieur Berowne to one
55   Lady Rosaline.
PRINCESS O, thy letter, thy letter! He's a good friend of   *To Rosaline*
      mine.—
      Stand aside, good bearer.— Boyet, you can carve: *Takes the letter*
      Break up this capon.   *and gives it to Boyet*

---

25 mercy i.e. the princess   **26 then** i.e. when the princess hunts, because she is merciful   **27 credit**
reputation   **28 Not ... do't** i.e. if she fails to hit a deer, she can claim it was out of pity   **31 out of**
without   **32 Glory** the desire to for glory/boastful spirit   **33 outward part** superficial attribute   **35 As** just
as   **36 my ... ill** means me no harm/towards whom I do not essentially mean harm   **37 curst** shrewish
self-sovereignty self-discipline   **42 member ... commonwealth** ordinary person   **43 God dig-you-den**
God give you good evening (i.e. any time after noon)   **46 heads** may pun on 'maidenheads'   **48 thickest**
fattest   **57 carve** cut up/make courteous gestures   **58 Break up** cut up   **capon** chicken (i.e. love letter)

BOYET I am bound to serve.

60   This letter is mistook: it importeth none here.
          It is writ to Jaquenetta.

PRINCESS We will read it, I swear.
          Break the neck of the wax, and everyone give ear.

BOYET (*Reads*) 'By heaven, that thou art fair, is most
65   infallible: true that thou art beauteous, truth itself that
     thou art lovely. More fairer than fair, beautiful than
     beauteous, truer than truth itself, have commiseration
     on thy heroical vassal. The magnanimous and most
     illustrate King Cophetua set eye upon the pernicious
70   and indubitate beggar Zenelophon, and he it was that
     might rightly say, *Veni, vidi, vici*, which to annothanize
     in the vulgar, — O base and obscure vulgar! —
     videlicet, he came, see and overcame. He came, one;
     see, two; overcame, three. Who came? The king. Why
75   did he come? To see. Why did he see? To overcome. To
     whom came he? To the beggar. What saw he? The
     beggar. Who overcame he? The beggar. The
     conclusion is victory. On whose side? The king. The
     captive is enriched. On whose side? The beggar's. The
80   catastrophe is a nuptial. On whose side? The king's. No,
     on both in one, or one in both. I am the king, for so
     stands the comparison: thou the beggar, for so
     witnesseth thy lowliness. Shall I command thy love?
     I may. Shall I enforce thy love? I could. Shall I entreat
85   thy love? I will. What shalt thou exchange for rags?
     Robes. For tittles? Titles. For thyself? Me. Thus
     expecting thy reply, I profane my lips on thy foot, my
     eyes on thy picture, and my heart on thy every part.
     Thine, in the dearest design of industry, Don Adriano
90   de Armado.

              Thus dost thou hear the Nemean lion roar
              Gainst thee, thou lamb, that standest as his
                   prey.

---

60 is mistook has been delivered to the wrong person   **importeth** concerns   **63 neck … wax** i.e. wax seal
(recalls wringing the neck of a **capon**)   **give ear** listen   **65 infallible** certain   **67 commiseration** pity
68 vassal servant/slave   **69 illustrate** illustrious, renowned   **pernicious** wicked (possibly Armado's error
for 'penurious')   **70 indubitate** undoubted   **71 Veni, vidi, vici** 'I came, I saw, I conquered' (Latin), Julius
Caesar's famous phrase   **annothanize** explain; perhaps a fusion of 'anatomize' and 'annotate'   **72 vulgar**
vernacular   **73 videlicet** 'namely' (Latin)   **see** saw   **74 overcame** conquered; possibly goes on to assume
sexual connotations   **80 catastrophe** conclusion   **83 lowliness** poverty, low status   **86 tittles** insignificant particles   **87 expecting** awaiting   **profane** desecrate   **88 thy picture** (mental) image   **89 dearest
… industry** most heartfelt intention of industrious gallantry   **91 Nemean lion** slain by Hercules as the first
of his twelve labours

Submissive fall his princely feet before,
And he from forage will incline to play.
95   But if thou strive, poor soul, what art thou
then?
Food for his rage, repasture for his den.'
PRINCESS What plume of feathers is he that indited this
letter?
What vane? What weathercock? Did you ever hear
better?
BOYET I am much deceived but I remember the style.
100   PRINCESS Else your memory is bad, going o'er it erewhile.
BOYET This Armado is a Spaniard that keeps here in court,
A phantasime, a Monarcho, and one that makes sport
To the prince and his book-mates.
PRINCESS Thou fellow, a word.   *To Costard*
105   Who gave thee this letter?
COSTARD I told you: my lord.
PRINCESS To whom shouldst thou give it?
COSTARD From my lord to my lady.
PRINCESS From which lord to which lady?
110   COSTARD From my lord Berowne, a good master of mine,
To a lady of France that he called Rosaline.
PRINCESS Thou hast mistaken his letter.— Come, lords,
away.—
Here, sweet, put up this: 'twill be thine another day.   *To Rosaline*
Exeunt [all but Boyet, Rosaline,
Maria and Costard]
BOYET Who is the shooter? Who is the shooter?
115   ROSALINE Shall I teach you to know?
BOYET Ay, my continent of beauty.
ROSALINE Why, she that bears the bow.
Finely put off!
BOYET My lady goes to kill horns, but if thou marry,
120   Hang me by the neck, if horns that year miscarry.
Finely put on!
ROSALINE Well, then, I am the shooter.

---

93 **Submissive fall** if you fall submissively   94 **forage** hunting   95 **strive** resist   96 **repasture** food
97 **plume of feathers** showy idiot   **indited** composed   98 **vane** weathervane (i.e. changeable)   99 **but I**
if I do not   100 **Else** otherwise   **going o'er** reading/climbing over (generating a pun on **style**/stile)
erewhile a short time ago   101 **keeps** lodges   102 **phantasime** one full of fantasies   **Monarcho**
nickname of a pretentious Italian who frequented the Elizabethan court   103 **To** for   **book-mates** fellow
students   112 **mistaken** wrongly delivered   113 **up** away   **thine** i.e. your turn   114 **shooter** archer, i.e.
who is to shoot next (puns on 'suitor')   116 **continent** container   118 **put off** evaded   119 **horns** i.e.
deer   120 **horns** i.e. cuckold's horns (which supposedly grew on the head of a man with an unfaithful
wife)   **miscarry** are scarce   121 **put on** hit

BOYET And who is your deer?

ROSALINE If we choose by the horns, yourself come not
near.

125   Finely put on indeed!

MARIA You still wrangle with her, Boyet, and she strikes
at the brow.

BOYET But she herself is hit lower: have I hit her now?

ROSALINE Shall I come upon thee with an old saying

130   that was a man when King Pepin of France was a
little boy, as touching the hit it?

BOYET So I may answer thee with one as old, that was a
woman when Queen Guinevere of Britain was a little
wench, as touching the hit it.

135 **ROSALINE** Thou canst not hit it, hit it, hit it,
Thou canst not hit it, my good man.

BOYET I cannot, cannot, cannot,
An I cannot, another can.

Exeunt [Rosaline and Katherine]

COSTARD By my troth, most pleasant: how both did fit it!

140 **MARIA** A mark marvellous well shot, for they both did
hit it.

BOYET A mark! O, mark but that mark! A mark, says my
lady.

Let the mark have a prick in't, to mete at, if it may be.

MARIA Wide o'th'bow hand! I'faith your hand is out.

COSTARD Indeed, a must shoot nearer, or he'll ne'er hit
the clout.

145 **BOYET** An if my hand be out, then belike your hand is in.

COSTARD Then will she get the upshoot by cleaving the
pin.

MARIA Come, come, you talk greasily, your lips grow foul.

COSTARD She's too hard for you at pricks, sir. Challenge
her to bowl.

---

123 deer puns on 'dear'   **124 If … near** i.e. not you; Rosaline dismisses Boyet either because he has a
cuckold's horns or lacks the (suggestively phallic) horns of a mature deer   **126 strikes … brow** takes aim at
the deer's head/accuses you of cuckoldry   **128 lower** i.e. in the heart/genitals   **hit her** scored wittily/
sexually   **129 come upon** answer (perhaps with sexual connotations)   **130 a man** i.e. old   **King Pepin**
eighth-century king   **131 hit it** name of a popular song and dance (plays on sense of 'sex')   **133 Queen
Guinevere** wife of King Arthur, who was unfaithful to her husband   **138 An if**   **139 fit it** unite lyrics and
metre (plays on sense of 'have sex')   **140 mark** target   **141 mark but** only take note of   **142 mark** target/
female genitals   **prick** bull's-eye/penis   **mete** aim (puns on 'mate')   **143 Wide o'th'bow hand!** wide of
the mark on the left side (**bow** plays on sense of 'vagina')   **out** inaccurate/out of practice   **144 shoot** plays
on sense of 'ejaculate'   **clout** cloth patch at the centre of the target (plays on sense of 'vulva')   **145 out** i.e.
of practice in archery/sexually   **in** i.e. in practice   **146 upshoot** best shot/ejaculation   **cleaving the pin**
splitting the peg at the centre of the target/stimulating his penis   **148 hard** good/sexually impenetrable
pricks archery targets/penises   **bowl** play at bowls (possible play on 'masturbate you')

BOYET I fear too much rubbing. Goodnight, my good owl.

                                [Exeunt Boyet and Maria]

150 **COSTARD** By my soul, a swain, a most simple clown!

       Lord, Lord, how the ladies and I have put him down!

       O my troth, most sweet jests, most incony vulgar wit,

       When it comes so smoothly off, so obscenely, as it

          were, so fit.

       Armado o'th't'other side — O, a most dainty man!

155   To see him walk before a lady and to bear her fan!

       To see him kiss his hand, and how most sweetly a will

          swear!

       And his page o't'other side, that handful of wit!

       Ah, heavens, it is most pathetical nit!   *Shout within*

       Sola, sola!   *Exit [Costard, running]*

[Act 4 Scene 2]   *running scene 4 continues*

Enter Dull, Holofernes the pedant, and Nathaniel

NATHANIEL Very reverend sport, truly, and done in the
      testimony of a good conscience.

HOLOFERNES The deer was, as you know, *sanguis*, in
      blood, ripe as a pomewater, who now hangeth like a

5   jewel in the ear of *caelo*, the sky, the welkin, the
      heaven, and anon falleth like a crab on the face of
      terra, the soil, the land, the earth.

NATHANIEL Truly, Master Holofernes, the epithets are
      sweetly varied, like a scholar at the least: but, sir, I

10   assure ye, it was a buck of the first head.

HOLOFERNES Sir Nathaniel, *haud credo*.

DULL 'Twas not a 'auld grey doe', 'twas a pricket.

HOLOFERNES Most barbarous intimation! Yet a kind of
      insinuation, as it were, *in via*, in way, of explication,

---

149 rubbing of the bowling ball against impediments/masturbatory friction   **owl** 'to take owl' was to take offence; pronounced to rhyme with **bowl** it puns on 'hole' (vagina)   **150 clown** rustic   **152 incony** fine, pronounced 'incunny', perhaps punning on 'coney'/French *con* ('cunt')   **vulgar** common, probably Costard's mistake for the opposite   **153 obscenely** malapropism, perhaps for 'seemly', appropriate for the preceding dialogue; there may also be innuendo in **comes so smoothly off** and **so fit**   **154 dainty** fastidious/ elegant   **158 pathetical nit** touching little fellow   **159 Sola** a hunting cry   **4.2** *pedant* schoolteacher   **1 reverend** worth respect   **in the testimony** with the warrant   **3** *sanguis*, **in blood** in finest condition   **4 pomewater** large juicy apple   **now** at one moment   **6 anon** at the next moment   **crab** crab-apple   **9 at the least** to say the least   **10 buck ... head** five-year-old male deer (i.e. having just grown antlers)   **11** *haud credo* 'I do not believe it' (Latin; Dull understands 'old grey doe')   **12 pricket** two-year-old male deer   **13 intimation** intrusion   **14 insinuation** introduction   **explication** detailed description

15   *facere*, as it were, replication, or rather, *ostentare*, to
        show, as it were, his inclination, after his undressed,
        unpolished, uneducated, unpruned, untrained, or
        rather, unlettered, or ratherest unconfirmed fashion,
        to insert again my *haud credo* for a deer.

20 **DULL** I said the deer was not a *haud credo*, 'twas a pricket.
    HOLOFERNES Twice-sod simplicity, *bis coctus*!
        O thou monster Ignorance, how deformed dost thou
        look!

    NATHANIEL Sir, he hath never fed of the dainties that are
25   bred in a book. He hath not eat paper, as it were. He
        hath not drunk ink. His intellect is not replenished,
        he is only an animal, only sensible in the duller parts.
        And such barren plants are set before us that we
            thankful should be,
        Which we of taste and feeling are, for those parts that
            do fructify in us more than he.
30   For as it would ill become me to be vain, indiscreet, or a
            fool,
        So were there a patch set on learning, to see him in a
            school.
        But *omne bene*, say I, being of an old father's mind,
        Many can brook the weather that love not the wind.

    DULL You two are bookmen: can you tell by your wit
35   What was a month old at Cain's birth that's not five
        weeks old as yet?

    HOLOFERNES *Dictynna*,   goodman   Dull.   *Dictynna*,
        goodman Dull.

    DULL What is *dictima*?

40 **NATHANIEL** A title to Phoebe, to Luna, to the moon.
    HOLOFERNES The moon was a month old when Adam
            was no more,
        And raught not to five weeks when he came to

---

15 *facere* 'to make' (Holofernes sprinkles his speech with Latin terms)   **replication** reply   **16 after** in
keeping with   **undressed** unkempt   **17 untrained** uninstructed/poorly managed horticulturally
18 unlettered illiterate   **ratherest** most of all   **unconfirmed** inexperienced/ignorant
19 insert introduce/substitute intrusively   **21 Twice-sod** doubly boiled   ***bis coctus*** 'twice cooked'   **24 of**
on   **25 eat** eaten   **27 sensible** capable of perception   **29 Which** as   **feeling** sensitivity   **fructify** bear
fruit   **31 So … learning** it would be like trying to educate a fool/clumsily patching learning's fabric
32 *omne bene* 'all is well'   **of … mind** in agreement with one of the Church Fathers (early Christian
authorities)   **33 Many … wind** i.e. one has to put up with what one can't change   **brook** endure
35 Cain's birth i.e. at the beginning of creation (Cain was Adam and Eve's son)   **37 *Dictynna*** one of the
names of the Roman moon goddess   **goodman** title for someone below the rank of gentleman
40 Phoebe, to Luna other names for the moon goddess   **41 no more** no older   **42 raught** reached
fivescore one hundred (five times twenty)

fivescore.

Th'allusion holds in the exchange.

DULL 'Tis true indeed: the collusion holds in the exchange.

45 **HOLOFERNES** God comfort thy capacity! I say, th'allusion
holds in the exchange.

DULL And I say, the pollution holds in the exchange, for
the moon is never but a month old: and I say beside
that, 'twas a pricket that the princess killed.

50 **HOLOFERNES** Sir Nathaniel, will you hear an extemporal
epitaph on the death of the deer? And, to humour the
ignorant, called I the deer the princess killed a pricket.

NATHANIEL *Perge*, good Master Holofernes, *perge*, so it
shall please you to abrogate scurrility.

55 **HOLOFERNES** I will something affect the letter, for it
argues facility.

The preyful princess pierced and pricked a pretty
pleasing pricket,

Some say a sore, but not a sore, till now made sore
with shooting.

The dogs did yell, put 'L' to sore, then sorrel jumps from
thicket.

Or pricket sore, or else sorrel, the people fall a-hooting.

60 If sore be sore, then L to sore makes fifty sores o'sorrel.

Of one sore I an hundred make by adding but one
more 'L'.

NATHANIEL A rare talent.

DULL If a talent be a claw, look how he claws him with a   *Aside*
talent.

43 **Th'allusion ... exchange** the riddle remains valid even if one substitutes Cain's name for Adam's
44 **collusion** verbal trick (unwittingly correct as this is a malapropism for **allusion**)   45 **comfort**
help   **capacity** mental ability   47 **pollution** corruption (of what he has said); another malapropism for
allusion   50 **extemporal** improvised   53 *Perge* 'proceed'   54 **abrogate scurrility** do away with coarse
language   55 **something ... letter** make some use of alliteration   **argues facility** demonstrates linguistic
fluency   56 **preyful** killing much prey/intent on hunting/sexually hungry   **pricket** two-year-old male deer,
with play on 'penis'   57 **say** say it was   **sore** four-year-old male deer, with play on 'vulva'   **sore**
wounded, with play on 'sexually infected'   **shooting** being shot at/ejaculating   58 **'L'** sound of the dogs'
yelling/letter 'L'   **sorrel** three-year-old male deer/L added to **sore**/sore penis (an 'ell' was a measure of length
and euphemism for 'penis')   **thicket** plays on sense of vagina/pubic hair   59 **Or ... sorrel** i.e. whatever
kind of deer it was   **fall a-hooting** begin calling out   60 **sore be sore** the deer is wounded   **fifty sores** L
is the Roman numeral for fifty; the **sores** in this sequence also carry connotations of sexual disease   **o'** out
of   61 **Of ... 'L'** adding another 'L' (fifty) makes one hundred deer   **more 'L'** possible pun on 'moral'
(hidden meaning)   63 **talent** alternative spelling for 'talon'   **claws** scratches/flatters

65   HOLOFERNES This is a gift that I have, simple, simple: a
     foolish extravagant spirit, full of forms, figures, shapes,
     objects, ideas, apprehensions, motions, revolutions.
     These are begot in the ventricle of memory, nourished in
     the womb of pia mater, and delivered upon the
70   mellowing of occasion. But the gift is good in those
     in whom it is acute, and I am thankful for it.
     NATHANIEL Sir, I praise the Lord for you; and so may my
     parishioners, for their sons are well tutored by you,
     and their daughters profit very greatly under you.
75   You are a good member of the commonwealth.
     HOLOFERNES *Mehercle*, if their sons be ingenious, they
     shall want no instruction. If their daughters be
     capable, I will put it to them. But *vir sapit qui pauca
     loquitur*. A soul feminine saluteth us.
     Enter Jaquenetta and the Clown [Costard]
80   JAQUENETTA God give you good morrow, Master Person.
     NATHANIEL Master Person, *quasi* pierce-one? And if one
     should be pierced, which is the one?
     COSTARD Marry, Master Schoolmaster, he that is likest
     to a hogshead.
85   HOLOFERNES Of piercing a hogshead! A good lustre of
     conceit in a turf of earth, fire enough for a flint, pearl
     enough for a swine: 'tis pretty, it is well.
     JAQUENETTA Good Master Parson, be so good as read me   *Gives*
     this letter. It was given me by Costard, and sent me   *letter to*
90   from Don Armado. I beseech you read it.   *Holofernes*
     HOLOFERNES *Fauste, precor gelida quando pecus omne sub
     umbra ruminat,* — and so forth. Ah, good old Mantuan,
     I may speak of thee as the traveller doth of Venice:
     Venetia, Venetia,
95   *Chi non ti vede non ti pretia.*

---

65 HOLOFERNES in the following sequence Shakespeare seems to have muddled the names of the
schoolmaster and the curate, leading the early editions to assign the speeches incorrectly; all editions,
including this one, correct for clarity   **66 foolish** simple/trifling   **forms** images   **figures** rhetorical devices
67 apprehensions conceptions   **motions** inward promptings   **revolutions** reflections   **68 begot** conceived   **ventricle** brain cavity   **69 pia mater** membrane covering the brain/brain   **upon ... occasion**
when the time is right   **74 profit** benefit/increase (due to pregnancy)   **under you** under your teaching/
underneath you (sexually)   **76 Mehercle** 'by Hercules'   **ingenious** clever/intelligent   **77 want** lack
78 capable able to learn/have sex   **put ... them** with sexual connotations   **vir ... loquitur** 'he's a wise
man who says little' (proverbial)   **81 quasi** 'as if'   **83 likest** most like   **84 hogshead** large cask for drink   **85 Of ...
hogshead** broaching a cask/getting drunk   **lustre of conceit** spark of wit   **86 turf of earth** i.e. person
close to the soil   **91 Fauste ... ruminat** 'Faustus, while all the cattle are chewing the cud in the cool shade,
I pray you ...' (opening of the poet **Mantuan's** first eclogue, a well-known work at the time)   **94 Venetia ...
pretia** 'Venice, he that does not see thee does not esteem thee' (Italian proverb)

Old Mantuan, old Mantuan! Who understandeth
thee not, loves thee not? Ut, re, sol, la, mi, fa. Under   *Sings*
pardon, sir, what are the contents? Or rather, as
Horace says in his— What, my soul, verses?
100 **NATHANIEL** Ay, sir, and very learned.
HOLOFERNES Let me hear a staff, a stanza, a verse. *Lege,*
domine.
NATHANIEL 'If love make me forsworn, how shall I   *Reads*
    swear to love?
    Ah, never faith could hold, if not to beauty
    vowed.
105 Though to myself forsworn, to thee I'll
    faithful prove.
    Those thoughts to me were oaks, to thee
    like osiers bowed.
    Study his bias leaves and makes his book
    thine eyes,
    Where all those pleasures live that art
    would comprehend.
    If knowledge be the mark, to know thee
    shall suffice:
110 Well learnèd is that tongue that well can
    thee commend,
    All ignorant that soul that sees thee
    without wonder,
    Which is to me some praise that I thy parts
    admire.
    Thy eye Jove's lightning bears, thy voice his
    dreadful thunder,
    Which not to anger bent, is music and
    sweet fire.
115 Celestial as thou art, O, pardon, love, this
    wrong,
    That sings heaven's praise with such an
    earthly tongue.'
HOLOFERNES You find not the apostrophus, and so miss   *Takes the*
    the accent. Let me supervise the canzonet. Here are   *letter*

---

97 **Ut … fa** either notes of a scale or snatch of tune   **Under pardon** begging your pardon   **99 Horace**
Latin poet of the first century BC   **101 staff** stanza   *Lege, domine* 'read, master'   **106 oaks** i.e. firm
osiers pliant willows   **107 Study … eyes** i.e. the student abandons his inclination and makes your eyes
his subject for study   **108 art** scholarship   **109 mark** target/vagina   **112 Which is** for which is owed
parts physical or mental attributes   **113 Jove** Roman king of the gods   **114 bent** inclined
117 apostrophus apostrophe   **118 accent** correct emphasis   **supervise** look over   **canzonet** short
song/poem

only numbers ratified, but for the elegancy, facility,
120   and golden cadence of poesy, *caret*. Ovidius Naso
was the man: and why indeed 'Naso', but for
smelling out the odoriferous flowers of fancy, the jerks
of invention? *Imitari* is nothing: so doth the hound his
master, the ape his keeper, the tired horse his rider.
125   But, damosella virgin, was this directed to you?

JAQUENETTA Ay, sir, from one Monsieur Berowne, one of
the strange queen's lords.

HOLOFERNES I will overglance the superscript: 'To the
snow-white hand of the most beauteous Lady
130   Rosaline.' I will look again on the intellect of the
letter, for the nomination of the party writing to the
person written unto: 'Your ladyship's in all desired
employment, Berowne.'

NATHANIEL Sir Holofernes, this Berowne is one of the
135   votaries with the king; and here he hath framed a
letter to a sequent of the stranger queen's, which
accidentally, or by the way of progression, hath
miscarried. Trip and go, my sweet, deliver this paper
into the hand of the king: it may concern much. Stay
140   not thy compliment: I forgive thy duty, adieu.

JAQUENETTA Good Costard, go with me. Sir, God save your
life.

COSTARD Have with thee, my girl.

Exit [Costard with Jaquenetta]

NATHANIEL Sir, you have done this in the fear of God, very
145   religiously: and as a certain father saith—

HOLOFERNES Sir tell me not of the father, I do fear
colourable colours. But to return to the verses: did
they please you, Sir Nathaniel?

NATHANIEL Marvellous well for the pen.

150   **HOLOFERNES** I do dine today at the father's of a certain
pupil of mine, where if, before repast, it shall please you
to gratify the table with a grace, I will, on my privilege

---

119 numbers ratified metrically correct lines   **120 *caret*** (it is) 'lacking'   **Ovidius Naso** Roman poet Ovid
(*Naso* means 'large-nosed')   **122 odoriferous** sweet-smelling   **fancy** imagination   **jerks** sharp speeches
123 *Imitari* 'to imitate'   **125 damosella** damsel   **127 strange** foreign   **128 overglance** look over
superscript address   **130 intellect** meaning, contents   **131 nomination** name   **132 all desired
employment** any service you wish to put me to   **135 framed** composed   **136 sequent** attendant
137 way of progression process of delivery   **138 Trip and go** move nimbly (phrase from a popular
song)   **139 concern much** be of great importance   **Stay … compliment** don't wait upon etiquette
140 forgive thy duty excuse the necessary courtesies   **143 Have with thee** I'll go with you   **145 father**
Church Father   **147 colourable colours** plausible explanations (offered by the Church Fathers)   **149 pen**
calligraphy/style

I have with the parents of the foresaid child or pupil,
undertake your *ben venuto*, where I will prove those
155   verses to be very unlearnèd, neither savouring of
poetry, wit, nor invention. I beseech your society.

NATHANIEL And thank you too, for society, saith the text,
is the happiness of life.

HOLOFERNES And, certes, the text most infallibly
160   concludes it.— Sir, I do invite you too: you shall   *To Dull*
not say me nay. *Pauca verba.*— Away, the gentles are
at their game, and we will to our recreation. *Exeunt*

[Act 4 Scene 3]   *running scene 4 continues*

Enter Berowne, with a paper in his hand, alone

BEROWNE The king, he is hunting the deer: I am coursing
myself. They have pitched a toil: I am toiling in a pitch,
pitch that defiles. Defile, a foul word. Well, set thee
down, sorrow, for so they say the fool said, and so say
5   I, and I the fool. Well proved, wit! By the lord, this love
is as mad as Ajax: it kills sheep, it kills me — I a sheep.
Well proved again o'my side. I will not love; if I do,
hang me. I'faith, I will not. O, but her eye, — by this
light, but for her eye, I would not love her — yes, for
10   her two eyes. Well, I do nothing in the world but lie,
and lie in my throat. By heaven, I do love, and it hath
taught me to rhyme and to be melancholy. And here is
part of my rhyme, and here my melancholy. Well, she
hath one o'my sonnets already. The clown bore it, the
15   fool sent it, and the lady hath it. Sweet clown, sweeter
fool, sweetest lady! By the world, I would not care a
pin, if the other three were in. Here comes one with a
paper. God give him grace to groan!

He stands aside. The King entereth [with a paper]

KING Ay me!

---

154 undertake … *venuto* ensure your welcome   **156 society** company   **157 text** i.e. the Bible (possibly
Ecclesiastes 4:8–12)   **159 certes** certainly   **160 concludes** resolves   **161 *Pauca verba*** 'few words'
gentles gentlefolk   **162 game** sport/hunting/love play   **4.3 1 coursing** hunting (may pun on 'cursing')
2 pitched a toil set up a net   **toiling … pitch** struggling amongst the sticky thoughts of love   **3 defiles**
pollutes, fouls   **set thee down** settle in   **5 I I am**   **mad … sheep** when not given the armour of the dead
Achilles, **Ajax** attacked a flock of sheep thinking they were the enemy   **6 mad … sheep** when not given
the armour of the dead Achilles, **Ajax** attacked a flock of sheep thinking they were the enemy   **11 lie …**
throat tell enormous lies   **17 in** in love   **18 groan** i.e. for love

20   **BEROWNE** Shot, by heaven! Proceed, sweet Cupid, thou   *Speaks*
      hast thumped him with thy bird-bolt   *aside through the rest of*
      under the left pap. In faith, secrets!   *the scene*
      KING 'So sweet a kiss the golden sun gives not   *Reads*
      To those fresh morning drops upon the rose,
25   As thy eye-beams, when their fresh rays have smote
      The night of dew that on my cheeks down flows.
      Nor shines the silver moon one half so bright
      Through the transparent bosom of the deep,
      As doth thy face through tears of mine give light.
30   Thou shin'st in every tear that I do weep,
      No drop but as a coach doth carry thee:
      So ridest thou triumphing in my woe.
      Do but behold the tears that swell in me,
      And they thy glory through my grief will show.
35   But do not love thyself: then thou wilt keep
      My tears for glasses, and still make me weep.
      O queen of queens, how far dost thou excel,
      No thought can think, nor tongue of mortal tell.'
      How shall she know my griefs? I'll drop the paper.
40   Sweet leaves, shade folly. Who is he comes here?
      Enter Longaville [with a paper]   *The King steps aside*
      What, Longaville, and reading? Listen, ear.
      BEROWNE Now, in thy likeness, one more fool appear!
      LONGAVILLE Ay me, I am forsworn!
      BEROWNE Why, he comes in like a perjure, wearing
      papers.
45   **KING** In love, I hope. Sweet fellowship in shame!   *Speaks aside*
      BEROWNE One drunkard loves another of the name.   *through the rest*
      LONGAVILLE Am I the first that have been perjured so?   *of the scene*
      BEROWNE I could put thee in comfort: not by two that I
      know.
      Thou makest the triumviry, the corner-cap of society,
50   The shape of Love's Tyburn that hangs up simplicity.
      LONGAVILLE I fear these stubborn lines lack power to
      move.

---

21 **bird-bolt** blunt arrow for shooting birds   22 **under ... pap** i.e. where the heart is   **pap** breast
25 **eye-beams** the eyes were thought to emit beams of light   26 **night of dew** nightly tears   28 **deep**
sea   36 **glasses** mirrors   **still** continually   42 **thy** i.e. the king's   44 **perjure** perjurer, oath-breaker
wearing papers perjurers were punished by having to wear papers stating their offence   46 **another ...**
name i.e. another drunkard   49 **triumviry** triumvirate (i.e. trio)   **corner-cap** three- or four-cornered cap
worn by clergymen and academics   **society** fellowship   50 **Tyburn** place of execution where triangular
gallows stood   **simplicity** folly   51 **stubborn** stiff, rough   **move** i.e. persuade Maria to love him

'O sweet Maria, empress of my love',   *Reads*

These numbers will I tear and write in prose.   *Tears paper*

BEROWNE O, rhymes are guards on wanton Cupid's hose:

55   Disfigure not his shop.

LONGAVILLE This same shall go.

He reads the sonnet

'Did not the heavenly rhetoric of thine eye,

Gainst whom the world cannot hold argument,

Persuade my heart to this false perjury?

60   Vows for thee broke deserve not punishment.

A woman I forswore, but I will prove,

Thou being a goddess, I forswore not thee.

My vow was earthly, thou a heavenly love:

Thy grace being gained cures all disgrace in me.

65   Vows are but breath, and breath a vapour is:

Then thou, fair sun, which on my earth dost shine,

Exhal'st this vapour-vow, in thee it is.

If broken then, it is no fault of mine:

If by me broke, what fool is not so wise

70   To lose an oath to win a paradise?'

BEROWNE This is the liver vein, which makes flesh a deity,

A green goose a goddess. Pure, pure idolatry.

God amend us, God amend! We are much out

o'th'way.

LONGAVILLE By whom shall I send this? Company? Stay.

Enter Dumaine [with a paper]   *Longaville steps aside*

75   **BEROWNE** All hid, all hid: an old infant play.

Like a demigod here sit I in the sky,

And wretched fools' secrets heedfully o'er-eye.

More sacks to the mill. O heavens, I have my wish!

Dumaine transformed! Four woodcocks in a dish!

80   **DUMAINE** O most divine Kate!

BEROWNE O most profane coxcomb!

DUMAINE By heaven, the wonder of a mortal eye!

BEROWNE By earth, she is not, corporal: there you lie.

DUMAINE Her amber hairs for foul hath amber quoted.

---

53 numbers verses/lines of poetry   **54 guards** decorations/defences   **hose** breeches   **55 shop** codpiece
64 grace favour   **67 Exhal'st** draws up (the sun was thought to draw vapours from the earth)   **70 To** as
to   **71 liver vein** style of the lover (the **liver** was thought to be the seat of passion)   **72 green goose** silly
young girl/new prostitute   **73 out o'th'way** gone astray   **75 infant play** child's game   **77 heedfully o'er-
eye** observe attentively   **78 sacks . . . mill** cause for laughter (proverbial)   **79 woodcocks** proverbially
stupid birds   **81 coxcomb** fool (literally, fool's cap)   **83 corporal** officer (in Cupid's army); plays on
'corporeal'   **84 for . . . quoted** makes real amber seem ugly in comparison   **quoted** cited

85 BEROWNE An amber-coloured raven was well noted.
    DUMAINE As upright as the cedar.
    BEROWNE Stoop, I say.
        Her shoulder is with child.
    DUMAINE As fair as day.
90 BEROWNE Ay, as some days, but then no sun must shine.
    DUMAINE O that I had my wish!
    LONGAVILLE And I had mine! *Aside*
    KING And I mine too, good lord! *Aside*
    BEROWNE Amen, so I had mine! Is not that a good word?
95 DUMAINE I would forget her, but a fever she
      Reigns in my blood and will remembered be.
    BEROWNE A fever in your blood? Why then incision
      Would let her out in saucers. Sweet misprision!
    DUMAINE Once more I'll read the ode that I have writ.
100 BEROWNE Once more I'll mark how love can vary wit.
    DUMAINE 'On a day — alack the day! —*Reads his sonnet*
        Love, whose month is ever May,
        Spied a blossom passing fair
        Playing in the wanton air:
105   Through the velvet leaves the wind,
        All unseen, can passage find.
        That the lover, sick to death,
        Wish himself the heaven's breath.
        "Air", quoth he, "thy cheeks may blow,
110   Air, would I might triumph so!
        But, alack, my hand is sworn
        Ne'er to pluck thee from thy thorn.
        Vow, alack, for youth unmeet,
        Youth so apt to pluck a sweet.
115   Do not call it sin in me,
        That I am forsworn for thee:
        Thou for whom Jove would swear
        Juno but an Ethiope were,
        And deny himself for Jove,
120   Turning mortal for thy love." '
        This will I send, and something else more plain,

---

85 An … noted punning on **foul** as 'fowl'. Berowne sarcastically applauds Dumaine's identification of Katherine's dark (**raven**) hair as amber-coloured   **87 Stoop** curved/come down to earth   **88 with child** i.e. round   **94 good word** i.e. Amen/kind of me   **95 a** as a   **97 incision** cutting for letting blood   **98 in saucers** into receptacles/by the saucerful   **misprision** error   **100 vary wit** inspire new forms of expression/decrease intelligence   **103 passing** surpassingly   **104 wanton** playful   **107 That** so that **sick to death** made ill from longing (**death** possibly plays on sense of 'orgasm')   **113 unmeet** unfitting **114 pluck a sweet** plays on sense of 'take virginity, have sex'   **118 Juno** Roman queen of the gods, wife of Jove   **Ethiope** Ethiopian (i.e. dark-complexioned, thought to be unattractive)   **119 for** to be

That shall express my true love's fasting pain.
O, would the king, Berowne, and Longaville
Were lovers too! Ill, to example ill,
125   Would from my forehead wipe a perjured note,
For none offend where all alike do dote.
LONGAVILLE Dumaine, thy love is far from charity,   *Comes forward*
That in love's grief desirest society.
You may look pale, but I should blush, I know,
130   To be o'erheard and taken napping so.
KING Come, sir, you blush: as his your case is such,   *Comes forward*
You chide at him, offending twice as much.
You do not love Maria? Longaville
Did never sonnet for her sake compile,
135   Nor never lay his wreathèd arms athwart
His loving bosom to keep down his heart?
I have been closely shrouded in this bush
And marked you both and for you both did blush.
I heard your guilty rhymes, observed your fashion,
140   Saw sighs reek from you, noted well your passion.
'Ay me', says one, 'O Jove!' the other cries,
One, her hairs were gold, crystal the other's eyes:
You would for paradise break faith and troth,   *To Longaville*
And Jove, for your love, would infringe an oath.   *To Dumaine*
145   What will Berowne say when that he shall hear
Faith infringèd which such zeal did swear?
How will he scorn? How will he spend his wit?
How will he triumph, leap and laugh at it!
For all the wealth that ever I did see,
150   I would not have him know so much by me.
BEROWNE Now step I forth to whip hypocrisy.   *Comes forward*
Ah, good my liege, I pray thee pardon me.
Good heart, what grace hast thou, thus to reprove
These worms for loving, that art most in love?
155   Your eyes do make no coaches. In your tears
There is no certain princess that appears.
You'll not be perjured, 'tis a hateful thing,
Tush, none but minstrels like of sonneting.
But are you not ashamed? Nay, are you not,

---

124 example provide precedent for   **125 perjured note** paper pinned to perjurer describing his offence   **126 dote** love dearly   **127 charity** Christian love (as opposed to amorous love)   **128 That** you who **society** company   **130 taken napping** caught unawares   **131 such** i.e. the same   **135 wreathèd** folded (sign of melancholy)   **athwart** across   **137 closely** secretly   **139 fashion** behaviour   **140 reek** emanate   **143 troth** good faith, a pledge   **147 spend** expend/exhaust   **150 by** about   **153 grace** privilege   **154 worms** wretches   **155 coaches** alludes to the coach image in the king's poem **158 minstrels** musicians, entertainers   **sonneting** sonnet-composition

160   All three of you, to be thus much o'ershot?
       You found his mote, the king your mote did see,   *To Longaville*
       But I a beam do find in each of three.
       O, what a scene of fool'ry have I seen,
       Of sighs, of groans, of sorrow and of teen!
165   O me, with what strict patience have I sat,
       To see a king transformèd to a gnat!
       To see great Hercules whipping a gig,
       And profound Solomon tuning a jig,
       And Nestor play at push-pin with the boys,
170   And critic Timon laugh at idle toys.
       Where lies thy grief? O, tell me, good Dumaine;
       And gentle Longaville, where lies thy pain?
       And where my liege's? All about the breast?
       A caudle, ho!
175   **KING** Too bitter is thy jest.
       Are we betrayed thus to thy over-view?
       BEROWNE Not you to me, but I betrayed by you:
       I, that am honest, I, that hold it sin
       To break the vow I am engagèd in,
180   I am betrayed by keeping company
       With men like you, men of inconstancy.
       When shall you see me write a thing in rhyme?
       Or groan for Joan? Or spend a minute's time
       In pruning me? When shall you hear that I
185   Will praise a hand, a foot, a face, an eye,
       A gait, a state, a brow, a breast, a waist,
       A leg, a limb—   *Starts to leave*
       KING Soft! Whither away so fast?
       A true man or a thief that gallops so?
190   **BEROWNE** I post from love. Good lover, let me go.
       Enter Jaquenetta [with a letter] and Clown [Costard]
       JAQUENETTA God bless the king!
       KING What present hast thou there?
       COSTARD Some certain treason.
       KING What makes treason here?
195   **COSTARD** Nay, it makes nothing, sir.

---

160 **o'ershot** in error/off course (literally, to have overshot the target)   161 **mote** speck of dust/fault
162 **beam** large object/major fault   164 **teen** grief   166 **gnat** i.e. insignificant thing   167 **gig** spinning-
top   168 **profound** wise   **tuning a jig** singing a lively song/dancing   169 **Nestor** Trojan leader, famed for his
wisdom   **push-pin** children's game   170 **Timon** Athenian notorious for his misanthropy   **idle toys** trivial
games/concerns   174 **caudle** medicinal gruel   176 **over-view** inspection   178 **honest** honourable
184 **pruning me** preening myself   186 **state** posture/bearing   188 **Soft!** Wait a moment!   189 **true**
honest   190 **post** ride quickly (away)   192 **present** gift/written document   194 **makes treason** is
treason doing

KING If it mar nothing neither,
    The treason and you go in peace away together.
JAQUENETTA I beseech your grace, let this letter be read.   *Gives letter*
    Our person misdoubts it: 'twas treason, he said.   *to the King*
200 **KING** Berowne, read it over—   *Gives the letter to Berowne*
    Where hadst thou it?   *To Jaquenetta*
JAQUENETTA Of Costard.   *[Berowne] reads the letter*
KING Where hadst thou it?
COSTARD Of Dun Adramadio, Dun Adramadio.   *Berowne tears the letter*
205 **KING** How now? What is in you? Why dost thou tear it?
BEROWNE A toy, my liege, a toy. Your grace needs not fear
    it.
LONGAVILLE It did move him to passion, and therefore let's
    hear it.
DUMAINE It is Berowne's writing and here is his name.   *Gathers the*
BEROWNE Ah, you whoreson loggerhead! You were born *pieces and reads*
210   to do me shame.—   *them*
    Guilty, my lord, guilty. I confess, I confess.   *To Costard*
KING What?
BEROWNE That you three fools lacked me fool to make up
    the mess:
    He, he, and you — and you, my liege — and I,
215   Are pick-purses in love, and we deserve to die.
    O, dismiss this audience and I shall tell you more.
DUMAINE Now the number is even.
BEROWNE True, true: we are four.
    Will these turtles be gone?
220 **KING** Hence, sirs, away!   *To Costard and Jaquenetta*
COSTARD Walk aside the true folk and let the traitors stay.
    [Exeunt Costard and Jaquenetta]
BEROWNE Sweet lords, sweet lovers, O, let us embrace!
    As true we are as flesh and blood can be,
    The sea will ebb and flow, heaven show his face:
225   Young blood doth not obey an old decree.
    We cannot cross the cause why we are born:
    Therefore of all hands must we be forsworn.
KING What, did these rent lines show some love of thine?

---

196 mar spoil (proverbial: 'to make or mar')   **199 person** parson (i.e. Nathaniel)   **misdoubts** distrusts
206 toy trifle   **207 passion** powerful emotion   **209 whoreson** bastard (son of a whore)   **loggerhead**
blockhead   **213 mess** four dining companions   **215 pick-purses** pickpockets   **219 turtles** turtle-doves –
i.e. lovers   **220 sirs** address acceptable for both men and women   **221 Walk ... folk** i.e. the honest people
will leave   **226 cross** thwart   **cause ... born** i.e. fate   **227 of all hands** in any case   **228 rent** torn

BEROWNE 'Did they', quoth you? Who sees the heavenly
    Rosaline,
230   That, like a rude and savage man of Ind,
    At the first opening of the gorgeous east,
    Bows not his vassal head, and strucken blind,
    Kisses the base ground with obedient breast?
    What peremptory eagle-sighted eye
235   Dares look upon the heaven of her brow
    That is not blinded by her majesty?
KING What zeal, what fury hath inspired thee now?
    My love, her mistress, is a gracious moon,
    She, an attending star, scarce seen a light.
240 **BEROWNE** My eyes are then no eyes, nor I Berowne.
    O, but for my love, day would turn to night!
    Of all complexions the culled sovereignty
    Do meet as at a fair in her fair cheek,
    Where several worthies make one dignity,
245   Where nothing wants that want itself doth seek.
    Lend me the flourish of all gentle tongues —
    Fie, painted rhetoric! O, she needs it not,
    To things of sale a seller's praise belongs:
    She passes praise, then praise too short doth blot.
250   A withered hermit, fivescore winters worn,
    Might shake off fifty, looking in her eye.
    Beauty doth varnish age as if new-born,
    And gives the crutch the cradle's infancy.
    O, 'tis the sun that maketh all things shine.
255 **KING** By heaven, thy love is black as ebony.
    BEROWNE Is ebony like her? O word divine!
    A wife of such wood were felicity.
    O, who can give an oath? Where is a book?
    That I may swear beauty doth beauty lack
260   If that she learn not of her eye to look.
    No face is fair that is not full so black.

---

230 **rude** ignorant, rough   **savage** uncivilized   **Ind** India   231 **opening** dawning   232 **vassal** submissive   234 **peremptory** determined   **eagle-sighted** eagles were supposed to be able to look directly into the sun   237 **fury** frenzy   239 **She** i.e. Rosaline   **attending** attendant   **scarce . . . light** barely visible   241 **but** were it not   **my love** i.e. the woman I love   242 **the culled sovereignty** those chosen as the best   244 **worthies** beings of excellence   **dignity** (supreme) excellence   245 **wants** is lacking   **want** desire   246 **gentle** well-born   247 **Fie** expression of disgust   **painted** artificial   248 **of** for   249 **passes** surpasses   **then . . . blot** thus any praise is inadequate and defames her   250 **fivescore winters worn** a hundred years old   252 **varnish** improve, give lustre to   253 **the crutch** i.e. old age   **cradle's infancy** youth   255 **black as ebony** dark/unattractive   257 **were felicity** would be bliss   258 **book** i.e. Bible   260 **If . . . look** unless beauty learns how to look from Rosaline's eye   261 **fair** beautiful/pale   **full so black** so completely dark-complexioned

KING O paradox! Black is the badge of hell,
    The hue of dungeons and the school of night,
    And beauty's crest becomes the heavens well.
265 BEROWNE Devils soonest tempt, resembling spirits of light.
    O, if in black my lady's brows be decked,
    It mourns that painting and usurping hair
    Should ravish doters with a false aspect,
    And therefore is she born to make black fair.
270   Her favour turns the fashion of the days,
    For native blood is counted painting now,
    And therefore red that would avoid dispraise
    Paints itself black, to imitate her brow.
DUMAINE To look like her are chimney-sweepers black.
275 LONGAVILLE And since her time are colliers counted
       bright.
KING And Ethiops of their sweet complexion crack.
DUMAINE Dark needs no candles now, for dark is light.
BEROWNE Your mistresses dare never come in rain,
    For fear their colours should be washed away.
280 KING 'Twere good, yours did, for, sir, to tell you plain,
    I'll find a fairer face not washed today.
BEROWNE I'll prove her fair, or talk till doomsday here.
KING No devil will fright thee then so much as she.
DUMAINE I never knew man hold vile stuff so dear.
285 LONGAVILLE Look, here's thy love: my foot and her   *Shows his shoe*
       face see.
BEROWNE O, if the streets were pavèd with thine eyes,
    Her feet were much too dainty for such tread.
DUMAINE O, vile! Then, as she goes, what upward lies
    The street should see as she walked overhead.
290 KING But what of this? Are we not all in love?
BEROWNE O, nothing so sure, and thereby all forsworn.
KING Then leave this chat, and good Berowne, now prove
    Our loving lawful, and our faith not torn.
DUMAINE Ay, marry, there, some flattery for this evil.

---

263 **hue** complexion/colour   **school** academy (though some editors emend to 'scowl' or 'stole')
264 **beauty's crest** i.e. the sun   **becomes** graces, befits   265 **resembling . . . light** when they pose as
angels   267 **It** i.e. she/her beauty   **that** the fact that   **painting . . . hair** cosmetics and wigs   268 **doters**
infatuated fools   **false aspect** deceptive appearance   270 **favour . . . days** face inverts what is
conventionally thought beautiful   271 **native blood** natural redness, a rosy complexion   **counted
painting** considered artificial (i.e. to be rouge)   272 **red** natural rosiness   **dispraise** disparagement
275 **colliers** coal-vendors   276 **crack** boast   278 **come in** expose themselves to   279 **colours** cosmetics/
sparse natural colour   283 **then** i.e. on **doomsday**   284 **vile** worthless/unattractive   285 **here's** i.e.
Longaville's shoe   287 **dainty** light, delicate/refined   288 **goes** walks   **what upward lies** i.e. what is up
her skirt   292 **prove** demonstrate using logic   294 **there** that's the point   **flattery . . . evil** pleasing self-
deception to justify our oath-breaking

295   **LONGAVILLE** O, some authority how to proceed.
        Some tricks, some quillets, how to cheat the devil.
    DUMAINE Some salve for perjury.
    BEROWNE O, 'tis more than need.
        Have at you then, affection's men at arms.
300   Consider what you first did swear unto:
        To fast, to study, and to see no woman —
        Flat treason against the kingly state of youth.
        Say, can you fast? Your stomachs are too young,
        And abstinence engenders maladies.
305   // And where that you have vowed to study, lords, //
        // In that each of you have forsworn his book. //
        // Can you still dream and pore and thereon look? //
        // For when would you, my lord, or you, or you, //
        // Have found the ground of study's excellence //
310   // Without the beauty of a woman's face? //
        // From women's eyes this doctrine I derive: //
        // They are the ground, the books, the academes //
        // From whence doth spring the true Promethean fire. //
        // Why, universal plodding poisons up //
315   // The nimble spirits in the arteries, //
        // As motion and long-during action tires //
        // The sinewy vigour of the traveller. //
        // Now, for not looking on a woman's face, //
        // You have in that forsworn the use of eyes //
320   // And study too, the causer of your vow, //
        // For where is any author in the world //
        // Teaches such beauty as a woman's eye? //
        // Learning is but an adjunct to ourself //
        // And where we are our learning likewise is. //
325   // Then when ourselves we see in ladies' eyes, //
        // With ourselves, //
        // Do we not likewise see our learning there? //
        O, we have made a vow to study, lords,
        And in that vow we have forsworn our books,
330   For when would you, my liege, or you, or you,
        In leaden contemplation have found out
        Such fiery numbers as the prompting eyes

---

296 quillets subtle distinctions/quibbles   **297 salve** healing ointment   **298 need** necessary
299 Have at you let me at it/here goes   **affection's … arms** love's soldiers   **302 state** majesty/status
305 And where … the following twenty-three lines are enclosed within solidi because, although they
appear in the early printed texts, they seem to be Shakespeare's first draft of the lines that follow; they should
be cut in performance   **313 Promethean fire** i.e. illumination (Prometheus stole fire from the gods to give
to mankind)   **332 fiery numbers** passionate poems

Of beauty's tutors have enriched you with?
Other slow arts entirely keep the brain,
335   And therefore, finding barren practisers,
Scarce show a harvest of their heavy toil.
But love, first learnèd in a lady's eyes,
Lives not alone immurèd in the brain
But with the motion of all elements
340   Courses as swift as thought in every power
And gives to every power a double power,
Above their functions and their offices.
It adds a precious seeing to the eye:
A lover's eyes will gaze an eagle blind.
345   A lover's ear will hear the lowest sound,
When the suspicious head of theft is stopped.
Love's feeling is more soft and sensible
Than are the tender horns of cockled snails.
Love's tongue proves dainty Bacchus gross in taste.
350   For valour, is not Love a Hercules,
Still climbing trees in the Hesperides?
Subtle as Sphinx, as sweet and musical
As bright Apollo's lute, strung with his hair.
And when Love speaks, the voice of all the gods
355   Make heaven drowsy with the harmony.
Never durst poet touch a pen to write
Until his ink were tempered with love's sighs.
O, then his lines would ravish savage ears
And plant in tyrants mild humility.
360   From women's eyes this doctrine I derive:
They sparkle still the right Promethean fire,
They are the books, the arts, the academes,
That show, contain and nourish all the world,
Else none at all in aught proves excellent.
365   Then fools you were these women to forswear,
Or, keeping what is sworn, you will prove fools.
For wisdom's sake, a word that all men love,

---

334 **slow arts** dull or more serious learning   **keep** occupy   335 **barren** unresponsive, unfruitful
338 **immurèd** walled up   340 **Courses** runs/chases   **power** faculty/function   342 **Above … offices**
beyond their ordinary abilities   346 **the … stopped** even the alert thief hears nothing   347 **sensible**
sensitive   348 **cockled** having a shell   349 **Bacchus** Roman god of wine   **gross** inferior, coarse
350 **For** as for   351 **climbing … Hesperides** Hercules' eleventh labour was to pick the golden apples from
the garden of the Hesperides   352 **Subtle** wily   **Sphinx** mythological creature who killed anyone who
couldn't answer her riddle   353 **Apollo** Greek sun god, also god of music   356 **durst** dares
357 **tempered** blended   361 **still … fire** continually with the heavenly fire stolen by Prometheus
362 **academes** academies   364 **Else** otherwise   **aught** anything

Or, for love's sake, a word that loves all men,
Or, for men's sake, the authors of these women,
370   Or, women's sake, by whom we men are men,
Let's once lose our oaths to find ourselves,
Or else we lose ourselves to keep our oaths.
It is religion to be thus forsworn,
For charity itself fulfils the law,
375   And who can sever love from charity?

KING Saint Cupid, then! And, soldiers, to the field!

BEROWNE Advance your standards, and upon them, lords.
Pell-mell, down with them! But be first advised
In conflict that you get the sun of them.

380   **LONGAVILLE** Now to plain dealing: lay these glozes by.
Shall we resolve to woo these girls of France?

KING And win them too: therefore let us devise
Some entertainment for them in their tents.

BEROWNE First, from the park let us conduct them thither.
385   Then homeward every man attach the hand
Of his fair mistress: in the afternoon
We will with some strange pastime solace them,
Such as the shortness of the time can shape,
For revels, dances, masks and merry hours
390   Forerun fair Love, strewing her way with flowers.

KING Away, away! No time shall be omitted
That will betime, and may by us be fitted.

BEROWNE *Allons! Allons!* Sowed cockle reaped no corn,
And justice always whirls in equal measure:
395   Light wenches may prove plagues to men forsworn,
If so, our copper buys no better treasure.   *Exeunt*

---

368 loves is loved by/inspires love in/is a friend to   **369 authors** creators   **370 whom** may pun on
'womb'   **371 once** for once/only once   **373 religion** within the boundaries of our beliefs   **374 charity** ...
law biblical allusion: 'he that loveth another hath fulfilled the law' (Romans 13:8)   **377 Advance your
standards** raise up your flags (with phallic connotations)   **upon them** to them (with sexual
connotations)   **378 Pell-mell** with no regard for order/at close quarters (sexual connotations)   **be first
advised** first take care   **379 get ... them** make sure the sun is in their eyes (thus giving you the advantage;
puns on '(be)get the son')   **380 dealing** puns on sense of 'having sex'   **glozes** elaborate speeches
385 attach seize (legal term)   **387 strange** novel, unusual, exceptional   **solace** entertain   **390 Forerun**
run before   **392 betime** happen   **fitted** used appropriately   **393 *Allons!*** 'Let's go!' (French)   **Sowed ...
corn** wheat won't be harvested if weeds are planted   **394 whirls ... measure** is distributed evenly
395 Light merry/frivolous/promiscuous   **396 copper** small coins   **treasure** vaginal connotations (**plagues**
in previous line suggests sexual disease)

Act 5 [Scene 1]

Enter [Holofernes] the Pedant, [Nathaniel the] Curate and
Dull [the Constable]

HOLOFERNES *Satis quod sufficit.*

NATHANIEL I praise God for you, sir. Your reasons at
dinner have been sharp and sententious, pleasant
without scurrility, witty without affection, audacious
5   without impudency, learnèd without opinion, and
strange without heresy. I did converse this *quondam*
day with a companion of the king's, who is intituled,
nominated, or called, Don Adriano de Armado.

HOLOFERNES *Novi hominem tanquam te*: his humour is
10   lofty, his discourse peremptory, his tongue filed, his
eye ambitious, his gait majestical, and his general
behaviour vain, ridiculous, and thrasonical. He is too
picked, too spruce, too affected, too odd, as it were, too
peregrinate, as I may call it.

15   **NATHANIEL** A most singular and choice epithet.

Draws out his table-book

HOLOFERNES He draweth out the thread of his verbosity
finer than the staple of his argument. I abhor such
fanatical phantasimes, such insociable and point-
20   device companions, such rackers of orthography, as
to speak 'dout', fine, when he should say 'doubt',
'det', when he should pronounce 'debt': d, e, b, t, not d,
e, t. He clepeth a calf 'cauf', half 'hauf', neighbour
vocatur 'nebour', neigh abbreviated 'ne'. This is
25   abhominable, which he would call 'abominable'. It
insinuateth me of insanie. *Ne intelligis, domine?* To
make frantic, lunatic.

NATHANIEL *Laus Deo, bone intelligo.*

5.1   1 *Satis quod sufficit* 'what is provided is sufficient' (i.e. 'enough is as good as a feast')   **2 reasons**
observations   **3 dinner** main meal eaten in the middle of the day   **sententious** full of wise remarks
4 affection affectation   **audacious** bold   **5 opinion** arrogance   **6 strange** new   *quondam* (the) 'other'
7 intituled entitled   **8 nominated** named   **9** *Novi . . . te* 'I know the man as well as I know you'
10 peremptory determined   **filed** smooth   **12 thrasonical** boastful   **13 picked** fastidious
14 peregrinate affectedly foreign (i.e. with the manner of one who has travelled)   **16** *table-book*
notebook   **18 staple** fibre/material   **argument** subject matter   **19 fanatical** extravagant/flamboyant
phantasimes fantastical people   **insociable** unsociable   **point-device** over-precise   **20 rackers of**
orthography torturers of correct spelling   **21 fine** thinly/affectedly; alternatively, a misprint for '*sine b*'
('without the letter *b*')   **23 clepeth** calls   **24** *vocatur* 'is called'   **25 abhominable** plays on the popular
misconception that the word was derived from Latin *ab homine* – i.e. 'away from man/unnatural'
26 insinuateth suggests, i.e. drives me to   **insanie** insanity   *Ne intelligis, domine?* 'Do you understand,
sir?'   **28** *Laus . . . intelligo* 'Praise God, I understand well'

HOLOFERNES *Bone? 'Bone'* for *'bene'*, Priscian a little
30   scratched, 'twill serve.
Enter [Armado the] Braggart, [Moth, his] Boy [and Costard]
NATHANIEL *Videsne quis venit?*
HOLOFERNES *Video et gaudeo.*
ARMADO Chirrah!
HOLOFERNES *Quare* 'chirrah', not 'sirrah'?
35   **ARMADO** Men of peace, well encountered.
HOLOFERNES Most military sir, salutation.
MOTH They have been at a great feast of languages, and   *Aside to*
        stolen the scraps.   *Costard*
COSTARD O, they have lived long on the alms-basket of   *To Moth*
40   words. I marvel thy master hath not eaten thee for a
        word, for thou art not so long by the head as
        honorificabilitudinitatibus. Thou art easier swallowed
        than a flap-dragon.
MOTH Peace! The peal begins.
45   **ARMADO** Monsieur, are you not lettered?   *To Holofernes*
MOTH Yes, yes: he teaches boys the hornbook. What is a
        b spelled backward with the horn on his head?
HOLOFERNES Ba, *pueritia*, with a horn added.
MOTH Ba, most silly sheep with a horn. You hear his
50   learning.
HOLOFERNES *Quis, quis,* thou consonant?
MOTH The last of the five vowels, if you repeat them, or
        the fifth, if I.
HOLOFERNES I will repeat them: a, e, i—
55   **MOTH** The sheep. The other two concludes it: o, u.
ARMADO Now, by the salt wave of the *Mediterraneum,* a
        sweet touch, a quick venue of wit! Snip, snap, quick
        and home! It rejoiceth my intellect: true wit!
MOTH Offered by a child to an old man — which is wit-old.

---

29 **Priscian … scratched** i.e. your Latin is slightly wrong (**Priscian** was an ancient grammarian whose
works were still used in the sixteenth century)   31 *Videsne quis venit*? 'Do you see who is coming?'
32 *Video et gaudeo* 'I see and I rejoice'   33 **Chirrah!** either mispronunciation of 'sirrah' or the Greek *chaere*
('hail')   34 *Quare* 'why'   39 **alms-basket** charity basket of food for the poor   40 **eaten … word** puns on
pronunciation of Moth's name as *mot* ('word' in French)   41 **long … head** tall
42 *honorificabilitudinitatibus* state of being honoured, supposedly the longest word in Latin   43 **flap-
dragon** edible object, such as a raisin (plucked from burning brandy and swallowed as part of the game of
flap-dragon)   44 **peal** loud uproar/bell-ringing   45 **lettered** educated (Moth understands 'literate')
46 **hornbook** paper displaying the alphabet, numbers, prayers etc. protected by a thin layer of horn
48 *pueritia* 'childishness', i.e. child   49 **Ba** sound made by a sheep   **silly** foolish   51 *Quis* 'who'
consonant nonentity, since it cannot be sounded without vowels   54 **i** interrupted by Moth, Holofernes
inadvertently identifies himself (I) as the **sheep**   55 **concludes it** finishes the list/proves my point   **o, u** i.e.
'oh you/ewe'   56 *Mediterraneum* Mediterranean   57 **touch** hit (scored against an opponent)   **venue**
thrust (in fencing)   **Snip, snap** remarking on Moth's quick wit; 'snip-snap' is also 'smart repartee'
58 **home** on the target   59 **wit-old** pun on 'wittold' or 'wittol' – i.e. a contented cuckold

60   **HOLOFERNES** What is the figure? What is the figure?

    MOTH Horns.

    HOLOFERNES Thou disputes like an infant. Go, whip thy
        gig.

    MOTH Lend me your horn to make one and I will whip
65   about your infamy *manu cita*. A gig of a cuckold's horn.

    COSTARD An I had but one penny in the world, thou
        shouldst have it to buy gingerbread. Hold, there is the
        very remuneration I had of thy master, thou halfpenny
        purse of wit, thou pigeon-egg of discretion. O, an the
70   heavens were so pleased that thou wert but my
        bastard, what a joyful father wouldst thou make me!
        Go to, thou hast it *ad dunghill*, at the fingers' ends, as
        they say.

    HOLOFERNES O, I smell false Latin: 'dunghill' for *unguem*.

75   **ARMADO** Arts-man, preambulate. We will be singled
        from the barbarous. Do you not educate youth at the
        charge-house on the top of the mountain?

    HOLOFERNES Or *mons*, the hill.

    ARMADO At your sweet pleasure, for the mountain.

80   **HOLOFERNES** I do, *sans* question.

    ARMADO Sir, it is the king's most sweet pleasure and
        affection to congratulate the princess at her pavilion
        in the posteriors of this day, which the rude
        multitude call the afternoon.

85   **HOLOFERNES** The posterior of the day, most generous sir,
        is liable, congruent and measurable for the
        afternoon. The word is well culled, choice, sweet
        and apt, I do assure you, sir, I do assure.

    ARMADO Sir, the king is a noble gentleman, and my
90   familiar, I do assure ye, very good friend. For what is
        inward between us, let it pass. I do beseech thee,
        remember thy courtesy: I beseech thee, apparel thy
        head. And among other important and most serious
        designs, and of great import indeed too — but let that
95   pass, for I must tell thee it will please his grace, by the

---

60 figure figure of speech **61 Horns** i.e. of cuckoldry **62 disputes** reason **63 gig** spinning-top
65 *manu cita* 'with a ready hand' **68 halfpenny** i.e. little **69 pigeon-egg** i.e. small egg
discretion good judgement **70 wert** were **72 *ad dunghill*** corruption of *ad unguem*, i.e. 'to the fingernail',
exact in detail **75 Arts-man** scholar **preambulate** (let us) walk **76 barbarous** uncivilized
77 charge-house school **78 *mons*** plays on *mons veneris*, pubic mound **80 *sans*** 'without' (French)
82 affection desire **congratulate** pay respects to **83 posteriors** buttocks, i.e. later parts **rude**
ignorant **85 generous** noble **86 liable** apt **congruent** suitable **measurable** fitting **87 culled**
chosen **90 familiar** close friend **91 inward** private **92 courtesy** manners (in wearing your hat)
apparel cover **94 designs** plans **95 by the world** mild oath

world, sometime to lean upon my poor shoulder and
with his royal finger thus dally with my excrement,
with my mustachio. But, sweet heart, let that pass. By
the world, I recount no fable: some certain special
100   honours it pleaseth his greatness to impart to Armado,
a soldier, a man of travel, that hath seen the world —
but let that pass. The very all of all is — but, sweet
heart, I do implore secrecy — that the king would have
me present the princess, sweet chuck, with some
105   delightful ostentation, or show, or pageant, or antic, or
firework. Now, understanding that the curate and
your sweet self are good at such eruptions and sudden
breaking out of mirth, as it were, I have acquainted
you withal, to the end to crave your assistance.

110   **HOLOFERNES** Sir, you shall present before her the Nine
Worthies. Sir Nathaniel, as concerning some
entertainment of time, some show in the posterior
of this day, to be rendered by our assistants, at the
king's command and this most gallant, illustrate
115   and learned gentleman, before the princess, I say
none so fit as to present the Nine Worthies.

NATHANIEL Where will you find men worthy enough to
present them?

HOLOFERNES Joshua, yourself. Myself, Judas Maccabaeus,
120   and this gallant gentleman, Hector. This swain, because   *Indicates*
of his great limb or joint, shall pass Pompey the Great.   *Don*
The page, Hercules.   *Armado*

ARMADO Pardon, sir, error: he is not quantity enough for
that Worthy's thumb. He is not so big as the end of his
125   club.

HOLOFERNES Shall I have audience? He shall present
Hercules in minority: his enter and exit shall be
strangling a snake, and I will have an apology for that
purpose.

---

97 excrement that which grows out of the body, such as hair and nails; also, faeces   **98 sweet heart** i.e.
dear friend   **99 recount no fable** am not telling untruths   **102 all of all** essence   **104 chuck** chick (term
of endearment)   **105 ostentation** public display   **antic** extravagant spectacle   **106 firework** i.e. firework
display   **109 withal** with this   **end** purpose   **110 Nine Worthies** popular subject for entertainments,
featuring three Jews (Joshua, David and Judas Maccabaeus), three pagans (Hector of Troy, Alexander the
Great and Julius Caesar), and three Christians (Arthur, Charlemagne and Godfrey of Bouillon).
112 entertainment spending   **114 illustrate** illustrious   **120 swain** i.e. Costard   **121 great . . . joint** i.e. he
has a big build (possible phallic joke)   **pass** pass for/represent   **Pompey the Great** famous Roman general
of the first century BC   **125 club** play on penis size   **126 have audience** be heard   **127 in minority** as a
child   **enter** entrance   **128 strangling a snake** as a baby, Hercules strangled two snakes sent by Juno to
kill him   **apology** formal explanation

130 MOTH An excellent device! So, if any of the audience hiss,
        you may cry 'Well done, Hercules! Now thou crushest
        the snake!' That is the way to make an offence
        gracious, though few have the grace to do it.

     ARMADO For the rest of the Worthies?

135 HOLOFERNES I will play three myself.

     MOTH Thrice-worthy gentleman.

     ARMADO Shall I tell you a thing?

     HOLOFERNES We attend.

     ARMADO We will have, if this fadge not, an antic. I beseech
140   you, follow.

     HOLOFERNES *Via*, goodman Dull! Thou hast spoken no
        word all this while.

     DULL Nor understood none neither, sir.

     HOLOFERNES *Allons*! We will employ thee.

145 DULL I'll make one in a dance, or so, or I will play
        On the tabor to the Worthies, and let them dance the
        hay.

     HOLOFERNES Most Dull, honest Dull! To our sport, away!
                                                        Exeunt

[Act 5 Scene 2]   *running scene 6*

Enter Ladies [the Princess, Katherine, Rosaline and Maria]

     PRINCESS Sweet hearts, we shall be rich ere we depart,
        If fairings come thus plentifully in.
        A lady walled about with diamonds!
        Look you what I have from the loving king.   *Shows a jewel*

5   ROSALINE Madame, came nothing else along with that?

     PRINCESS Nothing but this? Yes, as much love in rhyme
        As would be crammed up in a sheet of paper
        Writ on both sides the leaf, margent and all,
        That he was fain·to seal on Cupid's name.

10   ROSALINE That was the way to make his godhead wax,
        For he hath been five thousand years a boy.

     KATHERINE Ay, and a shrewd unhappy gallows too.

---

130 **device** scheme   138 **attend** listen   139 **fadge** works out, succeeds   141 *Via* 'come along'
145 **make one** take part   146 **tabor** small drum   **hay** winding country dance   5.2   2 **fairings** gifts
3 **A ... diamonds!** presumably an ornamental lady's portrait surrounded by diamonds   8 **margent**
margin   9 **fain ... name** obliged to place his seal over Cupid's name (as he had written everywhere)
10 **godhead** i.e. Cupid's   **wax** grow (puns on the **wax** of the **seal**; plays on idea of an enlarging penis)
11 **five ... boy** a child since the world was created   12 **shrewd** cunning/mischievous   **unhappy** trouble-
causing   **gallows** someone who deserves to be hanged

ROSALINE You'll ne'er be friends with him: a killed your
    sister.

KATHERINE He made her melancholy, sad, and heavy,
15   And so she died: had she been light, like you,
    Of such a merry, nimble, stirring spirit,
    She might ha' been a grandam ere she died.
    And so may you, for a light heart lives long.

ROSALINE What's your dark meaning, mouse, of this light
    word?

20 **KATHERINE** A light condition in a beauty dark.

ROSALINE We need more light to find your meaning out.

KATHERINE You'll mar the light by taking it in snuff:
    Therefore I'll darkly end the argument.

ROSALINE Look what you do, you do it still i'th'dark.

25 **KATHERINE** So do not you, for you are a light wench.

ROSALINE Indeed I weigh not you, and therefore light.

KATHERINE You weigh me not? O, that's you care not for
    me.

ROSALINE Great reason, for past care is still past cure.

PRINCESS Well bandied both. A set of wit well played.
30   But Rosaline, you have a favour too.
    Who sent it? And what is it?

ROSALINE I would you knew.
    An if my face were but as fair as yours,
    My favour were as great. Be witness this: *Shows a love*
35   Nay, I have verses too, I thank Berowne.   *token and a letter*
    The numbers true, and, were the numbering too,
    I were the fairest goddess on the ground.
    I am compared to twenty thousand fairs.
    O, he hath drawn my picture in his letter!

40 **PRINCESS** Anything like?

ROSALINE Much in the letters, nothing in the praise.

PRINCESS Beauteous as ink: a good conclusion.

KATHERINE Fair as a text B in a copy-book.

---

13 a … sister i.e. she died for love   **14 heavy** sorrowful   **15 light** merry/light-hearted/promiscuous
17 grandam grandmother   **19 dark** hidden   **mouse** term of affection   **light word** frivolous talk/word
'light'   **20 condition** disposition   **22 taking … snuff** trimming the wick/taking offence (proverbial)
23 darkly obscurely/enigmatically   **24 Look what** whatever   **do it** plays on sense of 'have sex'   **25 light
wench** i.e. unchaste   **26 not** i.e. not the same as   **27 weigh** esteem   **that's** that means   **28 past … cure**
there's no point worrying about what can't be helped (proverbial); some editors transpose 'care' and 'cure'
29 bandied exchanged, tossed to and fro   **set** game (of tennis/wit)   **30 favour** love token   **32 would** wish
36 numbers true poetic metre correct   **numbering** enumeration/calculation   **38 fairs** beautiful women
41 letters lettering   **praise** content   **43 text B** elaborately written capital B, possibly for 'black' or
'Berowne'   **copy-book** writing practice book

ROSALINE 'Ware pencils, how? Let me not die your debtor,
45   My red dominical, my golden letter.
O, that your face were not so full of O's!
PRINCESS A pox of that jest and I beshrew all shrews.
But, Katherine, what was sent to you from fair
Dumaine?
50 KATHERINE Madam, this glove.   *Shows a glove*
PRINCESS Did he not send you twain?
KATHERINE Yes, madam, and moreover
Some thousand verses of a faithful lover,
A huge translation of hypocrisy,
55   Vilely compiled, profound simplicity.
MARIA This and these pearls to me sent Longaville. *Shows a letter*
The letter is too long by half a mile.   *and a pearl necklace*
PRINCESS I think no less. Dost thou not wish in heart
The chain were longer and the letter short?
60 MARIA Ay, or I would these hands might never part.
PRINCESS We are wise girls to mock our lovers so.
ROSALINE They are worse fools to purchase mocking so.
That same Berowne I'll torture ere I go.
O that I knew he were but in by th'week!
65   How I would make him fawn and beg and seek
And wait the season and observe the times
And spend his prodigal wits in bootless rhymes
And shape his service wholly to my device
And make him proud to make me proud that jests!
70   So pert aunt like would I o'ersway his state
That he should be my fool and I his fate.
PRINCESS None are so surely caught, when they are
    catched,
As wit turned fool. Folly, in wisdom hatched,
Hath wisdom's warrant and the help of school
75   And wit's own grace to grace a learnèd fool.

---

44 'Ware beware   pencils fine paintbrushes   Let . . . debtor i.e. I'll not owe you an insult, I'll get my own
back (proverbial)   45 red dominical red lettering used to mark Sundays of the church year in calendars
golden also used to mark Sundays or Easter, or a reference to Katherine's hair   46 O's possibly small scars
caused by smallpox   47 pox curse (may pick up on the idea of smallpox scars)   beshrew curse
shrews vexatious, scolding women   51 twain two   54 translation expression   55 simplicity foolishness/
lack of skill   60 would wish   these . . . part perhaps Maria has bound the chain around her hands
62 purchase deserve, earn   64 in by th'week fully ensnared   66 the season for the right time   observe
the times keep to the rules   67 prodigal lavish, excessive   bootless useless   69 make . . . jests make
him feel grateful even for Rosaline's proud mockery of him   70 pert aunt like Folio's 'pertaunt' (Quarto
'perttaunt') is unexplained: perhaps 'like a lively older woman' (or with French *tante* for 'aunt'?), though
many emendations have been proposed, including 'planet-like', 'fortune-like' and 'pair-taunt-like'
(supposedly a strong hand at cards)   o'ersway overrule   71 his fate controller of his destiny   72 surely
securely   74 warrant authorization

ROSALINE The blood of youth burns not with such excess
    As gravity's revolt to wantonness.
MARIA Folly in fools bears not so strong a note
    As foolery in the wise, when wit doth dote,
80   Since all the power thereof it doth apply
    To prove, by wit, worth in simplicity.
Enter Boyet
PRINCESS Here comes Boyet, and mirth is in his face.
BOYET O, I am stabbed with laughter! Where's her grace?
PRINCESS Thy news, Boyet?
85 **BOYET** Prepare, madam, prepare!
    Arm, wenches, arm! Encounters mounted are
    Against your peace. Love doth approach disguised,
    Armed in arguments: you'll be surprised.
    Muster your wits, stand in your own defence,
90   Or hide your heads like cowards and fly hence.
PRINCESS Saint Denis to Saint Cupid! What are they
    That charge their breath against us? Say, scout, say.
BOYET Under the cool shade of a sycamore
    I thought to close mine eyes some half an hour,
95   When, lo, to interrupt my purposed rest,
    Toward that shade I might behold addressed
    The king and his companions. Warily
    I stole into a neighbour thicket by,
    And overheard what you shall overhear:
100   That, by and by, disguised they will be here.
    Their herald is a pretty knavish page,
    That well by heart hath conned his embassage.
    Action and accent did they teach him there:
    'Thus must thou speak', and 'thus thy body bear'.
105   And ever and anon they made a doubt
    Presence majestical would put him out,
    'For', quoth the king, 'an angel shalt thou see,
    Yet fear not thou, but speak audaciously.'
    The boy replied, 'An angel is not evil:

---

77 gravity seriousness/respectability **wantonness** foolish, uncontrolled, desirous behaviour **78 note** stigma/reproach **79 dote** behave foolishly **80 all … simplicity** the wise man will use his intelligence to demonstrate the wisdom of folly **86 Arm** prepare (for combat) **Encounters mounted are** skirmishes are prepared **88 surprised** ambushed **89 Muster** assemble (like troops) **91 Saint Denis** patron saint of France **to** against **92 charge** load/fire **breath** i.e. words **scout** spy **93 sycamore** tree associated with melancholy **95 purposed** intended **96 might behold addressed** saw approaching **98 by nearby** **99 overhear** hear told again **100 by and by** shortly **102 conned** learned **embassage** message **103 Action** appropriate gestures **accent** verbal delivery **105 ever and anon** every now and then **made a doubt** voiced their fear (that) **106 majestical** regal **put him out** disconcert him/make him forget his lines

110 I should have feared her had she been a devil.'
With that, all laughed and clapped him on the
    shoulder,
Making the bold wag by their praises bolder.
One rubbed his elbow thus, and fleered and swore
A better speech was never spoke before.
115 Another, with his finger and his thumb
Cried, '*Via!* We will do't, come what will come.'
The third he capered, and cried, 'All goes well.'
The fourth turned on the toe, and down he fell.
With that they all did tumble on the ground,
120 With such a zealous laughter, so profound,
That in this spleen ridiculous appears,
To check their folly, passion's solemn tears.
PRINCESS But what, but what, come they to visit us?
BOYET They do, they do, and are apparelled thus:
125 Like Muscovites or Russians, as I guess.
Their purpose is to parley, to court and dance,
And every one his love-feat will advance
Unto his several mistress, which they'll know
By favours several which they did bestow.
130 **PRINCESS** And will they so? The gallants shall be tasked,
For, ladies, we will every one be masked,
And not a man of them shall have the grace,
Despite of suit, to see a lady's face.
Hold, Rosaline, this favour thou shalt wear,
135 And then the king will court thee for his dear.
Hold, take thou this, my sweet, and give me thine,
So shall Berowne take me for Rosaline.   *The Princess and Rosaline*
                                                    exchange favours
And change your favours too, so shall your loves
Woo contrary, deceived by these removes.   *Katherine*
140 **ROSALINE** Come on, then, wear the favours most in sight.   *and Maria*
KATHERINE But in this changing what is your intent? *exchange favours*
PRINCESS The effect of my intent is to cross theirs:
They do it but in mocking merriment,
And mock for mock is only my intent.

112 **wag** mischievous young man   113 **rubbed his elbow** gesture of satisfaction   **fleered** grinned
115 **with … thumb** i.e. snapping his fingers   116 *Via!* 'Come along!'   117 **capered** leaped/danced
joyfully   118 **turned … toe** pirouetted   121 **spleen ridiculous** ludicrous fit of merriment   122 **check**
restrain/reprimand   125 **Like … guess** no rhyme for this line, so a line may be missing   126 **parley** enter
into conversation   127 **love-feat** perhaps a misprint for 'love-suit'   128 **several** individual   130 **gallants**
fine gentlemen/suitors   **tasked** tested   132 **grace** privilege   133 **Despite of suit** in spite of entreaty
134 **Hold … dear** these two lines might be a first draft of the two that follow   138 **change** exchange
139 **removes** exchanges   140 **most in sight** conspicuously   142 **cross** thwart

145   Their several counsels they unbosom shall
        To loves mistook, and so be mocked withal
        Upon the next occasion that we meet,
        With visages displayed to talk and greet.
ROSALINE But shall we dance, if they desire us to't?
150 **PRINCESS** No, to the death, we will not move a foot,
        Nor to their penned speech render we no grace,
        But while 'tis spoke each turn away her face.
BOYET Why, that contempt will kill the speaker's heart
        And quite divorce his memory from his part.
155 **PRINCESS** Therefore I do it, and I make no doubt
        The rest will e'er come in, if he be out.
        There's no such sport as sport by sport o'erthrown,
        To make theirs ours and ours none but our own.
        So shall we stay, mocking intended game,
160   And they, well mocked, depart away with shame.
                                    [*Trumpets*] *sound*
BOYET The trumpet sounds: be masked. The maskers
        come.   *The Ladies mask*
Enter Blackamoors with music, the boy [Moth] with a
speech, and the rest of the Lords [King, Berowne, Longaville
and Dumaine] disguised [in Russian costumes and masks]
MOTH All hail, the richest beauties on the earth!
BEROWNE Beauties no richer than rich taffeta.   *Aside?*
MOTH A holy parcel of the fairest dames.
165   That ever turned their —
                        The Ladies turn their backs to him
                        backs — to mortal views.
BEROWNE Their *eyes*, villain, their *eyes*!   *Aside to Moth*
MOTH That ever turned their *eyes* to mortal views! Out ...
BOYET True. Out indeed.
MOTH Out of your favours, heavenly spirits, vouchsafe
170   Not to behold—
BEROWNE *Once* to behold, rogue.   *Aside to Moth*
MOTH Once to behold with your sun-beamèd eyes ...
        With your sun-beamèd eyes ...

---

145 counsels private intentions   **unbosom** disclose   **146 loves mistook** i.e. the wrong women   **withal** with this   **148 visages displayed** faces visible, i.e. unmasked   **150 to the death** i.e. we'd rather fight to the death   **151 penned** composed   **render** yield   **grace** favour   **153 kill ... heart** discourage his affection   **154 part** remembered lines/intentions   **156 be out** has forgotten his lines   **158 theirs ours** i.e. their fun our amusement   **159 intended** their intended   ***Blackamoors*** attendants costumed and/or made-up to look like black men   **163 taffeta** silk material, often used for making masks   **164 parcel** small group   **167 Out ...** i.e. Moth has forgotten his lines; ellipsis used when speaker dries, dash when interrupted   **169 vouchsafe** permit, deign

BOYET They will not answer to that epithet.
175   You were best call it 'daughter-beamèd eyes'.
MOTH They do not mark me and that brings me out.
BEROWNE Is this your perfectness? Be gone, you rogue!

[*Exit Moth*]

ROSALINE What would these strangers? Know their   *Pretends to be*
    minds, Boyet.   *the Princess*
    If they do speak our language, 'tis our will
180   That some plain man recount their purposes
    Know what they would.
BOYET What would you with the princess?
BEROWNE Nothing but peace and gentle visitation.
ROSALINE What would they, say they?
185   **BOYET** Nothing but peace and gentle visitation.
ROSALINE Why, that they have, and bid them so be gone.
BOYET She says, you have it, and you may be gone.
KING Say to her, we 'have measured many miles
    To tread a measure with you on the grass'.
190   **BOYET** They say that they have measured many a mile
    To tread a measure with you on this grass.
ROSALINE It is not so. Ask them how many inches
    Is in one mile. If they have measured many,
    The measure then of one is easily told.
195   **BOYET** If to come hither you have measured miles,
    And many miles, the princess bids you tell
    How many inches doth fill up one mile.
BEROWNE Tell her we measure them by weary steps.
BOYET She hears herself.
200   **ROSALINE** How many weary steps,
    Of many weary miles you have o'ergone,
    Are numbered in the travel of one mile?
BEROWNE We number nothing that we spend for you.
    Our duty is so rich, so infinite,
205   That we may do it still without account.
    Vouchsafe to show the sunshine of your face,
    That we, like savages, may worship it.
ROSALINE My face is but a moon, and clouded too.

---

174 epithet description   **175 daughter-beamèd** punning on sun-/son-beamèd   **176 brings me out**
makes me forget my lines   **177 perfectness** being word-perfect   **178 What … strangers?** What do these
foreigners want?   **minds** intentions   **180 plain** plain-spoken/honest   **183 gentle visitation** a courteous,
friendly visit   **188 measured** traversed   **189 tread a measure** dance a stately dance   **194 measure**
quantity/measurement   **told** counted/said   **202 travel** journeying/labour (travail)   **203 number** ac-
count/count up   **205 still** always   **account** estimate, counting/debt   **208 My … moon** i.e. her face
shines with light reflected from the princess/is changeable   **clouded** i.e. masked

KING Blessèd are clouds, to do as such clouds do!
210 Vouchsafe, bright moon, and these thy stars, to shine,
Those clouds removed, upon our wat'ry eyne.
ROSALINE O vain petitioner! Beg a greater matter:
Thou now requests but moonshine in the water.
KING Then, in our measure vouchsafe but one change.
215 Thou bid'st me beg: this begging is not strange.
ROSALINE Play, music, then! Nay, you must do it soon.   *Music plays*
Not yet? No dance! Thus change I like the moon.
KING Will you not dance? How come you thus estranged?
ROSALINE You took the moon at full, but now she's
changed.
220 KING Yet still she is the moon, and I the man.
ROSALINE The music plays, vouchsafe some motion to it.
Our ears vouchsafe it.
KING But your legs should do it.
ROSALINE Since you are strangers and come here by
chance,
225 We'll not be nice: take hands. We will not dance.   *Offers her hand*
KING Why take you hands, then?
ROSALINE Only to part friends.
Curtsy, sweet hearts, and so the measure ends.   *Music stops*
KING More measure of this measure. Be not nice.
230 ROSALINE We can afford no more at such a price.
KING Price yourselves: what buys your company?
ROSALINE Your absence only.
KING That can never be.
ROSALINE Then cannot we be bought. And so, adieu.
235 Twice to your visor and half once to you.
KING If you deny to dance, let's hold more chat.
ROSALINE In private then.
KING I am best pleased with that.   *They talk apart*
BEROWNE White-handed mistress, one sweet word with   *To the*
thee.   *Princess*
240 PRINCESS Honey and milk and sugar: there is three.   *Pretends to*
be Rosaline

---

209 do ... do i.e. be as close to the ladies' faces as the masks are   210 stars i.e. the other ladies
211 eyne eyes   213 moonshine ... water i.e. something insubstantial   214 change round of dancing
215 strange unusual (plays on sense of 'foreign')   218 estranged apart/aloof; puns on strange   220 she
... man i.e. they belong together, being moon and man in the moon (no rhyme word for 'moon': a line may
be missing)   221 The ... it some editors assign this line to the king   motion movement   225 nice shy/
fussy/whimsical   229 More measure a greater quantity   231 Price 'price' and 'prize' sounded the same
235 Twice ... you possibly refers to Rosaline's curtsies – two to the king's visor, but only half of one to his
face   236 deny refuse   240 three i.e. sweet words for Berowne

BEROWNE Nay then, two treys, and if you grow so nice,
　　　Metheglin, wort and malmsey. Well run, dice!
　　　There's half-a-dozen sweets.
PRINCESS Seventh sweet, adieu.
245　　Since you can cog, I'll play no more with you.
BEROWNE One word in secret.
PRINCESS Let it not be sweet.
BEROWNE Thou griev'st my gall.
PRINCESS Gall! Bitter.
250　**BEROWNE** Therefore meet.　　　　　　　　　　*They talk apart*
DUMAINE Will you vouchsafe with me to change a word?　　*To Maria*
MARIA Name it.　　　　　　　　　　*Pretends to be Katherine*
DUMAINE Fair lady—
MARIA Say you so? Fair lord.
255　　Take you that for your 'fair lady'.
DUMAINE Please it you,
　　　As much in private, and I'll bid adieu.　　　　*They talk apart*
KATHERINE What, was your vizard made without a　　　*Pretends*
　　　tongue?　　　　　　　　　　　　　　　*to be Maria*
LONGAVILLE I know the reason, lady, why you ask.
260　**KATHERINE** O for your reason! Quickly, sir, I long.
LONGAVILLE You have a double tongue within your
　　　mask
　　　And would afford my speechless vizard half.
KATHERINE 'Veal', quoth the Dutchman. Is not 'veal' a
　　　calf?
LONGAVILLE A calf, fair lady?
265　**KATHERINE** No, a fair lord calf.
LONGAVILLE Let's part the word.
KATHERINE No, I'll not be your half.
　　　Take all, and wean it, it may prove an ox.
LONGAVILLE Look, how you butt yourself in these sharp
　　　mocks.
270　　Will you give horns, chaste lady? Do not so.
KATHERINE Then die a calf before your horns do grow.

---

241 **treys** threes (in gambling)　**nice** coy　242 **Metheglin** strong spiced Welsh mead　**wort** sweet
unfermented beer　**malmsey** strong sweet red wine　**run** played/fallen　243 **sweets** i.e. sweet words
245 **cog** cheat (like a gambler)　248 **griev'st** vex　**gall** sore spot/bile　250 **meet** fitting　251 **change**
exchange　256 **Please it you** if it pleases you　258 **vizard** visor　**tongue** leather strap held in the mouth
to keep the visor secure/reference to Longaville's silence　261 **double tongue** i.e. your tongue and the
mask's tongue/duplicitous tongue　262 **afford. . .half** i.e. end my silence/reveal your identity
263 **'Veal'** Dutch pronunciation of 'well' (i.e. assessment of Longaville's **reason**); added to Katherine's last
spoken word, '**long**', it provides the name of her wooer　**calf** stupid person, implying Longaville is
one　266 **part** divide　267 **half** co-sharer/partner (in marriage)　268 **wean** raise　**prove an ox** become a
fool　269 **butt** strike　270 **give horns** attack/cuckold your husband

LONGAVILLE One word in private with you ere I die.

KATHERINE Bleat softly then, the butcher hears you cry.   *They talk*

BOYET The tongues of mocking wenches are as keen   *apart*

275 As is the razor's edge invisible,

Cutting a smaller hair than may be seen,

Above the sense of sense, so sensible

Seemeth their conference. Their conceits have wings

Fleeter than arrows, bullets, wind, thought, swifter
    things.

280 **ROSALINE** Not one word more, my maids: break off, break
    off.

BEROWNE By heaven, all dry-beaten with pure scoff!

KING Farewell, mad wenches; you have simple wits.

                          Exeunt [King, Berowne, Longaville,
                                   Dumaine and Blackamoors]

PRINCESS Twenty adieus, my frozen Muscovites.   *The Ladies unmask*

Are these the breed of wits so wondered at?

285 **BOYET** Tapers they are, with your sweet breaths puffed
    out.

ROSALINE Well-liking wits they have: gross, gross, fat, fat.

PRINCESS O, poverty in wit, kingly-poor flout!

Will they not, think you, hang themselves tonight?

Or ever, but in vizards, show their faces?

290 This pert Berowne was out of countenance quite.

ROSALINE They were all in lamentable cases.

The king was weeping-ripe for a good word.

PRINCESS Berowne did swear himself out of all suit.

MARIA Dumaine was at my service, and his sword.

295 'No point', quoth I: my servant straight was mute.

KATHERINE Lord Longaville said I came o'er his heart:

And trow you what he called me?

PRINCESS Qualm, perhaps.

KATHERINE Yes, in good faith.

300 **PRINCESS** Go, sickness as thou art!

ROSALINE Well, better wits have worn plain statute-caps.

But will you hear? The king is my love sworn.

274 **keen** sharp/eager   277 **sense of sense** perception of the senses   **sensible** striking
278 **conference** conversation   **conceits** witty thoughts, quips   279 **Fleeter** swifter. nimbler
281 **dry-beaten** beaten. bruised   **scoff** mockery   285 **Tapers** candles   **with** by   286 **Well-liking**
thriving, plump   **gross** dull/plump   287 **kingly-poor flout** feeble insult from a king/majestically poor
mockery   290 **pert** lively   **out ... quite** completely disconcerted   291 **cases** states/masks
292 **weeping-ripe** ready to weep   293 **out ... suit** out of keeping with his love-suit (**suit** puns on sense of
'clothing')   295 **servant** servant in love/wooer   **straight** at once   296 **came o'er** overcame
297 **trow you** would you believe   298 **Qualm** sudden feeling of nausea/heart-burn   301 **plain statute-
caps** woollen knitted caps worn by those of lower social status

PRINCESS And quick Berowne hath plighted faith to me.
KATHERINE And Longaville was for my service born.
305 MARIA Dumaine is mine as sure as bark on tree.
BOYET Madam, and pretty mistresses, give ear:
    Immediately they will again be here
    In their own shapes, for it can never be
    They will digest this harsh indignity.
310 PRINCESS Will they return?
BOYET They will, they will, God knows,
    And leap for joy, though they are lame with blows:
    Therefore change favours, and, when they repair,
    Blow like sweet roses in this summer air.
315 PRINCESS How blow? How blow? Speak to be understood.
BOYET Fair ladies masked are roses in their bud:
    Dismasked, their damask sweet commixture shown,
    Are angels vailing clouds, or roses blown.
PRINCESS Avaunt, perplexity! What shall we do
320   If they return in their own shapes to woo?
ROSALINE Good madam, if by me you'll be advised
    Let's mock them still, as well known as disguised.
    Let us complain to them what fools were here,
    Disguised like Muscovites, in shapeless gear:
325   And wonder what they were and to what end
    Their shallow shows and prologue vilely penned,
    And their rough carriage so ridiculous,
    Should be presented at our tent to us.
BOYET Ladies, withdraw. The gallants are at hand.
330 PRINCESS Whip to our tents, as roes runs o'er land.
                    Exeunt [the Princess, Rosaline,
                          Katherine and Maria]
Enter the King and the rest [Berowne, Longaville and
Dumaine, as themselves]
KING Fair sir, God save you! Where's the princess?
BOYET Gone to her tent. Please it your majesty
    Command me any service to her?
KING That she vouchsafe me audience for one word.
335 BOYET I will, and so will she, I know, my lord.   *Exit*
BEROWNE This fellow pecks up wit as pigeons peas
    And utters it again when Jove doth please.

303 **quick** hasty **306 give ear** listen **308 In ... shapes** i.e. without disguises **309 digest** swallow/put
up with **313 repair** return **314 Blow** blossom (the princess plays on the sense of 'give blows')
317 damask red and white (variety of rose) **commixture** complexion/mingling **318 vailing** lowering/
yielding **319 Avaunt** begone **perplexity** riddler **322 as ... disguised** as much as we did when they
were in disguise **324 shapeless gear** unshapely clothes **325 end** purpose **327 rough carriage**
graceless behaviour **330 roes** female deer (puns on 'rose') **337 utters** speaks/offers for sale

He is wit's pedlar and retails his wares
At wakes and wassails, meetings, markets, fairs.
340   And we that sell by gross, the Lord doth know,
Have not the grace to grace it with such show.
This gallant pins the wenches on his sleeve.
Had he been Adam, he had tempted Eve.
He can carve too, and lisp. Why, this is he
345   That kissed away his hand in courtesy.
This is the ape of form, Monsieur the Nice,
That when he plays at tables chides the dice
In honourable terms. Nay, he can sing
A mean most meanly, and in ushering
350   Mend him who can. The ladies call him sweet.
The stairs, as he treads on them, kiss his feet.
This is the flower that smiles on everyone,
To show his teeth as white as whale's bone
And consciences that will not die in debt
355   Pay him the due of honey-tongued Boyet.
KING A blister on his sweet tongue, with my heart,
That put Armado's page out of his part!
Enter the Ladies [the Princess, Rosaline, Maria and
Katherine, with Boyet]
BEROWNE See where it comes! Behaviour, what wert thou
Till this madman showed thee? And what art thou
now?
360   KING All hail, sweet madam, and fair time of day!
PRINCESS 'Fair' in 'all hail' is foul, as I conceive.
KING Construe my speeches better, if you may.
PRINCESS Then wish me better, I will give you leave.
KING We came to visit you and purpose now
365   To lead you to our court. Vouchsafe it then.
PRINCESS This field shall hold me, and so hold your vow.
Nor God nor I delights in perjured men.
KING Rebuke me not for that which you provoke.
The virtue of your eye must break my oath.

---

339 wakes church festivals   **wassails** revels   **340 by gross** wholesale   **342 gallant** i.e. ladies' man
pins . . . **sleeve** makes the women dependent on him/collects them like favours   **343 Had** . . . **Eve** i.e. rather
than Eve tempting Adam as in the Bible   **344 carve** behave charmingly but affectedly   **lisp** talk in a
pretentious manner   **345 kissed** . . . **courtesy** wore his hand out with too many courteous kisses
346 ape of form imitator of etiquette   **Nice** fastidious   **347 tables** backgammon   **348 honourable**
polite   **349 mean** middle part (tenor or alto)   **meanly** well enough   **ushering** taking the part of the
gentleman usher, organizing ceremonies   **350 Mend** beat, improve on   **357 put** . . . **part** i.e. made Moth
forget his lines   **358 it** i.e. Boyet   **Behaviour** fine manners   **359 madman** i.e. Boyet   **361 'Fair'** . . . **foul** it
is false to call a hailstorm fair   **362 Construe** understand/interpret   **363 wish me** greet me with   **leave**
permission   **366 This** . . . **me** i.e. I will stay here   **hold** keep   **367 Nor** neither

370 **PRINCESS** You nickname virtue: 'vice' you should have
   spoke,
  For virtue's office never breaks men's troth.
  Now, by my maiden honour, yet as pure
  As the unsullied lily, I protest,
  A world of torments though I should endure,
375   I would not yield to be your house's guest,
  So much I hate a breaking cause to be
  Of heavenly oaths, vowed with integrity.
  KING O, you have lived in desolation here,
  Unseen, unvisited, much to our shame.
380 **PRINCESS** Not so, my lord. It is not so, I swear.
  We have had pastimes here and pleasant game:
  A mess of Russians left us but of late.
  KING How, madam? Russians?
  PRINCESS Ay, in truth, my lord.
385   Trim gallants, full of courtship and of state.
  ROSALINE Madam, speak true. It is not so, my lord.
  My lady, to the manner of the days,
  In courtesy gives undeserving praise.
  We four indeed confronted were with four
390   In Russian habit. Here they stayed an hour,
  And talked apace; and in that hour, my lord,
  They did not bless us with one happy word.
  I dare not call them fools; but this I think,
  When they are thirsty, fools would fain have drink.
395 **BEROWNE** This jest is dry to me. Fair gentle sweet,
  Your wits makes wise things foolish. When we greet,
  With eyes best seeing, heaven's fiery eye,
  By light we lose light. Your capacity
  Is of that nature that to your huge store
400   Wise things seem foolish and rich things but poor.
  ROSALINE This proves you wise and rich, for in my eye—
  BEROWNE I am a fool, and full of poverty.
  ROSALINE But that you take what doth to you belong,
  It were a fault to snatch words from my tongue.
405 **BEROWNE** O, I am yours, and all that I possess!
  ROSALINE All the fool mine?

---

370 nickname misname **371 office** function **372 yet** still **373 protest** declare **376 a ... Of** to be the reason for you breaking your **378 desolation** solitariness **382 but of late** only recently **385 Trim** smart **courtship** courtliness/wooing **state** stately appearance **387 to ... days** as is the current fashion **388 undeserving** undeserved **391 apace** quickly **392 happy** well-chosen/apt/agreeable **394 When ... drink** i.e. they are fools **395 dry** yields no result (plays on sense of **thirsty**) **396 When ... light** i.e. when we look directly at the sun, we are blinded by its light **398 capacity** intelligence **399 to** compared to **401 eye** organ of sight/opinion

BEROWNE I cannot give you less.

ROSALINE Which of the vizards was it that you wore?

BEROWNE Where? When? What vizard? Why demand you
    this?

410 **ROSALINE** There, then, that vizard; that superfluous case
    That hid the worse and showed the better face.

KING We are descried; they'll mock us now downright.   *Aside*

DUMAINE Let us confess and turn it to a jest.   *Aside*

PRINCESS Amazed, my lord? Why looks your highness
    sad?

415 **ROSALINE** Help, hold his brows! He'll swoon! Why look
    you pale?
    Sea-sick, I think, coming from Muscovy.

BEROWNE Thus pour the stars down plagues for perjury.
    Can any face of brass hold longer out?
    Here stand I lady, dart thy skill at me;

420   Bruise me with scorn, confound me with a flout,
    Thrust thy sharp wit quite through my ignorance,
    Cut me to pieces with thy keen conceit,
    And I will wish thee never more to dance,
    Nor never more in Russian habit wait.

425   O, never will I trust to speeches penned,
    Nor to the motion of a schoolboy's tongue,
    Nor never come in vizard to my friend,
    Nor woo in rhyme, like a blind harper's song!
    Taffeta phrases, silken terms precise,

430   Three-piled hyperboles, spruce affectation,
    Figures pedantical; these summer-flies
    Have blown me full of maggot ostentation.
    I do forswear them; and I here protest,
    By this white glove — how white the hand, God
    knows! —

435   Henceforth my wooing mind shall be expressed
    In russet yeas and honest kersey noes.
    And, to begin, wench — so God help me, law! —
    My love to thee is sound, *sans* crack or flaw.

---

410 **case** covering, i.e. mask   412 **descried** discovered   414 **Amazed** perplexed/dumbstruck
415 **brows** temples   416 **Muscovy** i.e. Russia   418 **face of brass** brazen manner/firm expression
419 **dart thy skill** hurl your judgement/wit   420 **confound** destroy/overthrow **flout** taunt   422 **keen
conceit** sharp wit   423 **wish** ask   424 **habit** outfit **wait** do service   426 **motion** movement
427 **friend** sweetheart   428 **harper's** harpist's   429 **Taffeta** i.e. elaborate **precise** fastidious
430 **Three-piled** luxuriously thick (like velvet)   431 **Figures** i.e. figures of speech **pedantical** pedantic/
excessively learned   432 **blown** swollen/deposited eggs/polluted   436 **russet** rustic/homely (homespun
reddish cloth) **kersey** plain (coarse cloth)   437 **law** la (i.e. 'indeed')   438 ***sans*** 'without' (French)

ROSALINE *Sans 'sans'*, I pray you.

440 BEROWNE Yet I have a trick
Of the old rage. Bear with me, I am sick.
I'll leave it by degrees. Soft, let us see:
Write, 'Lord have mercy on us' on those three.
They are infected, in their hearts it lies:

445 They have the plague, and caught it of your eyes.
These lords are visited, you are not free,
For the Lord's tokens on you do I see.

PRINCESS No, they are free that gave these tokens to us.

BEROWNE Our states are forfeit. Seek not to undo us.

450 ROSALINE It is not so, for how can this be true,
That you stand forfeit, being those that sue?

BEROWNE Peace! For I will not have to do with you.

ROSALINE Nor shall not, if I do as I intend.

BEROWNE Speak for yourselves. My wit is at an end.   *To the Lords*

455 KING Teach us, sweet madam, for our rude transgression
Some fair excuse.

PRINCESS The fairest is confession.
Were you not here but even now disguised?

KING Madam, I was.

460 PRINCESS And were you well advised?

KING I was, fair madam.

PRINCESS When you then were here,
What did you whisper in your lady's ear?

KING That more than all the world I did respect her.

465 PRINCESS When she shall challenge this, you will reject
her.

KING Upon mine honour, no.

PRINCESS Peace, peace, forbear.
Your oath once broke, you force not to forswear.

KING Despise me when I break this oath of mine.

470 PRINCESS I will: and therefore keep it.— Rosaline,
What did the Russian whisper in your ear?

ROSALINE Madam, he swore that he did hold me dear
As precious eyesight, and did value me
Above this world: adding thereto moreover

475 That he would wed me or else die my lover.

---

439 *Sans 'sans'* i.e. don't use affected French words   440 **trick** characteristic   441 **rage** madness/rash fever   442 **by degrees** little by little   443 **'Lord ... us'** written on the doors of plague victims as a warning   445 **of** from   446 **visited** afflicted   **free** uninfected   447 **Lord's tokens** signs of plague/love tokens given by the lords   448 **free** generous/uninfected   449 **states** honourable status/status as bachelors/estates   451 **sue** entreat/woo   452 **to do** sex/anything to do   458 **but even** just   460 **well advised** i.e. thinking wisely   464 **respect** value   465 **challenge** claim   467 **forbear** stop   468 **force ... forswear** will not hesitate to break it again

PRINCESS God give thee joy of him. The noble lord
Most honourably doth uphold his word.
KING What mean you, madam? By my life, my troth,
I never swore this lady such an oath.
480 **ROSALINE** By heaven, you did; and to confirm it plain,
You gave me this. But take it, sir, again.   *Shows the Princess'*
KING My faith and this the princess I did give.   *favour*
I knew her by this jewel on her sleeve.
PRINCESS Pardon me, sir, this jewel did she wear,
485 And Lord Berowne, I thank him, is my dear.—
What, will you have me or your pearl again?   *To Berowne*
BEROWNE Neither of either, I remit both twain.   *as she shows*
I see the trick on't. Here was a consent,   *Rosaline's favour*
Knowing aforehand of our merriment,
490 To dash it like a Christmas comedy.
Some carry-tale, some please-man, some slight zany,
Some mumble-news, some trencher-knight, some Dick
That smiles his cheek in years and knows the trick
To make my lady laugh when she's disposed,
495 Told our intents before, which once disclosed,
The ladies did change favours and then we,
Following the signs, wooed but the sign of she.
Now, to our perjury to add more terror,
We are again forsworn in will and error.
500 Much upon this 'tis.— And might not you   *To Boyet*
Forestall our sport, to make us thus untrue?
Do not you know my lady's foot by th'squier,
And laugh upon the apple of her eye?
And stand between her back, sir, and the fire,
505 Holding a trencher, jesting merrily?
You put our page out: go, you are allowed.
Die when you will, a smock shall be your shroud.
You leer upon me, do you? There's an eye

---

487 **either** the two **remit** give up 488 **on't** of it **consent** agreement 490 **dash** spoil **Christmas comedy** seasonal entertainment 491 **carry-tale** tell-tale **please-man** yes-man **slight** lowly **zany** clown's assistant 492 **mumble-news** gossip **trencher-knight** dinner-table hero/great eater **Dick** low fellow 493 **smiles … years** wrinkles his face with smiles **trick** knack (with sexual innuendo)
494 **disposed** inclined to be merry 497 **sign of she** outward symbol thought to represent our particular mistress 500 **Much … 'tis** it must have happened pretty much this way 502 **by th'squier** accurately 503 **laugh … eye** i.e. exchange laughter and knowing looks with her **apple** pupil 504 **stand … fire** i.e. act as her fire-guard (**stand** may play on sense of 'get an erection' and **fire** on sense of 'sexual passion', perhaps also with vaginal connotations) 505 **Holding a trencher** i.e. ready to be of service **trencher** plate 507 **Die** plays on sense of 'have an orgasm' **smock … shroud** you'll be buried like a woman **smock** woman's undergarment 508 **leer** look sideways

Wounds like a leaden sword.

BOYET   Full merrily hath
510   This brave manage, this career, been run.

BEROWNE Lo, he is tilting straight! Peace! I have done.

Enter Clown [Costard]

Welcome, pure wit! Thou partest a fair fray.

COSTARD O lord, sir, they would know
Whether the three Worthies shall come in or no.

515   BEROWNE What, are there but three?

COSTARD No, sir, but it is vara fine,
For every one pursents three.

BEROWNE And three times thrice is nine.

COSTARD Not so, sir — under correction, sir — I hope it is
not so.
520   You cannot beg us, sir, I can assure you, sir, we know
what we know.
I hope, sir, three times thrice, sir—

BEROWNE Is not nine?

COSTARD Under correction, sir, we know whereuntil it
doth amount.

525   BEROWNE By Jove, I always took three threes for nine.

COSTARD O lord, sir, it were pity you should get your
living by reckoning, sir.

BEROWNE How much is it?

COSTARD O lord, sir, the parties themselves, the actors, sir,
530   will show whereuntil it doth amount. For mine own
part, I am, as they say, but to perfect one man in one
poor man: Pompion the Great, sir.

BEROWNE Art thou one of the Worthies?

COSTARD It pleased them to think me worthy of Pompey
535   the Great. For mine own part, I know not the degree
of the Worthy, but I am to stand for him.

BEROWNE Go, bid them prepare.

COSTARD We will turn it finely off, sir, we will take some
care.   *Exit*

540   KING Berowne, they will shame us: let them not approach.

BEROWNE We are shame-proof, my lord, and 'tis some
policy

---

509 **Wounds** ... **sword** i.e. poses no threat of injury (**sword** may have phallic connotations)   510 **brave manage** fine gallop at full speed   **career** charge/gallop   511 **tilting straight** going straight back to his verbal jousting (plays on notion of a thrusting penis)   512 **Thou partest** you are breaking up   **fray** fight   513 **would** want to   516 **vara** very   517 **pursents** represents, acts   520 **beg us** i.e. take us for fools   523 **whereuntil** to what   526 **were** ... **get** would be a shame if you had to make   527 **reckoning** calculation   531 **perfect** i.e. perform, present   532 **Pompion** pumpkin; malapropism for 'Pompey'   535 **degree** rank   536 **stand for** represent   538 **turn** ... **off** pull off the performance well   541 **policy** clever device

To have one show worse than the king's and his
    company.

KING I say they shall not come.

PRINCESS Nay, my good lord, let me o'errule you now.

545   That sport best pleases that doth least know how:
    Where zeal strives to content and the contents
    Dies in the zeal of that which it presents,
    There form confounded makes most form in mirth
    When great things labouring perish in their birth.

550 **BEROWNE** A right description of our sport, my lord.   *To the King*

Enter Braggart [Armado]

ARMADO Anointed, I implore so much expense of thy
    royal sweet breath as will utter a brace of words.   *Armado and the*

PRINCESS Doth this man serve God?   *King talk apart*

BEROWNE Why ask you?

555 **PRINCESS** He speaks not like a man of God's making.

ARMADO That's all one, my fair, sweet, honey monarch,
    for, I protest, the schoolmaster is exceeding fantastical,
    too too vain, too too vain. But we will put it, as they
    say, to *fortuna de la guerra*. I wish you the peace of   *Gives him a*

560   mind, most royal couplement!   [*Exit*]   *paper,*

KING Here is like to be a good presence of Worthies. He *which the King*
    presents Hector of Troy, the swain Pompey the Great,   *looks over*
    the parish curate Alexander, Armado's page Hercules,
    the pedant Judas Maccabaeus.

565   'And if these four Worthies in their first show   *Reads*
       thrive,
    These four will change habits and present the
       other five.'

BEROWNE There is five in the first show.

KING You are deceived, 'tis not so.

BEROWNE The pedant, the braggart, the hedge-priest, the
    fool and the boy.

570   Abate throw at novum, and the whole world again
    Cannot prick out five such, take each one in's vein.

KING The ship is under sail and here she comes amain.

Enter [Costard as] Pompey

---

546 **zeal** fervent enthusiasm **content** please **contents** subject matter 547 **that** … **presents** the presentation 548 **There** … **mirth** the ruining of the presentation creates its own mirth 551 **Anointed** i.e. the king, anointed as monarch **expense** expenditure 552 **brace** pair 556 **one** the same (to me) 559 *fortuna* … *guerra* 'the chance of war' (Spanish) 560 **couplement** couple 561 **like** likely **presence** company 564 **pedant** schoolmaster 566 **habits** costumes 569 **hedge-priest** uneducated rural priest 570 **Abate** set aside **throw at novum** lucky throws in a dice game, in which throwing a five and nine won; the actors will perform the Nine Worthies with only five actors 571 **vein** mood/character 572 **amain** at full speed

COSTARD I Pompey am—

BEROWNE You lie, you are not he.

575 **COSTARD** I Pompey am—

BOYET With leopard's head on knee.

BEROWNE Well said, old mocker, I must needs be friends
with thee.

COSTARD I Pompey am, Pompey surnamed the Big—

580 **DUMAINE** The 'Great'.

COSTARD It is 'Great', sir—

Pompey surnamed the Great,

That oft in field,

With targe and shield,

585 Did make my foe to sweat.

And travelling along this coast, I here am come
by chance,

And lay my arms before the legs of this sweet
lass of France.—

If your ladyship would say, 'Thanks Pompey', I   *To the*
had done.   *Princess*

PRINCESS Great thanks, great Pompey.

590 **COSTARD** 'Tis not so much worth, but I hope I was
perfect. I made a little fault in 'Great'.

BEROWNE My hat to a halfpenny, Pompey proves the
best Worthy.

Enter Curate [Nathaniel] for Alexander

NATHANIEL When in the world I lived, I was the world's
commander:

595 By east, west, north and south, I spread my conquering
might.

My scutcheon plain declares that I am Alisander—

BOYET Your nose says no, you are not, for it stands too
right.

BEROWNE Your nose smells 'no' in this, most tender-
600 smelling knight.

PRINCESS The conqueror is dismayed.— Proceed, good
Alexander.

NATHANIEL When in the world I lived, I was the world's
commander—

---

576 leopard's head part of Pompey's costume, possibly painted on a shield   **577 must needs** must
584 targe light shield   **586 coast** area   **587 arms** weapons (plays on sense of 'limbs')   **591 perfect** i.e.
word perfect   **592 My ... halfpenny** I'll bet (anything)   *for* as   **596 scutcheon** shield painted with a coat
of arms   **598 right** straight; Alexander's head was supposed to lean to one side   **599 Your ... this**
Alexander was supposed to smell sweet; Berowne suggests Boyet's nose can tell this isn't really Alexander by
Nathaniel's odour   **tender-smelling** having a sensitive sense of smell

BOYET Most true, 'tis right: you were so, Alisander.

605 **BEROWNE** Pompey the Great—

COSTARD Your servant, and Costard.

BEROWNE Take away the conqueror, take away Alisander.

COSTARD O, sir, you have overthrown Alisander the   *To*
conqueror. You will be scraped out of the painted cloth   *Nathaniel*
610 for this. Your lion that holds his pole-axe sitting on a
close-stool will be given to Ajax. He will be the ninth
Worthy. A conqueror and afraid to speak? Run away
for shame, Alisander. There, an't shall please you, a   *Nathaniel*
foolish mild man, an honest man, look you, and soon   *steps back*
615 dashed. He is a marvellous good neighbour, in sooth,
and a very good bowler. But for Alisander, alas, you see
how 'tis — a little o'erparted. But there are Worthies a-
coming will speak their mind in some other sort.

PRINCESS Stand aside, good Pompey.   *Exit [Costard]*
Enter Pedant [Holofernes] for Judas and the boy [Moth] for
Hercules

620 **HOLOFERNES** Great Hercules is presented by this imp,
Whose club killed Cerberus, that three-headed *canus*,
And when he was a babe, a child, a shrimp,
Thus did he strangle serpents in his *manus*.
Quoniam he seemeth in minority,
625 *Ergo* I come with this apology.—
Keep some state in thy exit, and vanish.   *To Moth*
Exit boy [Moth]
Judas I am—

DUMAINE A Judas!

HOLOFERNES Not Iscariot, sir.

630 Judas I am, ycliped Maccabaeus.

DUMAINE Judas Maccabaeus clipped is plain Judas.

BEROWNE A kissing traitor. How art thou proved Judas?

HOLOFERNES Judas I am—

DUMAINE The more shame for you, Judas.

635 **HOLOFERNES** What mean you, sir?

BOYET To make Judas hang himself.

---

609 painted cloth the Nine Worthies were often depicted on painted hangings **610 lion ... close-stool**
Alexander's coat of arms as depicted in the Renaissance **pole-axe** battle-axe **611 close-stool** chamber-
pot within a seat (instead of throne) **Ajax** pun on 'a jakes' (i.e. toilet) **615 dashed** disheartened
617 o'erparted having too difficult a part to play **618 sort** manner **620 imp** child **621 Cerberus**
three-headed dog guarding the entrance to Hades, captured by **Hercules** as his final labour *canus* 'dog'
(Latin, actually *canis*) **623 *manus*** 'hands' **624 *Quoniam*** 'since' **in minority** a child **625 *Ergo***
'therefore' **626 state** dignity **628 A Judas!** i.e. a traitor **629 Iscariot** Judas Iscariot betrayed Christ;
Judas **Maccabaeus** was a military leader **630 ycliped** called **631 clipped** cut short/embraced **632 A**
kissing traitor Judas betrayed Jesus with a kiss **635 mean you** is your meaning/is your intention

HOLOFERNES Begin, sir: you are my elder.

BEROWNE Well followed: Judas was hanged on an elder.

HOLOFERNES I will not be put out of countenance.

640 BEROWNE Because thou hast no face.

HOLOFERNES What is this?   *Pointing to his face*

BOYET A cittern-head.

DUMAINE The head of a bodkin.

BEROWNE A death's face in a ring.

645 LONGAVILLE The face of an old Roman coin, scarce seen.

BOYET The pommel of Caesar's falchion.

DUMAINE The carved-bone face on a flask.

BEROWNE Saint George's half-cheek in a brooch.

DUMAINE Ay, and in a brooch of lead.

650 BEROWNE Ay, and worn in the cap of a tooth-drawer.
      And now forward, for we have put thee in
            countenance.

HOLOFERNES You have put me out of countenance.

BEROWNE False, we have given thee faces.

HOLOFERNES But you have out-faced them all.

655 BEROWNE An thou wert a lion, we would do so.

BOYET Therefore, as he is an ass, let him go.
      And so adieu, sweet Jude. Nay, why dost thou stay?

DUMAINE For the latter end of his name.

BEROWNE For the ass to the Jude? Give it him: Jud-as,
660   away!

HOLOFERNES This is not generous, not gentle, not
      humble.

BOYET A light for Monsieur Judas! It grows dark, he may
      stumble.   *Holofernes steps back*

665 PRINCESS Alas, poor Maccabaeus, how hath he been
      baited!

Enter Braggart [Armado as Hector]

BEROWNE Hide thy head, Achilles. Here comes Hector in
      arms.

---

637 Begin you go first (in hanging yourself)   **elder** senior/superior (Berowne picks up on 'type of tree on which Judas hanged himself')   **639 put ... countenance** made to lose composure (Berowne plays on sense of **face**)   **642 cittern-head** type of guitar with grotesquely carved head   **643 bodkin** hairpin with ornamental head   **644 death's ... ring** ring carved with death's head (a skull)   **645 scarce seen** almost worn away   **646 pommel** ornamental knob on a sword or dagger   **falchion** sword   **647 flask** powder-flask for gunpowder   **648 half-cheek** profile   **649 brooch ... tooth-drawer** tradesmen wore lead brooches to signify their trades   **651 put ... countenance** stopped you being disconcerted/given you a face   **654 out-faced them all** put them all to shame   **655 lion ... ass** in one of Aesop's fables the ass disguises himself as a lion by wearing its skin until he is betrayed by his braying   **658 latter end** second part (i.e. ass)
661 generous mannerly/noble   **gentle** courteous   **662 humble** polite   **663 light ... Judas** possible reference to the Judas candlestick, used at Easter in parish churches   **667 Achilles ... Hector** enemies in the Trojan war   **in arms** armed

DUMAINE Though my mocks come home by me, I will
670   now be merry.
KING Hector was but a Troyan in respect of this.
BOYET But is this Hector?
KING I think Hector was not so clean-timbered.
LONGAVILLE His leg is too big for Hector.
675 DUMAINE More calf, certain.
BOYET No, he is best endued in the small.
BEROWNE This cannot be Hector.
DUMAINE He's a god or a painter, for he makes faces.
ARMADO The armipotent Mars, of lances the almighty,
680   Gave Hector a gift—
DUMAINE A gilt nutmeg.
BEROWNE A lemon.
LONGAVILLE Stuck with cloves.
DUMAINE No, cloven.
685 ARMADO The armipotent Mars, of lances the almighty
     Gave Hector a gift, the heir of Ilion;
     A man so breathed that certain he would fight, yea
     From morn till night, out of his pavilion.
     I am that flower—
690 DUMAINE That mint.
LONGAVILLE That columbine.
ARMADO Sweet Lord Longaville, rein thy tongue.
LONGAVILLE I must rather give it the rein, for it runs
     against Hector.
695 DUMAINE Ay, and Hector's a greyhound.
ARMADO The sweet war-man is dead and rotten. Sweet
     chucks, beat not the bones of the buried. When we
     breathed he was a man. But I will forward with my
     device. Sweet royalty, bestow on me the sense of   *To the*
700   hearing.   *Princess*
[*Costard*] *steps forth*
PRINCESS Speak, brave Hector: we are much delighted.
ARMADO I do adore thy sweet grace's slipper.
BOYET Loves her by the foot.   *Aside to Dumaine*
DUMAINE He may not by the yard.   *Aside to Boyet*

---

669 home by me back to mock me   **671 Troyan** man of Troy/merry fellow   **673 clean-timbered** well-built   **675 calf** lower leg/fool   **676 endued** endowed   **small** i.e. thinnest part of the calf   **678 makes** creates/pulls   **679 armipotent** powerful in arms   **681 gilt** glazed   **684 cloven** split in two (sexually; punning on **lemon** as 'leman' or 'lover')   **686 Ilion** Troy   **687 breathed** exercised/fit   **688 pavilion** ceremonial tent used during tournaments   **692 rein** curb   **695 greyhound** i.e. fast runner   **696 war-man** warrior   **697 beat … buried** i.e. don't speak ill of the dead   **698 forward** advance   **699 device** performance   **703 foot** body part/measurement   **704 yard** three feet/penis

705 **ARMADO** This Hector far surmounted Hannibal.
      The party is gone—

   COSTARD Fellow Hector, she is gone. She is two months
      on her way.

   ARMADO What meanest thou?

710 **COSTARD** Faith, unless you play the honest Troyan, the
      poor wench is cast away: she's quick, the child brags
      in her belly already. 'Tis yours.

   ARMADO Dost thou infamonize me among potentates?
      Thou shalt die.

715 **COSTARD** Then shall Hector be whipped for Jaquenetta
      that is quick by him and hanged for Pompey that is
      dead by him.

   DUMAINE Most rare Pompey!

   BOYET Renowned Pompey!

720 **BEROWNE** Greater than great, great, great, great
      Pompey! Pompey the Huge!

   DUMAINE Hector trembles.

   BEROWNE Pompey is moved. More Ates, more Ates! Stir
      them, or stir them on!

725 **DUMAINE** Hector will challenge him.

   BEROWNE Ay, if a have no more man's blood in's belly
      than will sup a flea.

   ARMADO By the north pole, I do challenge thee.

   COSTARD I will not fight with a pole, like a northern man;
730   I'll slash, I'll do it by the sword. I pray you let me
      borrow my arms again.

   DUMAINE Room for the incensed Worthies.

   COSTARD I'll do it in my shirt.

   DUMAINE Most resolute Pompey!

735 **MOTH** Master, let me take you a buttonhole lower. Do   *To Armado*
      you not see, Pompey is uncasing for the combat.
      What mean you? You will lose your reputation.

   ARMADO Gentlemen and soldiers, pardon me. I will not
      combat in my shirt.

740 **DUMAINE** You may not deny it. Pompey hath made the
      challenge.

---

706 **gone** dead   707 **gone** pregnant (refers to Jaquenetta)   711 **cast away** ruined   **quick** pregnant
brags boasts (suggesting that Armado is the father)   713 **infamonize** slander   **potentates** monarchs
716 **quick** pregnant/living   **Pompey** i.e. the part of Pompey, played by Costard   723 **Ates** discordant
comments; Ate was the Roman goddess of vengeance   725 **challenge him** i.e. to a fight   726 **a have** he
has   727 **sup** feed   729 **pole ... man** raiders of the northern borders were known to fight with poles
731 **borrow ... again** use the weapons I had as Pompey   732 **Room** make room   735 **take ... lower** help
unbutton your doublet/humiliate you   736 **uncasing** undressing

ARMADO Sweet bloods, I both may and will.

BEROWNE What reason have you for't?

ARMADO The naked truth of it is, I have no shirt: I go
745   woolward for penance.

BOYET True, and it was enjoined him in Rome for want
of linen. Since when, I'll be sworn he wore none but
a dishclout of Jaquenetta's, and that he wears next
his heart for a favour.

Enter a Messenger, Monsieur Marcadé

750   **MARCADÉ** God save you, madam!

PRINCESS Welcome, Marcadé,
But that thou interrupt'st our merriment.

MARCADÉ I am sorry, madam, for the news I bring is
heavy in my tongue. The king your father—

755   **PRINCESS** Dead, for my life!

MARCADÉ Even so: my tale is told.

BEROWNE Worthies, away! The scene begins to cloud.

ARMADO For mine own part, I breathe free breath. I have
seen the day of wrong through the little hole of
760   discretion, and I will right myself like a soldier.

Exeunt Worthies

KING How fares your majesty?

PRINCESS Boyet, prepare. I will away tonight.

KING Madam, not so. I do beseech you, stay.

PRINCESS Prepare, I say. I thank you, gracious lords,
765   For all your fair endeavours, and entreat
Out of a new-sad soul that you vouchsafe
In your rich wisdom to excuse or hide
The liberal opposition of our spirits.
If over-boldly we have borne ourselves
770   In the converse of breath, your gentleness
Was guilty of it. Farewell worthy lord!
A heavy heart bears not a nimble tongue.
Excuse me so, coming too short of thanks
For my great suit so easily obtained.

---

742 **bloods** spirited men   745 **woolward** wearing wool next to the skin without a linen shirt
746 **enjoined** imposed on   **want** lack (i.e. Armado's shirtlessness is the result of poverty not religious
penance)   748 **dishclout** dishcloth, with play on menstrual rag   749 **favour** love token   *Marcadé* his
name can be associated with Mercury, messenger of the Roman gods and god of rhetoric; also with the
French *danse macabre* or 'dance of death'   756 **tale** news   758 **breathe free breath** am relieved   **I . . .
discretion** I have enough (if little) discretion to know I have behaved badly   760 **right** avenge/behave
(correctly)   767 **hide** overlook   768 **liberal** unrestrained   **opposition** antagonism   770 **the . . . breath**
i.e. conversation   **gentleness** nobility/courtesy   771 **guilty of** responsible for   773 **so** therefore

775   **KING** The extreme parts of time extremely forms
          All causes to the purpose of his speed,
          And often at his very loose decides
          That which long process could not arbitrate.
          And though the mourning brow of progeny
780   Forbid the smiling courtesy of love
          The holy suit which fain it would convince,
          Yet, since love's argument was first on foot,
          Let not the cloud of sorrow justle it
          From what it purposed: since to wail friends lost
785   Is not by much so wholesome-profitable
          As to rejoice at friends but newly found.
    PRINCESS I understand you not: my griefs are double.
    BEROWNE Honest plain words best pierce the ear of grief,
          And by these badges understand the king.
790   For your fair sakes have we neglected time,
          Played foul play with our oaths: your beauty, ladies,
          Hath much deformed us, fashioning our humours
          Even to the opposed end of our intents.
          And what in us hath seemed ridiculous —
795   As love is full of unbefitting strains,
          All wanton as a child, skipping and vain,
          Formed by the eye and therefore, like the eye,
          Full of straying shapes, of habits and of forms,
          Varying in subjects as the eye doth roll
800   To every varied object in his glance:
          Which parti-coated presence of loose love
          Put on by us, if in your heavenly eyes
          Have misbecomed our oaths and gravities,
          Those heavenly eyes, that look into these faults,
805   Suggested us to make. Therefore, ladies,
          Our love being yours, the error that love makes
          Is likewise yours. We to ourselves prove false
          By being once false forever to be true

---

775 **The . . . speed** i.e. when there is little time available decisions have to be made quickly   777 **his very loose** the very last moment (archery metaphor)   778 **process** proceedings   **arbitrate** conclude   779 **mourning . . . progeny** child's grief for a parent   780 **Forbid** denies   781 **holy suit** i.e. marriage   **fain** gladly   **convince** demonstrate   782 **on foot** i.e. begun   783 **justle** push   784 **wail** lament   **lost** dead   785 **wholesome-profitable** beneficial to well-being   787 **double** because her father is dead and she cannot understand him   789 **badges** outward signs/words   791 **foul play** unfairly   792 **deformed** disfigured   793 **opposed end** i.e. exact opposite   795 **unbefitting** inappropriate   **strains** features/impulses   796 **wanton** carefree/playful   **vain** foolish/silly   798 **straying** some editors emend to 'strange'   **shapes** appearances   **habits** ways of behaving/clothes   800 **his** its   801 **parti-coated** motley, patchwork (worn by fools)   **presence** appearance   **loose** unrestrained   802 **Put on** presented/worn   803 **misbecomed** been unbecoming to   805 **Suggested . . . make** tempted us to commit them   807 **prove false** i.e. by breaking their vows to pursue only learning   808 **true** i.e. faithful to the ladies

To those that make us both — fair ladies, you.
810   And even that falsehood, in itself a sin,
Thus purifies itself and turns to grace.
PRINCESS We have received your letters full of love,
Your favours, the ambassadors of love,
And in our maiden council rated them
815   At courtship, pleasant jest and courtesy,
As bombast and as lining to the time.
But more devout than this in our respects
Have we not been, and therefore met your loves
In their own fashion, like a merriment.
820   DUMAINE Our letters, madam, showed much more than
            jest.
LONGAVILLE So did our looks.
ROSALINE We did not quote them so.
KING Now, at the latest minute of the hour,
Grant us your loves.
825   PRINCESS A time, methinks, too short
To make a world-without-end bargain in.
No, no, my lord, your grace is perjured much,
Full of dear guiltiness, and therefore this:
If for my love, as there is no such cause,
830   You will do aught, this shall you do for me:
Your oath I will not trust, but go with speed
To some forlorn and naked hermitage,
Remote from all the pleasures of the world,
There stay until the twelve celestial signs
835   Have brought about their annual reckoning.
If this austere insociable life
Change not your offer made in heat of blood,
If frosts and fasts, hard lodging and thin weeds
Nip not the gaudy blossoms of your love,
840   But that it bear this trial and last love,
Then at the expiration of the year
Come challenge me, challenge me by these deserts,
And, by this virgin palm now kissing thine,   *Gives him her hand*
I will be thine. And till that instant shut

809 **both** i.e. oath-breakers and true to our word 814 **rated** assessed 815 **At** as no more than
816 **bombast ... time** i.e. ways of filling time **bombast** wool padding/speechifying 817 **devout**
committed/earnest **respects** deliberation/attention 818 **met** responded to 822 **quote** regard
826 **world-without-end** everlasting 828 **dear** dire/costly, valuable 829 **as** although **such cause**
reason (for you to) 830 **aught** anything 832 **forlorn** desolate **naked** austere 834 **until ... reckoning**
i.e. a year **signs** i.e. of the zodiac 836 **insociable** unsociable 838 **hard lodging** uncomfortable living
conditions **weeds** clothes 839 **Nip not** inhibit not the growth of **gaudy** flourishing, colourful
840 **last** remain 841 **expiration** end 842 **challenge** claim **deserts** deserving actions

845   My woeful self up in a mourning house,
      Raining the tears of lamentation
      For the remembrance of my father's death.
      If this thou do deny, let our hands part,
      Neither entitled in the other's heart.
850   KING If this, or more than this, I would deny,
      To flatter up these powers of mine with rest,
      The sudden hand of death close up mine eye!
      Hence, hermit, then — my heart is in thy breast.
      BEROWNE // And what to me, my love? And what to me? //
855   ROSALINE // You must be purgèd too, your sins are rack'd: //
      // You are attaint with faults and perjury. //
      // Therefore, if you my favour mean to get, //
      // A twelvemonth shall you spend and never rest, //
      // But seek the weary beds of people sick. //
860   DUMAINE But what to me, my love? But what to me?
      KATHERINE A wife? A beard, fair health and honesty:
      With three-fold love I wish you all these three.
      DUMAINE O, shall I say 'I thank you, gentle wife'?
      KATHERINE Not so, my lord. A twelvemonth and a day
865   I'll mark no words that smooth-faced wooers say.
      Come when the king doth to my lady come,
      Then if I have much love, I'll give you some.
      DUMAINE I'll serve thee true and faithfully till then.
      KATHERINE Yet swear not, lest ye be forsworn again.
870   LONGAVILLE What says Maria?
      MARIA At the twelvemonth's end
      I'll change my black gown for a faithful friend.
      LONGAVILLE I'll stay with patience, but the time is long.
      MARIA The liker you, few taller are so young.
875   BEROWNE Studies my lady? Mistress, look on me.
      Behold the window of my heart, mine eye:
      What humble suit attends thy answer there.
      Impose some service on me for thy love.
      ROSALINE Oft have I heard of you, my Lord Berowne,
880   Before I saw you, and the world's large tongue

---

849 entitled in having legal claim to   **851 flatter up** pamper   **852 The** may the   **854 And ... sick** these six lines are enclosed within solidi because they seem to be the first draft of the subsequent longer exchange between Berowne and Rosaline; they should be cut in performance   **865 mark no** pay no attention to **smooth-faced** plausible/youthful   **872 friend** i.e. lover/husband   **873 stay** wait   **874 The liker** that's more like; plays on **long** in 'Longaville'   **taller** braver; puns on sense of **long**   **875 Studies** reflects, muses **877 attends** awaits   **880 world's large tongue** i.e. widely distributed report

Proclaims you for a man replete with mocks,
Full of comparisons and wounding flouts,
Which you on all estates will execute
That lie within the mercy of your wit.
885　To weed this wormwood from your fruitful brain,
And therewithal to win me, if you please,
Without the which I am not to be won,
You shall this twelvemonth term from day to day
Visit the speechless sick and still converse
890　With groaning wretches, and your task shall be
With all the fierce endeavour of your wit
To enforce the painèd impotent to smile.

BEROWNE To move wild laughter in the throat of death?
　　It cannot be, it is impossible:
895　Mirth cannot move a soul in agony.

ROSALINE Why, that's the way to choke a gibing spirit,
　　Whose influence is begot of that loose grace
　　Which shallow laughing hearers give to fools.
　　A jest's prosperity lies in the ear
900　Of him that hears it, never in the tongue
　　Of him that makes it. Then, if sickly ears,
　　Deafed with the clamours of their own dear groans,
　　Will hear your idle scorns, continue then,
　　And I will have you and that fault withal.
905　But if they will not, throw away that spirit,
　　And I shall find you empty of that fault,
　　Right joyful of your reformation.

BEROWNE A twelvemonth? Well, befall what will befall,
　　I'll jest a twelvemonth in an hospital.

910　**PRINCESS** Ay, sweet my lord, and so I take my leave.　　*To the King*

KING No, madam, we will bring you on your way.

BEROWNE Our wooing doth not end like an old play:
　　Jack hath not Jill. These ladies' courtesy
　　Might well have made our sport a comedy.

915　**KING** Come, sir, it wants a twelvemonth and a day,
　　And then 'twill end.

BEROWNE That's too long for a play.

---

881 **replete with** full of　882 **comparisons** scoffing analogies　**flouts** insults　883 **estates** classes of people　**execute** inflict　885 **weed** root out　**wormwood** bitterness (medicinal herb)　886 **therewithal** along with that　888 **term** period of time　889 **still converse** continually associate　891 **fierce** vigorous/keen　892 **enforce** compel　**painèd impotent** helpless distressed　893 **move** arouse　**the … death** i.e. the dying　896 **gibing** scoffing　897 **loose grace** easy charm (with possible oxymoronic joke since **loose** can mean 'sinful' while **grace** often signifies 'virtue')　899 **prosperity** success　902 **Deafed** deafened　**dear** dire, terrible　904 **withal** as well　908 **befall … befall** what will be will be　911 **bring** escort　913 **courtesy** courteous behaviour

Enter Braggart [Armado]

ARMADO Sweet majesty, vouchsafe me—   *To the King*

PRINCESS Was not that Hector?

920 **DUMAINE** The worthy knight of Troy.

ARMADO I will kiss thy royal finger and take leave. I am a   *To the*
votary: I have vowed to Jaquenetta to hold the plough   *Princess*
for her sweet love three years.— But, most esteemed   *To the King*
greatness, will you hear the dialogue that the two
925 learnèd men have compiled in praise of the owl and the
cuckoo? It should have followed in the end of our
show.

KING Call them forth quickly: we will do so.

ARMADO Holla! Approach.

*Enter all [Holofernes, Nathaniel, Moth, Costard, Jaquenetta
and others. They stand in two groups]*

930 This side is Hiems, Winter. This Ver, the Spring. The
one maintained by the owl, th'other by the cuckoo.
Ver, begin.

[**THE SPRING GROUP** *sings] the song*

    When daisies pied and violets blue
    And cuckoo-buds of yellow hue
935   And lady-smocks all silver-white
    Do paint the meadows with delight,
    The cuckoo then on every tree
    Mocks married men; for thus sings he:
    'Cuckoo,
940   Cuckoo, cuckoo.' O word of fear,
    Unpleasing to a married ear.

    When shepherds pipe on oaten straws
    And merry larks are ploughmen's clocks,
    When turtles tread, and rooks and daws,
945   And maidens bleach their summer smocks,
    The cuckoo then, on every tree,
    Mocks married men, for thus sings he:
    'Cuckoo,
    Cuckoo, cuckoo.' O word of fear,
950   Unpleasing to a married ear.

---

922 hold the plough become a farmer (with sexual connotations)   **924 dialogue** scholarly debate   **two
learnèd men** i.e. Sir Nathaniel and Holofernes   **931 maintained** defended/represented   **933 pied**
multicoloured   **935 lady-smocks** cuckoo-flowers   **936 paint** adorn   **938 Mocks married men** i.e.
because his call sounds like 'cuckold' and because the **cuckoo** usurps the nests of other birds   **942 oaten
straws** straws from oat plants   **943 larks … clocks** because **ploughmen** rise early and **larks** are dawn
birds   **944 turtles** turtle-doves   **tread** mate   **daws** jackdaws

[THE WINTER GROUP *sings*]
            When icicles hang by the wall
            And Dick the shepherd blows his nail
            And Tom bears logs into the hall
            And milk comes frozen home in pail,
955   When blood is nipped and ways be foul,
            Then nightly sings the staring owl:
            'Tu-whit, tu-whoo.'
            A merry note,
            While greasy Joan doth keel the pot.

960   When all aloud the wind doth blow
            And coughing drowns the parson's saw
            And birds sit brooding in the snow
            And Marian's nose looks red and raw,
            When roasted crabs hiss in the bowl,
965   Then nightly sings the staring owl:
            'Tu-whit, tu-whoo.'
            A merry note,
            While greasy Joan doth keel the pot.
ARMADO The words of Mercury are harsh after the songs
970   of Apollo. You that way; we this way.
                                    Exeunt [*separately*]

---

952 blows his nail i.e. warms his hands by blowing on them/has nothing much to do   **955 nipped**
chilled   **ways be foul** paths are muddy   **959 greasy** covered with grease/fat/sweaty   **keel** stir/cool
961 parson's saw clergyman's maxims   **962 brooding** incubating eggs   **964 crabs** crab-apples   **bowl**
i.e. bowl of ale   **969 Mercury** messenger of the gods   **harsh** disagreeable, discordant   **970 Apollo** Greek
god of music   **You** may refer either to the audience, ladies or actors   **we** may refer either to the actors,
lords, or Armado and Jaquenetta

TEXTUAL NOTES

Q = First Quarto text of 1598
F = First Folio text of 1623
F2 = a correction introduced in the Second Folio text of 1632
Ed = a correction introduced by a later editor
SD = stage direction
SH = speech heading (i.e. speaker's name)
// // probable authorial first thoughts that should have been cut from the
    early printed editions

List of parts = Ed

1.1.27 quite = Q. *Not in* F **62 feast** = Ed. F = fast **72 and** = F. Q = but **111 That were to** =
F. *Not in* Q **gate** = F. Q = little gate **112 sit** = Q. F = fit **129 SH BEROWNE** = Ed. F
and Q *continue speech to Longaville* **132 court shall** = F. Q = Court can **153 speak** = Q.
F = break **184 tharborough** = F. Q = Farborough **254 continent** = Q. F =
Continet **266 keep** = Q. F = keeper **285 SH KING** = F *(Fer.)*. Q = *Ber.* **304 until
then, sit down** = F. Q = till then sit thee downe sorrow
1.2.3 SH MOTH = Ed. F = *Boy. (throughout)* **4 SH ARMADO** = Ed. F = *Brag. or Bra.
(throughout)* **10 señor** = Ed. F = signeur **14 epitheton** = F2. F = apathaton **27
ingenious** = Q. F = ingenuous **39 fits** = F. Q = fitteth **46 call** = F. Q = do call
86 maculate = Q. F = immaculate **94 blushing** = F2. F = blush-in **119 let him take**
= F. Q = suffer him to take **124 SH JAQUENETTA** = Ed. F = *Maid.
(throughout)* **130 that** = Q. F = what **135 SH COSTARD** = F. *Some eds reassign
to* DULL, *ignoring his exit at line 98* **138 SH COSTARD** = Ed. F = *Clo.
(throughout)* **143 SH ARMADO** = F = Clo. **152 to be too** = Q. F = to be **162
Samson was** = F. Q = was Sampson
2.1.13 SH PRINCESS = F2. F = *Queen* (F *has a redundant 'Prin.' at line 21)* **45 parts** = F. Q
= peerelsse **54 SH MARIA** = Ed. F = *Lad.*1 **57 SH KATHERINE** = Ed. F = *2.
Lad.* **61 he** = Q. F = she **66 if** = Q. F = as **81 SH MARIA** = F. Q = *Lord*
90 unpeopled = F. Q = unpeeled **117 SH ROSALINE** = F. *This and next six speeches
assigned to Kath. in* Q **145 repaid** = F = repaie **147 On** = Ed. F = One **172 would
I** = F. Q = I will **176 in** = F. Q = within **179 fair** = Q. F = farther **181 we shall** =
F. Q = shall we **184 SH BEROWNE** = Q. *This and next five speeches assigned to Boy*[*et*]
in F **188 fool** = Q. F = soule **194 *Non point*** = Ed. F = *No poynt* **199 Katherine** =
Ed. Q/F = Rosalin **217 Rosaline** = Ed. Q/F = Katherine **220 You** = F. Q = O
you **227 SH MARIA** = F. Q = *Lady Ka.* **228 SH BOYET** = Q. *Placed at next line in*
F **245 did** = Q. F = doe **255 whence** = F. Q = where **262 SH BOYET** = Q. F =
Bro.
3.1.1 SH ARMADO = Ed. F = *Brag. or Bra.* **9 master** = Q. *Not in* F **10 your feet** = F. F =
the feete **11 eyelids** = Q. F = eie **13 through the nose** = F2. F = through: nose **54 Thy**
= F. Q = The **73 O** = Q. F = Or **83 sain** = Q. F = faine **122 honours** = F. Q =
honour **128 One penny** = Ed. F = i.d. **130 French** = Q. F = a French **167 Signior
Junior** = Ed. F = signior *Iunios* **191 sue and** = F2. F = shue

4.1.1 SH PRINCESS = F2. F = *Qu. (throughout)* **14 again** = Q. F = then again **74 overcame** = Ed. F = covercame **90 Armado** = F2. F = Armatho **140 hit it** = Ed. F = hit **146 pin** = F2. F = is in **154 Armado o'th't'other** = Ed. F = *Armathor* ath to the side **158 SD** *Shout* = F2. F = *Shoote*

4.2.3 SH HOLOFERNES = Ed. F = *Ped.* **12 auld grey doe** = Ed. F = *haud credo* **29 of** = Ed. *Not in* F **34 by** = F. Q = me by **37** *Dictynna* = Ed. F = *Dictisima* **52 called I** = Ed. F = call'd **65 SH HOLOFERNES** = Ed. Q/F *reverse speech headings of Holofernes and Nathaniel in this and their next seven speeches* **69 pia mater** = Ed. F = primater **76 ingenious** = Ed. F = ingennous **78** *sapit* = Ed (Q2). F = *sapis* **81 pierce-one** = Ed. F = Person **91** *Fauste* = F2. F = *Facile* **97 loves thee not** = Q. F. *Not in* F **103 SH NATHANIEL** = Ed. *Not in* F **118 Here** = Ed. *(continuation of Holofernes' speech).* Q/F *assign to* Nath. **128 SH HOLOFERNES** = Ed. Q/F = *Nath.* **131 writing** = Ed. F = written **139 hand** = F. Q = royal hand **144 SH NATHANIEL** = Ed. F = *Hol.* **151 before** = Q. F = being

4.3.82 of = F. Q = in **93 I** = Ed. *Not in* F **102 ever** = Q. F = every **142 One** = Q. F = On **155 coaches** = Ed. F = couches **168 tuning** = F. Q = to tune **174 caudle** = Q. F = candle **177 to … by** = Ed. F = by … to **181 men like you, men** = Ed. F = men, like men **224 show** = Q. F = will shew **226 are** = F. Q = were **257 wood** = Ed. F = word **267 and** = Ed. *Not in* F **369 authors** = Ed. F = author **393** *Allons! Allons!* = Ed. F = Alone, alone

5.1.1 *quod* = Ed. F = *quid* **22 d, e, t** = Ed. F = det **26 insanie** = Ed. F = infamie **28** *bone* = Ed. F = *bene* **29** *Bone?* … *'bene'* = Ed. F = *Bome boon for boon* **57 venue** = Ed. F = vene we **65** *manu* = Ed. F = unum **87 choice** = F2. F = chose **93 important** = Ed. F = importunate **111 Nathaniel** = Ed. F = Holofernes *(Shakespeare confuses the names again)* **119 Judas … Hector** = Ed. F *transposes order of phrases and omits* Hector **144** *Allons* = Ed. F = Alone

5.2.46 not so = Q. *Not in* F **58 not wish** = Q. F = wish **77 wantonness** = F2. F = wantons be **82 is in** = Q. F = in **143 mocking** = F. Q = mockerie **152 her** = Ed. F = his **153 speaker's** = Q. F = Keepers **182 princess** *spelled* Princes *in* F **189 you on the** = F. Q = her on this **214 vouchsafe but** = F. Q = do but vouchsafe **255 Take you that** = F. Q = Take that **258 SH KATHERINE** = Ed. F = *Mari. or Mar. (throughout this exchange)* **336 pecks** = Q. F = picks **337 Jove** = F. Q = God **345 kissed … hand** = F. Q = kist his hand, a way **355 due** = Q. F = dutie **371 men's** = Q. F = men **373 unsullied** = F2. F = unsallied **390 Russian** = Q. F = Russia **395 Fair gentle** = F2. F = Gentle **408 was** = Q. F = what **412 are** = F. Q = were **430 affectation** = Ed. F = affection **458 you not** = F. Q = not you **510 manage** = Ed. F = manager **545 least** = F. Q = best **548 There** = Ed. F = Their **571 prick** = F. Q = picke **589 SH PRINCESS** = F2. F = *La.* **674 Hector** = F. Q = Hectors **697 When … man** = Q. *Not in* F **700 SD** *Costard* = Ed. F = *Berowne (probably error for* Clowne, *who is about to confront Armado over Jaquenetta's pregnancy)* **705–06** *set as SD in* F **730 pray** = F. Q = bepray **751 SH PRINCESS** = F2. F = *Qu. (throughout rest of scene)* **765 entreat** = Q. F = entreats **772 nimble** = Ed. F = humble **773 too** = Q. F = so **788 ear** = Q. F = ears **817 this in our** = Ed. F = these are our. Q = this our **853 hermit** = Ed. F = euer. Q = herrite **878 thy** = Q. F = my **923 years** = F. Q = yeere **969 SH ARMADO** = F. *Not in* Q, *where the Mercury/Apollo speech is set in large type with no speaker* **970 You that way** = F. *Not in* Q

SCENE-BY-SCENE ANALYSIS

ACT 1 SCENE 1

Lines 1–180: The King of Navarre reminds his friends, Berowne, Longaville and Dumaine, of their plans to make his court into 'a little academe, / Still and contemplative in living art'. He promises that this will ensure that they are renowned long after they are dead, giving them 'fame, that all hunt after in their lives', establishing the theme of learning and introducing the hunting imagery that runs throughout (usually associated with love, but symbolizing the pursuit of any desire, be it romantic, sexual or academic). It also establishes the theme of 'reputation', something many of the characters are either concerned with or judged by. The king reminds his friends that they have agreed to live in the court for three years and to abide by an oath that he asks them to sign. Longaville and Dumaine do so, but Berowne questions the severity of the conditions: they are 'not to see a woman' in that time, 'to touch no food' for 'one day in a week' and to sleep only 'three hours in the night'. Berowne's speech raises the motif of time and the recurrent images of light and dark as he complains that he has been used to sleep a lot more than this, sometimes making 'a dark night too of half the day'. His arguments show his quick wit and ability to reason, but the king claims that he is 'like an envious sneaping frost', destroying their plans before they are underway, and suggests that he leaves. Berowne says that he has 'sworn' to be part of the king's plans and so will stay, highlighting the importance of honour. Berowne reads the declaration by the king that 'no woman shall come within a mile' of the court and that no man shall talk with a woman during the three years or otherwise 'endure such public shame as the rest of the court shall possibly devise'. He points out that the king himself must break this 'article', as the 'French king's daughter' is due to arrive in Navarre to talk with the king on behalf of her 'decrepit, sick and bedrid father'. The king confesses that he had forgotten this, and declares that the princess must be allowed 'on mere necessity'. Berowne finally signs the oath and asks if there is to be no 'quick recreation' while they study. The king reminds him of the visiting Spaniard, Armado, whose flamboyance and fanciful language make him a figure of fun. Berowne comments that he is a man of 'fire-new words, fashion's own knight', one of many references to words and speech that highlight the play's obsession with language. They agree that Armado and 'Costard the swain' shall be their 'sport'.

Lines 181–305: Dull brings in Costard and delivers a letter to the king from Armado. Comedy is created through Dull and Costard's incorrect use of language, which contrasts with Berowne's verbal dexterity. The king and his friends are pleased at the prospect of a ridiculous letter from Armado, and Costard explains that the 'contempts' (contents) concern him. With several comic interruptions from Costard, the king reads the letter aloud, revealing Armado's pompous and long-winded style. This includes a pedantry over detail and the over-use of synonyms, such as 'viewest, beholdest, surveyest or see'st', typical of the play's self-consciously over-written style. Armado reports that he saw Costard in the king's park, where he 'sorted and consorted' with Jaquenetta, thereby breaking the king's recently declared law. He has sent Costard for punishment. The king declares that Costard will 'fast a week with bran and water' and tells Berowne to deliver him back to Armado, who shall be Costard's 'keeper'.

ACT 1 SCENE 2

Armado confesses to his page, Moth, that he loves Jaquenetta. Their exchange is full of verbal ambiguities that illustrate Moth's superior wit. In addition to his intricate wordplay, Moth's asides also generate humour as he reveals his low opinion of his master and his scorn that Armado is in love with 'a light wench'. Dull brings in Costard and Jaquenetta and explains that Armado is in charge of Costard and that Jaquenetta is to serve at the lodge. Armado tells Jaquenetta that he loves her, but she responds with contempt and leaves. Armado tells Moth to take Costard away. Alone, he considers his feelings and decides to 'turn sonnet', declaring: 'Devise, wit: write, pen, for I am for whole volumes in folio'. This draws attention to the conventions of romantic love, which are explored throughout the play, and highlights the written word as an aspect of language.

ACT 2 SCENE 1

Lines 1–91: The Princess of France arrives outside the court with her train. Lord Boyet encourages her to 'summon up' her 'dearest spirits', as she will need them in dealing with the King of Navarre. Status and honour are emphasized as he talks of the princess as 'precious in the world's esteem' and reminds her that she is dealing with 'matchless Navarre', reinforcing the issue of reputation that was established in Act 1. The ambiguity of the term 'matchless' also evokes the king's unmarried state and establishes expectations for the development of the romantic plotline. Boyet's speech introduces a recurrent motif concerned with wealth and value ('precious', 'inheritor', 'owe', 'dowry', and 'dear'), reminding us that there is always a financial as well as romantic aspect to a potential match. Having heard of the king's vow that 'No woman may approach his silent court', the princess sends Boyet to tell the king that she is waiting. While Boyet is away, the princess asks her attending ladies if they know any of the king's 'vow-fellows'. Reflecting the careful structuring of the romantic plotline, each of the ladies knows one of the lords: Maria speaks of Longaville, 'a man of sovereign parts', Katherine describes Dumaine, 'a well-accomplished youth', and Rosaline praises Berowne's wit and his 'sweet and voluble' 'discourse'. The princess declares that they must all be in love. Boyet returns to report that the king intends to 'lodge' the princess 'in the field', 'Like one that comes here to besiege his court', an example of the military imagery that is often used as a metaphor for courtship.

Lines 92–183: The king welcomes the princess. Their verbal sparring establishes her as his intellectual equal. She gives him a letter from her father and, while he reads it, Berowne and Rosaline also engage in a brief battle of wits. The letter concerns the disputed loan of 'a hundred thousand crowns' and the rights to the province of Aquitaine. The princess claims that she can produce the documentation that proves her father 'faithfully' paid Navarre, but Boyet tells them that the packet containing the papers will not arrive until the next day. The king ceremoniously welcomes the princess to wait in lodging that will be provided for her outside of the court. He leaves, taking Longaville and Dumaine with him.

Lines 184–274: Berowne and Rosaline flirt briefly before he follows the others. Dumaine returns and asks Boyet who Katherine is. After he has left, Longaville also comes back and asks 'what is she in the white?' and Boyet identifies Maria. Finally, Berowne returns and asks Boyet for Rosaline's name, and inquires if she is 'wedded'. Once the French party is alone, Maria and Boyet banter and the princess suggests that instead of 'jangling' with each other, they should engage in a 'civil war of wits' with 'Navarre and his bookmen'. In a speech that typifies the play's inquiry into sight and observation, Boyet expresses the opinion that the king is in love with the princess, claiming that 'all eyes saw his eyes enchanted with gazes'. The ladies all tease Boyet, calling him a 'love-monger' and 'Cupid's grandfather'.

ACT 3 SCENE 1

Lines 1–123: Sustaining his role of 'lover', Armado asks Moth to sing for him (music, like poetry, is one of the conventional expressions of romantic love). Armado's 'romance' however, is comically undermined by Jaquenetta's previous contempt and the fact that she is, as Moth continually points out, of low status and questionable virtue. Moth demonstrates his intellectual superiority over his master, who cannot follow his quick wit and whose own attempts to appear learned are made ridiculous by comparison, as Moth insults him as an 'ass' and Jaquenetta as a 'hackney'. Moth fetches Costard and, after a confusing conversation, Armado gives Costard some money and sets him free on the condition that he delivers a letter to Jaquenetta. Armado and Moth leave.

Lines 124–192: Berowne finds Costard and pays him to deliver a letter to Rosaline. Costard agrees and sets off to deliver both letters. Alone, Berowne muses on how he used to be scornful of love, but now finds himself attracted to Rosaline. His speech simultaneously acknowledges and challenges the conventions of romantic love. In keeping with tradition, it is a highly stylized poetic declaration, but this is undermined by a generic self-consciousness as Berowne refers to 'Don Cupid, / Regent of love-rhymes' and acknowledges various traditional images of love poetry. The subversion of conventional romance is emphasized by Berowne's apparent reluctance to be in love and his less than enthusiastic description of Rosaline, whose eyes are like 'two pitch-balls stuck in her face'. Eventually, however, he resigns himself to traditional lover-like behaviour, declaring that he will 'love, write, sigh, pray, sue and groan'.

ACT 4 SCENE 1

The princess and her attendants are out hunting. She demonstrates her wit as she discusses the struggle for power between the genders, an idea that becomes the focus of much of the action from here onwards. The hunting/courtship metaphor is sustained, as is the theme of reputation as the princess acknowledges that she only hunts for the 'fame' and 'praise' that she will receive for killing the 'poor deer'. They are interrupted by Costard who gives the princess a letter, telling her that it is 'from Monsieur Berowne to one Lady Rosaline'. Unable to read, however, he gives her the letter from Armado to Jaquenetta instead. Boyet discovers the mistake and the princess tells Boyet to read the letter aloud. Armado's ridiculous style causes everyone much amusement. The princess leaves with most of her attendants. Boyet and Rosaline engage in a brief exchange of bawdy wit and Rosaline leaves, saying that Boyet cannot 'hit' her (either in wit, or sexually) and Boyet acknowledges this, but says that 'another can', meaning Berowne. Maria then banters with Boyet and Costard in an exchange that contains some barely-concealed innuendo, although Costard does not appear to understand all that passes, adding to the humour.

ACT 4 SCENE 2

Dull, Holofernes and Nathaniel discuss the hunt. The conversation illustrates two extremes of learning/understanding, as Dull fails to understand most of what is said and Holofernes and Nathaniel show off their knowledge and education. All characters generate humour, as Dull's misunderstanding creates confusion, and the others' pedantic nature makes them ridiculous (and perhaps demonstrates the outcome of a life devoted to learning with no actual 'living', such as the one proposed by the king). Costard and Jaquenetta interrupt and Jaquenetta asks them to read the letter that Costard has just delivered to her, believing it to be from Armado. Costard has, of course, confused the letters and Nathaniel consequently reads out Berowne's letter to Rosaline, which is a love sonnet. Holofernes analyses the technical merit of the poem and ignores its sentiment, again showing the distance between education and experience. When they realize that the letter is from Berowne to Rosaline, Nathaniel sends Jaquenetta to take it to the king.

ACT 4 SCENE 3

Lines 1–190: The hunting/courtship parallel is emphasized as Berowne observes that the king is 'hunting the deer' while he himself is 'coursing'. He expresses his reluctance to be in love, but acknowledges that he is, and that love has 'taught' him 'to rhyme and to be melancholy', an instance of learning through experience, rather than through books. The king enters, holding a paper, and Berowne hides to watch him. Sighing, the king reads a sonnet that he has written to the princess. As he finishes, he sees Longaville arrive and hides to watch him read aloud a sonnet that he has written to Maria. The comedy generated by the circumstances, with Berowne watching the king watching Longaville, is added to as Dumaine arrives and Longaville hides to watch him read a sonnet to Katherine. The comedy is heightened by their asides, particularly Berowne's cynical observations on the effects of love. Berowne's comment that he alone sees everyone else, 'Like a demigod' watching over 'wretched fools' secrets' creates awareness of observation/spectatorship as the theatre audience becomes vicariously involved in the process of concealment, observation and reaction. Once Dumaine has read his sonnet, Longaville comes forward and tells him that he overheard and would 'blush' to be 'taken napping' in this way. At this point, the king comes forward and tells Longaville not to 'chide' Dumaine, as he has overheard him declare his love for Maria. He berates them for breaking their oaths and claims that Berowne will 'scorn' and 'triumph' at them both, adding that he is glad that Berowne does not 'know so much' of him. Berowne steps out at this point to 'whip hypocrisy' and reveals that he has seen all three of them declare their love. He claims that he has been 'betrayed' by them all and that he is 'honest' and has kept the oath. Jaquenetta and Costard enter, bringing Berowne's letter to Rosaline to give to the king.

Lines 191–396: The king gives the letter to Berowne to read aloud, but Berowne, recognizing it, tears it up. Everyone is surprised, but when Dumaine gathers the pieces of the letter he recognizes Berowne's writing. Berowne is forced to admit that he is also a 'fool' and asks that Costard and Jaquenetta leave so that he can tell his friends more. He confesses his love for Rosaline and the four men argue over which lady is the most beautiful. The king urges them to 'leave this chat' and asks Berowne to construct an argument to 'prove' that their love is 'lawful' and that they have not broken their oaths. They urge him to find 'Some salve for perjury' and Berowne makes a long speech that justifies their behaviour. He argues that their oath was 'Flat treason against the kingly state of youth' and claims that they would never have learned from their books what they have learned from 'the prompting eyes / Of beauty's tutors'. He argues that learning that solely occupies the brain is 'barren', but that love learned through experience, 'learnèd in a lady's eyes', stimulates the 'power' of all the faculties. The king declares 'soldiers, to the field!', reinforcing the earlier imagery paralleling love and battle, and they discuss how best to 'woo these girls of France'. Berowne suggests that they entertain them with 'revels, dances, masks and merry hours' and they go to prepare.

ACT 5 SCENE 1

Holofernes and Nathaniel criticize Armado for his 'verbosity', ironically analysing every aspect of his speech in their long-winded way. Armado arrives, accompanied by Moth and Costard. Holofernes, Nathaniel and Armado embark on a needlessly lengthy conversation, punctuated by Moth's witty interjections and asides as he observes that the three men have 'been at a great feast of languages, and stolen the scraps'. Armado announces that the king has charged him to produce some entertainment for the princess and that he has come to ask for their help. Holofernes suggests that they stage a pageant of 'the Nine Worthies' and Armado agrees.

ACT 5 SCENE 2

Lines 1–161: The ladies compare the favours and messages that the men have sent, criticizing the verses for being too long and mocking the senders. Boyet arrives, laughing, and tells the ladies to 'arm' themselves, as 'Love doth approach disguised'. He explains that he overheard the king and his companions planning to visit the ladies, disguised 'Like Muscovites or Russians', to 'parley, to court and dance'. Believing that the men 'do it but in mocking merriment', the princess decides to give back 'mock for mock'. She instructs her ladies to wear masks and to exchange favours, so that she will appear as Rosaline, and vice versa, and Katherine and Maria will be mistaken for each other. A trumpet announces the arrival of the men, who are disguised.

Lines 162–282: Moth delivers a greeting, interrupted by both Berowne and Boyet, and is ignored by the ladies. Rosaline, pretending to be the princess, instructs Boyet to ask what the 'strangers' want. Rosaline thwarts all attempts at gallantry or courtship by the king, cleverly parrying all his flattery and refusing to dance. Eventually, however, she agrees to speak with him and they draw aside, although the king still thinks that he is speaking to the princess. Sustaining the careful structuring of the play, Berowne speaks with the princess (believing that she is Rosaline), Dumaine talks with Maria (thinking that she is Katherine) and Longaville talks to Katherine (thinking that she is Maria). The women continue to rebuff the men's advances until Rosaline declares 'Not one word more.' Berowne observes that the men have been 'dry-beaten with pure scoff' and they leave.

Lines 283–511: The ladies are pleased by the success of their plan and continue to mock their suitors. Boyet suggests that the men will come back 'In their own shapes' and that, when they do, the ladies should pretend not to have recognized them earlier and 'complain to them what fools were here, / Disguised like Muscovites'. The ladies retire and the king and his companions return, without their disguises. The king asks Boyet to fetch the ladies and when they arrive he tries to persuade the princess to return with him to his court. She refuses, saying that she does not wish to cause him to break his oath. When he argues that they have 'lived in desolation' in the field, 'Unseen' and 'unvisited', she says that this is not so: they have just been visited by 'a mess of Russians'. Rosaline adds that the Russian were fools who did not speak 'one happy word'. When Rosaline asks Berowne which of the 'vizards' he wore, the men realize that they have been recognized all along. Berowne declares that he will never 'woo in rhyme again' or dress up his feelings in excessive language: 'Taffeta phrases, silken terms precise', but instead his 'wooing mind shall be expressed / In russet yeas and honest kersey noes'. The king confesses to the princess that he was there in disguise, but is confused when she asks Rosaline what he whispered in her ear, still believing that he had been speaking to the princess. The ladies reveal their 'disguises' (the switched favours) and Berowne realizes that the men have been outdone and accuses Boyet the 'carry-tale' of telling the ladies of their plan so that they could 'dash it like a Christmas comedy'.

Lines 512–749: Costard arrives to ask whether the pageant may begin and, despite the king's concern that the entertainment will 'shame' them in front of the ladies, Berowne sends Costard to fetch the actors. He argues that ''tis some policy / To have one show worse than the king's and his company'. The pageant, as a performance within a performance, draws our attention to issues of theatre and acting and consequently to the disguise and artifice in the wider play. The 'dual audience', like the one in Act 4 scene 3, reinforces the preoccupation with sight/observation. Comedy is generated not only by the ineptitude of the performance, but also by the comments of the onstage 'audience' who interrupt and mock the actors (although the princess tries to be kind and encouraging). The performance is interrupted by Costard announcing that Jaquenetta is pregnant by Armado, who denies it and challenges Costard. As they prepare to fight, however, he changes his mind, explaining that he has no shirt on and cannot disrobe. As they wrangle, a messenger, Monsieur Marcadé, arrives from the French court.

Lines 750–917: Marcadé tells the princess that her father has died, creating a moment of tragedy that seems in tension with the comic conventions of the play so far. She tells Boyet that they will leave that night and the king tries to persuade her to remain. His language, however, is too complicated, causing Berowne to comment that 'plain words best pierce the ear of grief' and to explain that they are all in love. The princess says that they all believed that the men only courted them as 'bombast and lining to the time', and thus met their loves in the same vein 'like a merriment'. The men claim that their 'letters' and their 'looks' 'showed much more than jest' and the king urges, 'at the latest minute of the hour', that the ladies grant them their loves. This reinforces the sense of the power of time, one of many motifs in this final scene that evoke those in Act 1 scene 1, creating a cyclical structure to the play. The princess' reference to 'frosts and fasts' that might 'nip' the love of the king, for example, echoes the king's comment about the 'sneaping frost' of Berowne's wit at the beginning of the play, and there are many references to sight/observation. Abstinence is also returned to, as the princess agrees that she will marry the king, but only if he will wait one year in 'austere unsociable life' to test his love for her. The other ladies impose similar conditions of waiting on their suitors: Rosaline, for example, instructs Berowne to use his wit to entertain 'the speechless sick'. In some ways, then, this cyclical nature pattern reflects the careful structuring throughout, but the balance is disturbed by a lack of resolution that undermines the traditional comedy genre, as Berowne comments: 'Our wooing doth not end like an old play: / Jack hath not Jill.'

Lines 918–970: Armado returns to take his leave, having vowed to Jaquenetta to 'hold the plough for her sweet love three years' (another unresolved courtship), and suggests that the king and his company might like to hear a 'dialogue' between the cuckoo and the owl, written by Nathaniel and Holofernes. The play ends with the dialogue (in the form of a song) contrasting spring and winter, which reflects the tensions of the play.

LOVE'S LABOUR'S LOST IN PERFORMANCE: THE RSC AND BEYOND

The best way to understand a Shakespeare play is to see it or ideally to participate in it. By examining a range of productions, we may gain a sense of the extraordinary variety of approaches and interpretations that are possible – a variety that gives Shakespeare his unique capacity to be reinvented and made 'our contemporary' four centuries after his death.

We begin with a brief overview of the play's theatrical and cinematic life, offering historical perspectives on how it has been performed. We then analyse in more detail a series of productions staged over the last half-century by the Royal Shakespeare Company. The sense of dialogue between productions that can only occur when a company is dedicated to the revival and investigation of the Shakespeare canon over a long period, together with the uniquely comprehensive archival resource of promptbooks, programme notes, reviews and interviews held on behalf of the RSC at the Shakespeare Birthplace Trust in Stratford-upon-Avon, allows an 'RSC stage history' to become a crucible in which the chemistry of the play can be explored.

Finally, we go to the horse's mouth. Modern theatre is dominated by the figure of the director, who must hold together the whole play, whereas the actor must concentrate on his or her part. The director's viewpoint is therefore especially valuable. Shakespeare's plasticity is wonderfully revealed when we hear directors of highly successful productions answering the same questions in very different ways.

FOUR CENTURIES OF *LOVE'S LABOUR'S*: AN OVERVIEW

Evidence about the play's earliest performances is scarce, consisting of little more than a few passing references and allusions.[1] The title page of the 1598 Quarto of *Love's Labour's Lost* claims that 'it was presented before her Highness this last Christmas' and, further, that it has been 'Newly corrected and augmented'. The latter claim suggests the possible existence of an earlier Quarto, in which case the reference to performance before Queen Elizabeth may have been carried over from the earlier Quarto rather than relate specifically to the Christmas period 1597–98. If there were two Quartos in quick succession, that would suggest considerable demand: as a rule, Shakespeare's comedies were reprinted far less often than his histories and tragedies.

In 1598 Francis Meres, in *Palladis Tamia: Wit's Treasury*, listed both *Love's Labour's Lost* and *Love's Labour's Won* as examples of Shakespeare's excellence as a writer of comedies. The same year, Robert Tofte published his poem of unrequited love, *Alba: The Month's Mind of a Melancholy Lover*, which seems to refer to a performance of the play:

> *Love's Labour Lost*, I once did see a play,
> Yclepèd so, so callèd to my pain,
> Which I to hear to my small joy did stay,
> Giving attendance on my froward dame.
> My misgiving mind presaging to me ill,
> Yet was I drawn to see it 'gainst my will.
>
> This play no play but plague was unto me,
> For there I lost the love I likèd most:
> And what to others seemed a jest to be,
> I that (in earnest) found unto my cost.
> To everyone (save me) 'twas comical,
> Whilst tragic-like to me it did befall.
>
> Each actor played in cunning wise his part,
> But chiefly those entrapped in Cupid's snare:
> Yet all was feignèd, 'twas not from the heart,

They seemed to grieve, but yet they felt no care.
  'Twas I that grief indeed did bear in breast,
  The others did but make a show in jest.

Yet neither feigning theirs, nor my mere truth,
Could make her once so much as for to smile:
Whilst she (despite of pity mild and ruth)
Did sit as scorning of my woes the while.
  Thus did she sit to see Love lose his love,
  Like hardened rock that force nor power can move.

The poem provides a rare and suggestive glimpse into what might be described as Elizabethan 'dating': a man taking his girlfriend to the theatre and finding his reaction to the play entangled with his own feelings.

A letter from Sir Walter Cope to Sir Robert Cecil in 1604 indicates the play was still in the repertory in the following decade. Richard Burbage, the leading actor with Shakespeare's company, recommended it as suitable entertainment for the new Queen, Anne, wife of James I:

> Sir – I have sent and been all this morning hunting for players, jugglers and such kind of creatures, but find them hard to find; wherefore leaving notes for them to seek me, Burbage is come, and says there is no new play that the queen hath not seen, but they have revived an old one, called *Love's Labour's Lost*, which for wit and mirth he says will please her exceedingly. And this is appointed to be played tomorrow night at my Lord of South-ampton's, unless you sent [a note] to remove the *corpus cum causa* to your house in Strand.[2]

The play was also performed at court in January 1605. The 1631 Quarto refers on the title page to the play 'As it was acted by his Majesty's Servants at the Blackfriars and the Globe', which confirms that it was performed publicly and that the King's Men continued to perform it after 1608, when they took over the smaller indoor Blackfriars Theatre. The theatres closed in 1642 during the Commonwealth. After the Restoration of the monarchy in 1660,

Love's Labour's Lost was assigned to Thomas Killigrew's company, but there is no record of its performance then for nearly two hundred years.

In 1762 an anonymous adaptation, *The Students*, was published, but there is no evidence of its performance, nor of any staging of a musical version that was commissioned by David Garrick in 1771. Various theories have been put forward to account for the play's lack of theatrical appeal to generations of directors and theatre-goers, chiefly its complex, often obscene, wordplay and lack of a conventional happy ending. For many years critical reception was likewise hostile, with certain scholars, such as Alexander Pope, asserting that it was not even by Shakespeare. Doctor Johnson defended the play as Shakespeare's work but drew attention to what he regarded as its shortcomings:

> In this play, which all the editors have concurred to censure and some have rejected as unworthy of our poet, it must be confessed that there are many passages mean, childish, and vulgar; and some which ought not to have been exhibited, as we are told they were, to a maiden queen. But there are scattered through the whole many sparks of genius; nor is there any play that has more evident marks of the hand of Shakespeare.[3]

It was not until 1839 that the play returned to the London stage, when the opera star Lucia Elizabeth Vestris and her husband, Charles James Mathews, inaugurated their management of Covent Garden with a spectacular production designed in collaboration with James Robinson Planché. Madame Vestris played Rosaline. Although a critical success, the riots which followed the closure of the theatre's shilling gallery brought its run to an end after only nine performances.

Samuel Phelps finally mounted a successful production at Sadler's Wells in 1857. Set in a picturesque medieval court with painted backdrops of 'wooded landscapes', it won critical acclaim. Phelps, who played Don Armado, was generally praised for his intelligent ensemble approach and his attention to detail. The play itself was finally rehabilitated: John Oxenford, in his review for

The Times, commented that he thought the play one 'over which a great deal of good acting may be diffused, for even the smallest parts are marked characters and some of them very strongly and very strangely defined . . . [Mr Phelps] has so well applied the talent of his company that there is not a single weakly acted part.'[4] His promptbook continued in use into the twentieth century. It was presented at the Old Vic in 1918, 1923 and 1928.

Augustin Daly directed a production in New York in 1891. The *New York Times* praised the acting and especially commended the set: 'Indeed, no handsomer setting of a play by Shakespeare was ever seen in this country – or in any other probably. Every picture is a noble example of the scene painter's art.'[5] There were Stratford-upon-Avon productions in 1885, 1907, 1925 and 1934. Meanwhile Barry Jackson directed a production at the Birmingham Rep in 1919, revived in 1925.

It was Tyrone Guthrie's 1932 production at the Westminster Theatre, London, however, which marks the turn in the play's theatrical fortunes. Using a heavily cut text and a single set, it was played at top speed with great verve, lasting an astonishing ninety minutes. Gordon Crosse describes how precisely the set and the actors' movements were controlled: 'with the king's pavilion draped in red on one side and the Princess's in green on the other, each group of characters dressed in the corresponding colour and keeping strictly to its own side in all entrances and exits'.[6] The production was re-staged at the Old Vic in 1936, but the colour scheme softened with costumes in pastel shades of pink, green and cream against an uncluttered set consisting of only a fountain, two tents on either side of the stage, and a wrought iron gate, topped by an arc of fresh leaves, that led into the domain of Navarre. The critic John Dover Wilson described the dramatic effect seeing this production had on his perception of the play: 'Mr Guthrie not only gave me a new play, the existence of which I had never suspected, which indeed had been veiled from men's eyes for three centuries, but he set me at a fresh standpoint of understanding and appreciation from which the whole of Shakespearian comedy might be reviewed in a new light.'

Crucially, Guthrie replaced the grand finales which had characterized the earlier productions of Vestris and Phelps:

> The extraordinary impression left upon the audience by the
> entrance of the black-clad messenger upon the court revels was
> the greatest lesson I took away with me from the Guthrie
> production. It made me see two things – (a) that however gay,
> however riotous a Shakespearian comedy, tragedy is always there,
> *felt*, if not seen; (b) that for all its surface lightness and frivolity, the
> play had behind it a serious mind at work, with a purpose.[7]

This emphasis on the play's darker elements was to be realized
most fully in Peter Brook's 1946 production at Stratford. Still in the
shadow of the Second World War, the twenty-year-old Brook made
his professional debut with this production. He recalled the rehearsal
process in detail in his book *The Empty Space* (1968). He emphasized
the play's painterly qualities by means of a set and costumes that
drew on Antoine Watteau's eighteenth-century 'fête champêtre'
paintings, with their sense of a gilded age tempered by a play of light
and dark. The production was an unqualified success and established
Brook's professional reputation. According to *The Times* (London),

> His presentment of the play as a masque of youthful affectations
> shows a remarkably complete grasp of its somewhat elusive
> values, and is, from first to last, consistent with itself. He has
> given its movement on the stage a puffball lightness, handled the
> chiaroscuro with delicate, imaginative expertness, and once or
> twice succeeds in fading out a scene in such a way that colour
> and grouping heighten its significance.[8]

Locating the production within the historical context of work at the
Stratford Memorial Theatre, theatre historian Sally Beauman argued
that the adjective 'Watteau-esque' most usually applied to the
production might work as an 'interesting correlative for the aristocratic
young lovers, journeying from illusion and artifice to greater maturity',
but was inadequate when applied to other characters:

> The production teemed with ideas that owed nothing to
> Watteau. The Princess was accompanied by a chalk-faced

commedia dell'arte clown, who never spoke; Constable Dull was a Punch-and-Judy policeman with a truncheon and a string of sausages; Armado was a sixteenth-century grandee whom Velazquez might have painted. The play began with insolent aplomb by confronting the audience with a gigantic drop on which was painted a great barred gate and the words of the King of Navarre's proclamation banning women, writ large like a song-scroll in a pantomime. The production was far more heretic, rag-bag, and anarchic than the adjective 'Watteau-esque'

2. Paul Scofield as Don Armado in Peter Brook's landmark 1946 production. How does humankind overcome 'devouring time'? Through 'fame' or philosophical study or love? Shakespeare meditates deeply on this question not only in the play, but also in his Sonnets, which he seems to have begun writing around the same time.

conveys. It was played fast, except for the famous long silence that greeted that messenger of death, Mercade; it had a delight in artifice as great as that of any of the characters, and it was funny, belying the play's reputation for difficult-to-comprehend jokes.[9]

A few years later, there was another highly successful production in London. Hugh Hunt's 1949 staging was the greatest success of the Old Vic season. The reviewer Lionel Hale described how in his view the director had

> put exactly the right movement into the play: it skates charmingly over the thin ice of the glittering words: and it is decorated throughout with a full invention but without any infuriating fuss. Mr Berkeley Sutcliffe's settings – lakes, summer houses, gay pavilions, and overhanging trees in the manner of an Elizabethan miniaturist – catch all the lyric quality of this 'April comedy.' His costumes have a sheen, a rich shimmer. He and Mr Hunt have worked rarely to make a success even of the scene when the King and his courtiers arrive disguised as Muscovites:

3. Painterly set and Elizabethan costume: the Old Vic production of 1949.

they have seen it as a picture. And, when we come to the 'elegiac close,' they have . . . made it a thing of pure enchantment.[10]

Despite the success of such productions, the play is still performed less frequently than the most of Shakespeare's plays. Most of the revivals in recent years have been staged by the Royal Shakespeare Company. These are discussed below in greater detail. In 1968 Laurence Olivier directed a production at the National Theatre in London, which critics complained lacked the vitality of earlier productions. Critic Helen Dawson thought the set, which had been much admired, problematic: 'The trees in the royal park may float rather captivatingly, but otherwise they are merely props in a chocolate box fairy glade. The décor, like the production, lacks the delicate shading of menace to hint at the darkness beneath the sparkling surface.'[11] London *Times* reviewer Irving Wardle thought the 'sumptuous blaze of Renaissance costumes' responsible for the slow pace of the production since it hampered the actors' movements, but he was mainly critical of the final scene: 'It is only in the great scene of Mercade's announcement of the King's death that the production falters. It is equal to the fantasy and the games, but not to the fact of death from which it turns away in favour of a Christmas card ending.'[12]

Critic and theatre director Charles Marowitz was more caustic, calling it 'slow-footed' and 'sugar-coated', 'a production that preens and cosmeticizes a play which can only work today if wrung firmly by the neck'. He went on to argue that it failed to make itself relevant to the times:

A play that concerns the sensual distractions of a band of men devoted to the rigors of scholarship would seem to be thumpingly appropriate in the late 1960s, but in opting for artifice and elegance, Olivier has sealed the play off from contemporary resonance. One is left with a lot of fussy staging, eccentric vocalism, and a Christmas-card finale which forcibly brings back the festering Old Vic days of the 1950s when Shakespeare was conceived entirely in terms of fudge sundaes and whipped cream.[13]

Successful productions have usually recognized the need to update the play, to transpose period and setting to give it a contemporary edge for modern audiences. The American Shakespeare Festival in Stratford, Connecticut, staged a production in 1968 directed by Michael Kahn that deliberately set out to satirize 1960s popular culture. The four young aristocrats from Navarre became

> versions of the Beatles, especially since they were pursued by teenyboppers and camera-flashing reporters as they arrived for the first scene. Like the Beatles, they escaped the modern world to go to India/Navarre where the long-haired and full-bearded King, accompanied by incense-bearers and a sitar player, wore a long white robe and, though noticeably younger than the Maharishi, obviously alluded to that cult figure.[14]

Kahn believed that 'Presenting the play in a contemporary setting created a world that was simultaneously glamorous and yet easy to make fun of', a world in which the satire of 'trendiness of language and feeling' would be immediately recognizable. The 2006 revival of this production included in the RSC's Complete Works Festival testified to its continuing vitality.

Karel Kriz staged a radical, innovative production at the National Theatre in Prague in 1987 in which the 'dominant element on stage was an ornate fire curtain'.[15] In 1989 Gerald Freedman directed *Love's Labor's Lost* as part of Joseph Papp's ambitious series of productions of Shakespeare in New York's Central Park. Freedman set his play in the 1930s, an era he believed 'when appearance was all' and used 'a row of confetti-like strips of colored paper for a curtain to suggest the festive nature of the goings-on'.[16] Trevor Nunn concluded his period as Artistic Director of Britain's National Theatre in 2003 with a production set in the early twentieth century: 'Nunn's most striking concept is to set this *Love's Labour's Lost* as a dream sequence on the battlefields of the First World War. Men about to die horribly are given a brief glimpse of the love they will never know.'[17]

The 1930s was the setting for Kenneth Branagh's film musical adaptation of 2000. Sympathetic to the concept, most critics found

4. Transposition to the counter-culture: Michael Kahn's revival of his 1960s production, played by the Shakespeare Theatre Company of Washington DC during the RSC's Complete Works Festival (2006).

its realization incomplete: 'The project was a promising possibility, not an instant sacrilege. The trouble is that the promise was not well-kept.'[18] As A. O. Scott suggested in the *New York Times*,

> There is no doubting Mr Branagh's sincere enthusiasm for the material, which is not only Shakespeare but also old newsreels, *Casablanca* and classic MGM musicals. He throws them together with the gusto of a man playing a tuba with a bass drum strapped to his back while his pet monkey leaps around with a squeeze box. It's not art exactly, or even music, but it's entertaining, albeit in an intermittently annoying kind of way.[19]

AT THE RSC

Designing Navarre

'Staging a play in which Coleridge found "little to interest as a dramatic representation" and which Dr Johnson thought "childish and vulgar" can be a stiff task', began one reviewer in response to

Terry Hands' RSC production of 1990.[20] Yet with its masques and pageant, and the awakening of the young men to the realities of love, the play offers itself to a very modern, even post-modern, self-conscious exploration of artifice and performance – both on stage in the action of the play, and in the theatre between the real audience and the actors.

Some directors and designers have begun from the (unsubstantiated) conjecture that the play might have been written 'for open air performance in a nobleman's garden'.[21] They have accordingly taken the opportunity to look at different types of acting space in a beautifully scenic but stylized way. Many have opted for set designs that, either through their painterly quality or their attempt to mimic reality, have emphasized the artificial nature of the world which the young men inhabit. Irving Wardle in *The Times* (London), writing about the 1973 David Jones production, explained how Timothy O'Brien and Tazeena Firth's set design consisted of

> a grassy floor with a pair of pole-like trees pushing upwards through a green canopy. The canopy is the main feature of the set: raked downwards to the back wall it forms a silken roof overprinted with magnified leaf photographs. Beautiful to look at, this also supplies a perfect visual metaphor for the play itself, which equally shows nature appearing through an artefact.[22]

One reason for the play's revived success on the stage is the almost artificial nostalgia or fairytale quality to this refuge for love, which for most of the play remains untouched by the cares of the real world. Populated with 'endearing rustics and academics who seem to be smiling out of an old-fashioned children's book',[23] the escapist quality of the play is part of its attraction. The design of the 1965 production directed by John Barton offered a reminder of reality in the lighting created by John Bradley, which illuminated the action as if it took place in a single day. This worked in juxtaposition to the highly stylized set:

The Sleeping Beauty-like wooded background of Sally Jacobs' set is dappled with bright morning sunshine in the early scenes, with the longer shadows of the afternoon following – both to be finally eclipsed by nightfall which, appropriately enough, coincides with the announcement of the French king's death and the play's consequent abrupt and final shift of mood.[24]

With its box hedges and couture costumes, the design suggested the garden architecture and formal dress of an aristocratic country house in a world dominated by artifice. The pretensions of the young men, and their attempt to avoid the real world, were played out in a leafy idyll, shattered only by the inescapable reality of Death. In the words of the review in the *Financial Times*,

> The King of Navarre's Court has put on black to signalise its withdrawal from pleasure and its three-year dedication to abstinence and study; and the trees in the King's park ... have turned black to match, and gloom over the revels in a rather forbidding way. The Court removes its mourning dress once the oaths of the courtiers have been broken; the trees are denied this privilege ... There isn't very much sparkle about King Ferdinand's Court. The King and his chums get the lion's share of such good poetry as there is in the play, but their sombre clothes seem to have reacted on their mood, and they revel, jest and make love in rather a subdued frame of mind.[25]

In 1973, Irving Wardle in *The Times* praised director David Jones for turning 'the play's stylistic artifice to dramatic advantage':

> From its opening mock-funeral procession – where the four votaries cast their gay clothes into an empty coffin – the production develops under the shadow of death. A joke to begin with, it imposes its lasting separation in the final scene, just as sex, begun as a holiday game, enmeshes them in harsh responsibilities.[26]

The onset of darker days is not always so blatantly advertised. Most productions opt for a softer, more autumnal feel – the stage often being littered with fallen leaves, as in John Barton's second production, played in 1978 and described in *Shakespeare Survey*:

> Enormous boughs of cascading autumnal leaves entirely enclosing a raked wooden forestage, behind which seats and a leaf-strewn floor suggested distant parkland. But there was no external glamour about the two courts, which seemed humbler, less formal, than usual: the lords took their oaths with little ceremony on a rustic seat; Rosaline cleaned the Princess's travelling boots and the travel-stained hem of her skirt in their first scene, and swept up autumn leaves with a broom in the last; the King and the Princess, especially, were very unelaborated, untidy even, in appearance, ordinary human beings rather than heads of state, especially when they first met, a rather endearing unimpressive, bespectacled pair: a long silence indicated sudden (to them embarrassing) mutual attraction.[27]

Barton's production was favourably received by audiences and critics alike, but some others in a similar vein have been less so: there is a risk of over-labouring the elegiac point. As the theatre historian Russell Jackson points out,

> Directors and (especially) designers who take their cue from the wistfulness of the ending are in danger of sentimentalising the whole performance. The autumnal languor that sometimes bathes productions of the play – in anticipation of the final scene – can work against the comedy itself. Directors sometimes use the quizzical and pathetic element in the endings of Shakespearean comedy as a pretext for being wise not merely after but during and (in the souvenir programmes) before the event.[28]

With regard to the onslaught of reality, we are left in no doubt at the end of the play that the young men are about to enter into a different form of education, based on real experience in the wider world. Whether or not love penetrates their artificially constructed refuge from life is a debatable matter, but set designs for *Love's Labour's Lost* often reflect the idea of romantic love. In 1984 a statue of Eros, the Greek god of love and sexual desire, dominated the set of Barry Kyle's production – a visually stunning design, suggestive of French Impressionist paintings, but which also pointed towards the battle between the sexes:

> We are in turn-of-the-century France, and against a distant prospect of silhouetted lovers strolling along a leafy lake-side, Bob Crowley has mounted dozens of parapluies on telescopic stems, thus cleverly creating an impression of mock battle-standards under which the lovers wage their struggle.[29]

5. Stage design assisting the comedy of deception and overhearing: Roger Rees as Berowne and Josette Simon as Rosaline in Barry Kyle's 1984 RSC production.

In 1990 Timothy O'Brien's set took the theme of French Impressionism further with 'a pointillist agglomeration of autumnal leaves – yellow, red, gold and brown – glinting in the dense greenery of a private idyllic forest'.[30] The production opened with a deliberate reference to one of the most controversial paintings from the early Impressionist movement. Critic Peter Holland described how:

> French impressionism turned three-dimensional, its trees and hedges vivid splashes of colour. The lords sat for the first scene picnicking, reading and sketching, in a tableau carefully arranged to remind the audience of Manet's *Déjeuner sur l'herbe*, though here with Manet's naked women conspicuous by their absence. By 2.1 the garden had been cordoned off with a sign 'Interdit aux femmes'.[31]

The idea of male education in isolation, combined with verbal exhibitionism and the immaturity of young men in the ways of love, prompted Ian Judge to put two and two together and set the play in an Oxford college. Peter Holland again:

> The loss of the court setting, as in Hands' production in 1991, was here more than offset by the immediately recognisable world of 'academe' in which young men, in single-sex colleges, had to balance their commitment 'to live and study here three years' (1.1.35) against such temptations as 'to see a woman in that term' (37). Nathaniel became a college chaplain, Holofernes a 'Professor of Latin' (according to the programme, Moth . . . a well-scrubbed student chorister and Costard a local delivery boy).[32]

Critic Stanley Wells elaborated further:

> The lodge in the royal park is a porter's lodge, and Don Adriano de Armado is not the only don on the horizon. John Gunter's charming basic set of stone walls and mullioned windows festooned with greenery adapts easily and wittily to suggest a variety of locations: a high-backed settle trundles on, and we are in a buttery bar . . . puffs of smoke plus a few sound effects and it is clear that the

Princess and her companions have arrived by train; Holofernes and Sir Nathaniel converse in deck chairs, while watching and applauding a cricket match that takes place somewhere in the auditorium; an awning descends to show that the entertainments of the last act are not unconnected with a May Ball.[33]

6. Edwardian Oxbridge: the Worthies plan their pageant in a cricket pavilion (directed by Ian Judge, 1993, RSC).

The Edwardian setting also offered an opportunity for a poignant reading, reminding the audience that the play is as much about loss as it is about love. Wells continues:

It is only with the ladies' rejection of their suitors' offers of love that the full point of the Edwardian setting becomes clear. We may have idly noticed that the sun has never ceased to shine: this has been a long hot summer. And as the ladies depart, leaving Berowne to lament that the delay of twelve months before their courtship can have a happy ending is 'too long for a play', the backdrop changes from the spires of Oxford to Flanders fields; we hear the noise of gunfire and of shells, and know that the idyll is over. The lights fade, the actors take a call, the audience applauds.

It may seem a portentous and forced ending, and unnecessary deflection from the shock that Shakespeare has already provided with the news of the King of France's death, but it makes an effective concluding *coup de théâtre*. At least it would have done if Ian Judge had had the courage to stop there, cutting what remains of the play. But no. The actors halt our applause, the dialogue resumes, and the evening ends with a trivializing setting of the songs for the owl and the cuckoo. With the final waltz number for the entire company, the actors waving to the audience as they depart, we are in the world of showbiz, of Edwardian musical comedy, in an evasion of the challenges of Shakespeare's own, highly original ending to one of his most brilliantly experimental plays.[34]

Words, Words, Words...

As comedy, *Love's Labour's Lost* displays a fascination with language as the tool of wit, learning and persuasion at all social levels.

According to John Pendergast, John Barton's 1978 interpretation suggested that

The linguistic acrobatics of the lower-class characters such as Moth and Costard were similar in spirit to those of the more sophisticated characters such as Berowne and Armado; although the upper-class characters may be more 'correct' when they speak archaically, they are experimenting with the possibilities of language in a manner similar to the lower-class characters and all the communication in the play is an attempt at sounding sophisticated... the language comes to serve the characters' personalities, rather than the reverse... For example, rhyming is used by the young men as part of their wooing yet it also suggests wit and immaturity. Armado and Holofernes are not nearly as witty as they think they are, and their speech habits reflect their pretentiousness and Old World ways.[35]

Despite all the lover's overblown rhetoric, Costard is the character that cuts to the chase when he tells us 'such is the simplicity of man to hearken after the flesh'. Robert Speaight remarked of John Barton's 1965 production:

> Mr Tim Wylton was quite rightly mounted on a farm-cart for this stupendous utterance, although his own authority was quite enough to articulate the wisdom of babes and sucklings. This Costard was much more than an endearing lout; he . . . communicated a kind of heroic happiness which suffused the whole play. Just as Feste acts as a go-between in *Twelfth Night*, counterpointing comedy with cynicism, and retiring at the end into solitude from which he emerged at the beginning, so Costard is a go-between in *Love's Labour's Lost*. But Costard is too wise for the intelligence of cynicism, and when the stage has emptied one sees him retiring with the other Worthies, perhaps for a drink at the Vicarage, perhaps for a drink at the schoolmaster's house, or perhaps for a drink at the pub. But wherever he is, he will not be alone, and we should like to be in his company, because he has said in one line what Berowne has said in twenty.[36]

Christopher Luscombe, who played Moth in 1993, thought that 'our Oxbridge setting . . . helped to take the curse off some of this elaborate wit. In academia such conversational cut-and-thrust seemed entirely natural. Friendships are forged in the delighted discovery of new vocabulary.'[37]

Kenneth Branagh played Navarre in the RSC's 1984–85 production and in 2000 was to direct a film version, again with an Oxbridge setting. He observed the dilemma for directors in tackling such a wordy play:

> The play is full of rhymed line endings. Verbally, or musically, it is a 'great feast of language'. This presents some difficulties for actors and producers. They have to decide whether to play the language to the hilt knowing that, because it is so dense, the audience isn't necessarily going to pick up everything, or whether to slow it down a bit in order to try to give away as much of the meaning as possible. This may be a reason why the

play has been neglected since Shakespeare's day really until this century.[38]

Ian Judge's 1993 production utilized the musicality of the language turning it into one of the production's assets, something which Branagh also did with his film, when he shot the play as a 1930s musical:

> A musical comedy without music is how one critic described *Love's Labour's Lost* . . . This Brideshead-style academia has pretty ballads, a turkey trot by [composer] Nigel Hess and a set of French misses in Poiret frocks.[39]

In 1984 the ridiculous song about the fox, the ape and the humble-bee was turned into 'a first-class music-hall routine'.[40] However, many critics felt that the final song was given a too sophisticated staging, over-elaborated by redundant stage business:

> This is rendered by an operatic singer who has already appeared between some of the scenes as one of a band of picturesque (and languorous) peasants, vocalising what sound like bits of the *Chants de l'Auvergne*. For the concluding lyrics the singer is accompanied by the rest of the cast, who provide such literal-minded illustrations as a sneezing peasant girl (Marian's nose is red and raw). The operatic voice is confident and accomplished, so that any sense of tentativeness is lost, and the music's sophistication makes it less credible than usual that the parson and the schoolmaster might have been responsible for the song.[41]

In 1965 and again in 1978, as Roger Warren notes in *Shakespeare Survey*, John Barton, emphasizing the language and its imagery, made the innovation of having the final songs spoken,

> Thereby throwing greater emphasis onto their vivid images of country life; but he extended the idea so that all the villagers echoed the 'Cuckoo' and 'Tu-whit, tu-who', and, even more important, the court led by the King and Princess joined in too, so that the stage became filled with harmonious echoes of country

sounds – exquisitely capped by the hooting of a real owl above their heads, magically reinforcing Shakespeare's own final emphasis upon the ordinary realities of country life. Such an extraordinarily complex scene, which takes the breath away with its combination of gaiety and sadness, its blending of affairs of state, of the heart, of the countryside, is Mr Barton's special territory as a director.[42]

One of the major strengths of Barton's 1978 production was the revelation that the extravagant language used by the characters is a form of verbal mask, an artificial front to their true feelings. The characters spoke in 'elegant, precious and self-conscious language not because Shakespeare is writing such language but because they are showing off, or defending themselves against feeling, or trying to communicate but tying themselves in knots while doing so'.[43]

This is especially true of the character Berowne, who gets the larger share of the play's poetry and wit. In David Jones' 1975 production Ian Richardson's central performance captured the essence of the play. He later revealed that it was his favourite part in the canon, believing that Berowne, the excellent wordsmith, was no other than Shakespeare himself. The part, he said, 'stands out above all the Shakespeare roles I've ever played, as being the one I love the most. Curiously enough it does seem to be the role that Shakespeare might have written for himself . . . Here is Shakespeare talking, here is the man himself with all his verbal quips.'[44]

Critic Michael Billington, in praise of Richardson, reported that 'you realise this is really a play about the process of growing-up; and that under its formality, artifice and endless topical allusions, it is a work that captures the very rhythm of life itself':

This transition from artifice, to true feeling is nowhere better illustrated than by Ian Richardson's masterly performance as Berowne. Whether breaking out in sighs that seem to hail from his bootstraps or tearing up the letter that reveals the breaking of his vows of study, he is frantic, word-drunk and possessed by the spirit of love. Yet in his great hymn to Cupid he drops all vocal artifice and when he declares to Rosalind, 'I am yours and all that I possess' you feel he has learnt the virtues of true sentiment and direct speech.[45]

Men in Love?

The lack of seriousness with which the young men take their oaths, the hapless bandying of the language and manners of courtly love, their genuine unkindness towards the participants of the pageant, might give a girl cause for concern. As director John Barton put it in his 1965 programme, 'ridiculous and impracticable' as the oath may be, 'it is an oath all the same, and a serious one. So when the King and the rest break it at the first sight of a woman's eyes, the girls are justified in questioning their oaths of love.'[46]

In his 1978 production Barton offered a 'new and most fruitful shift of emphasis'[47] by having the Princess of France and King of Navarre take a more prominent role, of equal importance to Rosaline and Berowne. He also deliberately cast against type with Richard Griffiths and Carmen Du Sautoy as an inelegant pair, instantly drawn to each other. These factors imbued the play with a warm-hearted basis that has not been surpassed by future productions:

[Carmen] Du Sautoy's Princess and Griffiths's King are obviously meant for each other, and they fall in love almost at first sight. When she says 'suddenly resolve me in my suit', she holds out the letter and there is a long pause. He fumbles for words – 'Madam, I will if suddenly I may' – and her answer, completely without sarcasm ... sounds as if she is struggling to put words together ... Characteristically, as the King reaches out for the letter from her father, she accidentally drops it; both she and the King bend over to pick up the letter, the Princess gets it and hands it over to him, but both are embarrassed by the small mishap ... He turns away to read the letter while she turns away – and takes off her glasses. The immediate falling in love of these two slightly clumsy and unromantic-looking people becomes very touching and creates a gentle tone for their relationship...so different from the elegant and usually self-assured rulers found in other productions.[48]

In their appearance and manner one was aware of the genuine emotion that was blooming between them. These were not people beguiled by the artifice of appearance but were soulmates, insecure in themselves and their positions, able to understand each other, and the difficulties of matching up to royal status.

The relationship between Rosaline and Berowne complemented that of the king and princess, further emphasizing the real passion burning beneath the words. As Warren notes in *Shakespeare Survey*, Michael Pennington's performance had 'an intense, almost erotic lyricism for the great defence of Love, which rightly became the climax of the first half. This scene typified the production's quality, building superbly from one humorous peak to another, without loss of humanity: the lords' poems were not guyed, but rather became the rapid, passionate release of pent-up desire.'[49]

In 1984 and 1990 there was a marked discrepancy between the maturity of the men and that of the women – the women appeared far more sophisticated and in control than the men who were portrayed as relatively immature. This left the audience with a large question mark over the issue of whether or not genuine feelings of love lay behind their declarations. In Barry Kyle's production (1984), Kenneth Branagh played Navarre as

A boyish, amiable monarch whose attempts to be strict with himself and his courtiers were doomed from the beginning. His shyness is soon overcome by his enthusiasm for the pursuit of the ladies...Against Emily Richard's Princess – older than Navarre and much more mature in her emotions – he seems like someone making the transition from adolescence to early manhood. In the last Stratford production (by John Barton) it was suggested that the Princess was about the same age as Navarre, if not a little younger...the Princess's self-confidence and maturity were in as critical a stage of development as Navarre's...Berowne (Roger Rees) obviously takes the prize for experience and self-knowledge, but his counterpart, Rosaline, is moody, withdrawn and something of an outsider amongst the women. Josette Simon plays her with an abrasive and uncompromising quality that goes so far as to imply absence of any warm feeling towards Berowne. As the only black woman in the court, she wears her hair in a severe, close-cropped style and is no less severe in her attitude to the men.[50]

The critic for the *Observer* also highlighted the isolation of Josette Simon's Rosaline: 'What she thinks of him we never find out, for . . . Simon plays her elegant and reserved, cold indeed, often at the edge of groups and sizing Berowne up with a wariness that argues an experience of pain unknown to the rest.'[51]

Similarly, in Terry Hands' 1990 production, Carol Royle as the princess came across as defensive against love. Her costuming with military overtones hinted at readiness for battle with the opposite sex. She was

> Cool and assured, wearing a gorgeous mauve dress with a huge hoop skirt, the bodice of the dress trimmed with military-looking stripes. Her parasol and her hoop always created space around her, making her virtually untouchable . . . Only at the end did she seem both composed and gentle in her treatment of the King, but since the composure had always been present, there was no noticeable change when she heard about her father's death.[52]

The very contrasting personality of Simon Russell Beale's king left a credibility gap which again hampered the audience's belief in the possibility of genuine emotion: 'if a production wants . . . to suggest at last that there may be some hope in these relationships, its presenting of the king as a more or less unmitigated chump and the princess as an astute operator, coolly aware of the power of her femininity, left one wondering what she saw in him'.[53] 'Gender confrontation was followed through to the end of the evening where the women were clearly embarrassed and ashamed of the men's vicious cynicism at the Pageant of the Nine Worthies, Simon Russell Beale's King sharing the women's distress.'[54]

In this production the artifice of the wooing rituals indicated that these immature men were in love with love rather than with the women as individuals. This interpretation was best demonstrated when the men went a-wooing in disguise but could not tell to which woman they were speaking:

> The four lords court the four ladies first as Muscovites, in which guise they are mockingly dismissed, and later in their own persons. Their emotional immaturity and the fact that they are essentially still acting parts are communicated by the ridiculous comic disguise. In Hands's production one was in a bear costume; in 1993 the men appeared as dancing Cossacks. They return to the game of courtship as themselves where Berowne is chastened into plain speech:

> Henceforth my wooing mind shall be expressed
> In russet yeas and honest kersey noes.[55]

Other relationships in the 1990 production further highlighted the young men's romantic posturing, especially the passionate portrayal of Don Armado by John Wood:

> From his first entrance, collapsing on to a heap of cushions, Wood's Armado was madly illogical with a grasshopper mind. Yet his devotion to Jaquenetta was affectingly obsessive, passionately excited by her easy display of sexuality, as he crawled around after her exit [in Act 1 scene 2], kissing the carpet wherever she had trodden ... As the stage cleared, Jaquenetta came on into the light previously occupied by Mercade, and Don Armado, happily ready for his three years' vow as a ploughman, kissed her, a tender act that the other nobles would never approach.[56]

In comparing the productions of Barton (1978), Kyle (1984) and Hands (1990), the theatre historian Miriam Gilbert explored the essential difference in their handling of love:

Kyle and Hands chose to underscore the sense in which the love is primarily an illusion at which we smile. If so, then the ending is less surprising and less painful than if the audience has been asked to believe, even fleetingly, in the reciprocal feelings of the men and women...the disparity between the emotional and social maturity of the Princess and that of the King [in 1990] makes it difficult to believe that the Princess ever feels, or could feel, anything for him. A schoolboy crush on an older and more sophisticated woman is plausible, but not a reciprocal feeling... Barton's solution – showing both men and women as insecure to some extent – allows the audience to see the possibility of reciprocal love developing even though we also understand that whatever these people feel for each other needs time for testing and for growth. Later productions have been less successful in conveying such a possibility.[57]

Peter Holland criticized Ian Judge's 1993 production for supplementing the lack of genuine emotion with an overbearing musical score, which only created an artificial illusion of love. Like the soundtrack to a Hollywood movie, the music indicated what the audience should be feeling, overcompensating for the director's lack of belief in the accessibility of Shakespeare's plot and characters:

> Ample resources of comedy must in *Love's Labour's Lost* be balanced by an understanding of love and this production signally failed to provide. Every expression of love was heavily underscored by Nigel Hess's overscored music swelling beneath; the young men's poems became songs and Don Armado's farewell to valour...and excess of musical ardour. The saccharine sentimentalism of musical pastiche smothered any possibility of accurate depiction of emotion under its clichés. Judge's versions of love were all of a piece with such faked romantic feeling.[58]

It appears that key to any successful production of *Love's Labour's Lost* is a sense of emotional reality. Directors avoiding the pitfalls of the language often miss the point that so much of what the characters say is full of 'airy nothings', evasion and intellectual posing. Dull's succinct reply to Holofernes' 'Thou hast spoken no word all this while', 'Nor understood none neither, sir', is often singled out as the greatest moment of hilarity in a production. The audience are relieved by his straightforward honesty and identify with him. It is the big moment of release from the verbal lunacy of the spheres of court and academia, love and intellect. As 'John Barton's [1978] production demonstrated ... ordinary theatregoers can respond to the verbal pyrotechnics of a set of wit well played even when the historical dimension eludes them'[59] – and sometimes because it eludes them. The conditions of the women at the end are not just a love test, but a test of language and humanity. With knowledge and language comes responsibility, and the educated young men have to learn to wield their linguistic powers, whether in

7. The men are constantly in competition with one another. The women are more successful because they always work together as a group. Boyet is their spokesman: from left, Rosaline (Janet Suzman), Maria (Katharine Barker), Boyet (Brewster Mason), Katherine (Jessica Claridge) and the Princess of France (Glenda Jackson) in John Barton's 1965 production.

matters of the heart or the head, with greater care: 'Gently but firmly, the men are sent away to learn something that the women have known all along: how to accommodate speech to facts and to emotional realities, as opposed to using it as a means of evasion, idle amusement, or unthinking cruelty.'[60]

THE DIRECTOR'S CUT: INTERVIEWS WITH TERRY HANDS AND LIZ SHIPMAN

Terry Hands, born 1941, studied at the University of Birmingham and the Royal Academy of Dramatic Art. In 1964 he established the Liverpool Everyman Theatre, then two years later he joined the Royal Shakespeare Company to run its touring group, Theatregoround. He become joint Artistic Director with Trevor Nunn in 1978, and was sole Artistic Director from 1986 to 1991. He has also directed many productions in Europe, notably at the Comédie-Française in Paris. His cycle of Shakespeare's history plays, with Alan Howard in leading roles, was among the highlights of the RSC in the 1970s. In 1997 he became Artistic Director of Clwyd Theatr Cymru. Here he discusses his RSC production, which opened in Stratford in 1990 and transferred to the Barbican in London in 1991.

Liz Shipman is co-founder and Associate Director of the Kings County Shakespeare Company (KCSC) in New York. She served as its Co-artistic Director from 1985 to 2001 and has directed many Shakespearean productions there. She also teaches in the Theatre Arts programme at the University of San Diego, specializing in a movement-based approach to acting. The production that she discusses here was performed as part of the 1998 Kings County Shakespeare Festival in Brooklyn, New York. Because the action is seemingly set entirely out of doors, *Love's Labour's Lost* is a play that has been peculiarly amenable to outdoor production.

Whereas most Shakespearean plays sweep across many locations, this one is confined in an enclosed space – an enclosure that seems very important to what the play is about. Directors and designers have recreated the 'little academe'

as, say, an eighteenth-century aristocratic *fête champêtre* (Peter Brook suggesting the paintings of Watteau) or – perhaps more predictably – an Oxford college. What did you and your designer go for, and why?

TH: *Love's Labour's Lost* is set in a park – an open space where gentry and villagers can meet easily and informally. The 'little academe' is an improvisation – as unexpected as it is improbable. It fails very quickly, and part of that failure is the reality of the country life that impinges upon it, and sex. In 1990 the designer Timothy O'Brien created a world that was inspired by Manet's *Déjeuner sur l'herbe*, but also, in its execution, by Signac, Seurat and Monet. His idea was that the world of nature should be represented as vibrantly as possible with colours mixing in the eye of the beholder rather than on the palette. If Navarre's artifice were to be overwhelmed by nature, then that nature should be overwhelming. Frankly I don't think the period matters much. The world is probably, and not for the last time, Charlecote [the aristocratic house and park just outside Stratford, that Shakespeare knew well].

LS: The production was set in the early twentieth century at Navarre's 'country estate'. It was presented in the round with each entrance (four voms*) leading to an outdoor courtyard of sorts. There was a large, central, raised hexagonal platform surrounded by three large movable benches that could be shifted in the space according to the needs of the scene. The entire space was a 'marbleized' white and extended throughout the audience areas. One of the four entrances into the courtyard arrived from the 'outer world'. One led to the king's parklands. One opened into the courtyard from the main house where Navarre and his close comrades reside. The last came from an outer building reserved for guests – Don Armado and Moth. The idea was that Navarre's estate was the centrepiece of the surrounding community. His grounds and park were open to the people, hence the traffic that passes through

---

* ['*Voms*' is a theatre term for openings, doors or passages through which stage entrances are made (from Latin *vomitorium*).]

during the events of the play. The playing area was open and expansive. Scenery was minimal – limited to a simple set element in each vom, such as a few broad steps flanked by urn-like planters, a garden gate, the suggestion of a large tree, and the set was dressed with occasional greenery. The overall impression was of lightness, warmth and springtime. Costumes were of natural fabrics and were in whites, creams and warm colours. The arrival of Marcadé in formal funereal black offered a stark contrast and, appropriately, signalled the end of illusions and youthful fancies and the re-emergence of reality. Our intent in setting the play in the graceful environs of a wealthy country estate just prior to the First World War was to capture the audience's imagination with a time within a not-too-distant past that stood on the edge of a major socio-political change – a time of promise that was interrupted by a tragic event that ended an 'age of innocence'. I felt that this setting was consistent with what I understand to be the themes central to the play.

This is the Shakespeare play that almost reminds us of a Mozart comic opera. It has a kind of musical structure, with all sorts of symmetries and counterpoints. A nineteenth-century production once combined it with the music of _Cosí fan tutte_ (which also has paired lovers and Muscovite disguises). And in Thomas Mann's great novel _Dr Faustus_, it is the play that the composer Leverkühn is turning into an opera. To approach it in a quasi-musical way, structurally, perhaps helps draw attention away from all the recondite language, the Elizabethan in-jokes. Did you have any thoughts along these lines?

TH: _Love's Labour's Lost_ is an early play with a tableau structure, clumsy in the beginning, but flowing once the whole world of village and courtier is established. The language again is early – experimental, but understandably real to those who speak it. A great deal depends upon the actors. It is a truism that a director has done 80 per cent of the production by the time the casting is finished. I was lucky. The 1990 cast included John Wood, Ralph

Fiennes, Simon Russell Beale, Paterson Joseph, Amanda Root, Carol Royle, Alex Kingston, Lloyd Hutchinson and David Troughton – all capable of bringing idiosyncratic emotional depth to reading the dictionary.

LS: Musicality, the rhythmical interplay of the text, the constant games of wordplay and combative wit combine to define the experience of hearing this play. The language of *Love's Labour's Lost* requires that particular attention be paid to rhythm, melody and timing. It is an intricate song and dance of words and interpersonal action. I found that the language stirred action and thus the KCSC production was full of movement. There was a sense that the characters and the action swept through the playing space – the text and the context mobilizing the actors. Time seemed to fly. There was a kind of building momentum that could only be interrupted by the arrival of Marcadé. I cast very large and masculine men as Navarre and his friends. Their interplay was sometimes very physical so that they were nimble physically as well as verbally. Even their commitment to the ideals of Navarre's 'little academe' was undertaken in a visceral manner, and yet the music of the interactive dialogue had to be maintained. I did make certain cuts in the text and with them some of the obscure references were eliminated. But, I find that when actors know and understand clearly what they are saying and what is being said to them and when they engage with the text actively, the meanings become quite clear, and even when the audience did not understand the exact frame of reference, they were able to understand the gist of it and certainly the intent of the character who spoke the words. Additionally, songs and instrumental music were an integral element in our production. A travelling musician character was ever-present, leading into and out of the scenes and accompanying all of the songs included throughout the text.

The poems and sonnets used in the wooings are tricky, aren't they? Sometimes they seem deliberately bad, sometimes not. For the more sophisticated members of Shakespeare's original audience, versed in all the Petrarchan love poetry of the age, a

lot of the fun would have come from this. Trickier for a modern audience who are unfamiliar with the poetic conventions which Shakespeare is working both with and against?

TH: The same is largely true of the competitive poems and sonnets. We know from performance which is gold and which pinchbeck. In any case there is invariably a commentary to guide us – whether it is Berowne's ribald observations on his fellows' efforts or the collective sigh that greets the best (Berowne's sonnet to Rosaline), read by Sir Nathaniel and heard by Holofernes, Costard and Jaquenetta. Part of Shakespeare's genius was his ability to combine thought with feeling – what T. S. Eliot called the association of sensibility. In the theatre the audience can take one or the other, or – if the actor is good enough – both.

8. Terry Hands' 1990 production: the King (Simon Russell Beale, left) and Berowne (Ralph Fiennes) consider the vow to abjure female company for the sake of academic study.

LS: I believe that the wooing poems are intended to be as ridiculous as the actors can make them. These are opportunities for lovers to show themselves as clowns. Their verses, though not as outrageous as Don Armado's, are quite as silly. Certainly the characters are gushing in the first throes of intense infatuation. Their verses, good or bad, are less important than the circumstances of the scene. The fact that the king, Longaville and Dumaine are unknowingly exposing themselves for their questionable poetry, their susceptibility to love and their oath-breaking in a single act makes this scene potentially hilarious. As they, in turn, are 'caught out', we revel in their public exposure and subsequent chagrin and we fully endorse the practical Berowne's justifications and the king's new 'plan of action'. Audiences love it, whether they are aware of the stylistic references or not. We have different audiences today, but the situation is a comically classic one that we love to savour.

It's his most courtly and self-consciously 'poetic' play, but also – when you really pick away at the double entendres – one of his rudest. Did that high/low juxtaposition help shape your production?

LS: Absolutely. I have heard this play described as lyrical and full of elegant poetry. Rhymes, yes. Plenty of verse, yes. And the place is at Navarre's court. But I do not experience the text as lyrical or courtly. I find it laced with testosterone, fully satirical in its point of view as it illuminates the blindness of youth and the follies of 'love'. In this play the clowns become lovers and the lovers become clowns. It's a game. It's fun. Politeness is a facade and wit is often quite rude. The base and the noble interact. Verse and prose can be spoken by either. It is informal in its seeming formality. The images and metaphors that leaven the script reference games, sports, warring and battles, hunting and pursuit. In this play, perhaps, the challenge is everything – an end in itself. It is all about the game – word games, games of disguise and the sport of falling in love. Sport is rough and competitive and played to win. If and when love is gained, the 'game' is over, but I think it is significant and perhaps hopeful when Berowne responds to the one-year waiting period set by the women at the end of the play by saying, 'That's too long for a play'. Is he also saying, 'we'll have to get serious and work at it because we can't keep the play or the game going that long'? Time will bear it out in the end. There is plenty of room for cynicism, but we can hope and imagine that at least some of the lovers end up marrying in one year's time.

Berowne is a jewel of a role, isn't it? What kind of discoveries did you and your actor make about his language – and maybe his nimble, improvisatory gifts? Some people have been tempted to see him as a Shakespearean self-portrait ...

TH: It is possibly as difficult to date a Shakespeare play as it is to interpret one. But somewhere around the composition of *Love's Labour's Lost* Shakespeare was either writing, or at least thinking of, plays like *Titus Andronicus* or even *Richard III*. Is it altogether fanciful to imagine that he himself was facing a career choice? Whether to be a 'court jester' like Berowne (and later Benedick [in *Much Ado About Nothing*]) the purveyor of wit and poetry to the aristocracy, or a major player in one of the new Elizabethan playhouses? It is to all our benefit that he chose the latter.

LS: Berowne is a realist, an observer, one who stands outside – usually immune to the follies of those around him. His wit derives from this ability to see the world as it is and to use humour as his response to it. He masks himself behind his wit. It is the tool of his detachment. That is until he meets his match in Rosaline. The actor (Ray Virta) I was fortunate enough to cast in the role was a natural wit and clown, able to move adroitly between the subtleties and the broader aspects of the character and the text. Mr Virta gave the character realistic form and substance based on the text and his own instincts. He was immensely helpful during the rehearsal period, especially when I was making cuts to move the action along. He seemed to have a deep understanding of who Berowne, the man, is. He knew that Berowne's rhetorical flourishes and game-loving wit had to be about who he is and how he lives in the world. One of Ray's mantras is 'sound is sense'. His pursuit of Berowne and his interpretation of the character began then with the sounds of his text.

Technically (not least as a living demonstration of the meaning of the phrase 'dramatic irony'), the multiple overhearing scene, in which the men are successively caught out professing the love they purport to disdain, is utterly brilliant – how did you stage it?

LS: Staging this scene was quite a challenge since it was presented in the round with very little by way of structural elements in the setting. The audience was seated on risers viewing the action from four sides. Each of the gentlemen hid, in his turn, within sight of the audience, but with the illusion that they were all hidden from each other. As each of the gentlemen arrived in the courtyard, his predecessor quickly found a clever hiding place. Berowne hid aloft (we imagined he had climbed a tree), moving up through the audience to the top corner of one of the risers. Navarre secreted himself behind one of the slightly oversized benches, which had been shifted to the outer edges of the space for this scene. Longaville slipped into one of the voms, or, if possible, into a vacant seat in the audience – hiding behind a book (his poetry journal). From these hiding places, the subsequent reveals flowed easily.

'Women on top': is that what it boils down to? There are certainly some very strong female parts ...

LS: Shakespeare's plays are full of strong female characters. In his comedies, they are often more savvy and realistic than their male counterparts. The princess and her ladies are portrayed as rather sophisticated, witty and somewhat worldly. Their repartee is both as biting and as well played as the men's. They are brought back to reality by Marcadé's news, but it is clear to me that their response to the gentlemen's final proposals would have been similar had they not received the tragic news. Although they too become enamoured with the young men and fully enjoy the 'chase', they are convinced that all the pleasurable love-sport was no more than that – sport. It is ironic that the would-be scholars in search of living life through idealizing Reason are completely unreasonable in their expectations of love and commitment at the end of the play. The women know better, as women often do . . . or do they?

In Shakespeare's writing of the script, he sometimes referred (in the speech headings) to Holofernes simply as 'Pedant' and Don Armado as 'Braggart': does that suggest that the comic characters are simply 'types'? One way of playing this kind of comic role is with a sort of Jonsonian monomania – find the 'humour', the quirk, and milk it for all it's worth. Or should all the characters be somehow 'rounded'?

TH: Despite his friendship with Ben Jonson, there is rarely anything Jonsonian in Shakespeare's writing. Jonson's characters don't change – the situation does. Shakespeare's characters, on the other hand, constantly develop. Holofernes and Don Armado – whether called 'Pedant' or 'Braggart' – are different people by the end of the play.

LS: Part of the fun of these stock-type characters is their illusions of themselves. The Pedant and the Curate fancy themselves possessed of 'great learning'. Don Armado cherishes the illusion that he is an accomplished swordsman and soldier, and that he is an intimate of the king. Costard is a classic clown. These are givens in the script. However, for my taste, three-dimensional characters are always more involving. We absolutely worked to achieve this in our production. We might look at almost all of the characters in this play as 'types'. More central to the telling of the story, I think, is the acknowledgement and exploration of the many masks and self-delusions that abound. Just about everyone is operating under some illusion about him- or herself veiled in hidden agenda, masked, disguised – giving an impression perhaps, but born of self-delusion. Berowne realizes the king's enterprise is a gamble, but goes ahead anyway – he hides behind the illusion of wit. The princess hides behind the illusion of her own power, wit and importance. Navarre and his followers seek the illusion of fame/eternal life. Boyet finds his illusion of worth in his manipulations of the courtships and his biting wit. The French ladies delude themselves in their blind attraction to unready partners. They become lost in a game that they wish were not a game and they perhaps hope will have a surprise ending. Moth masks his disdain for his master and lives dishonestly, as he gives the illusion that he is wise and a 'truth-teller'. Jaquenetta is the only person physically altered by the experience, or is she simply creating the illusion that Don Armado is the father of her child? How could the most impotent of characters be the one real begetter in this play, which is the epitome of a false pregnancy? *Love's Labour's Lost* is dream/illusion versus reality – the ultimate reality being death.

What did you do with the pageant of the Nine Worthies? Structurally, and with its onstage audience, there are resemblances to 'Pyramus and Thisbe' in *A Midsummer Night's Dream*. But it's tougher to get the audience into this one, not least since not many of them will know anything about the Worthies.

TH: The pageant of the Nine Worthies reveals not only the unworthiness of the performers, but unworthiness within the aristocratic audience commenting upon them. It is a typical Shakespearean tribute to his chosen profession and a reminder to the young aristocrats that generosity is learned not born.

LS: Is it important that an audience know the mythology behind 'Pyramus and Thisbe' in order for them to enjoy the Mechanicals' rendition of their story? Is it not the silly and lovable clowns who make us laugh at their vain attempts at putting on a play of their own devising? In *Love's Labour's Lost*, the Nine Worthies pageant never quite gets off the ground for it is a device that provides a playground of wit for the onstage audience. What is most important, I believe, is that the 'Worthies' be as ridiculously costumed and portrayed as possible and that their performance be as broad and yet sincere as it can be. Their function is to be the object of the playful (and often acerbic) derision of the men as they show off their witty repartee. We used the central hexagonal platform as the Worthies' stage, with the onlookers seated or standing at the outer edges of the play area. The pageant played 'in the round', just as our play did. Although I cut some of the lines and with them some of the more obscure references, the scene was left virtually intact. As we worked on it, we discovered that this scene needs to be simply staged, to move quickly, and that rhythm is of the essence. The interplay between the courtiers and the clowns and the rapid-fire exchanges must be precisely timed. As I worked on it, I began to wonder whether the numerous interruptions that the presenters of the pageant undergo might even be a foreshadowing of the 'interruption' that ultimately ends the play.

Monsieur Marcadé, messenger of death. He changes the tone, doesn't he? How harsh was your ending?

TH: 'The words of Mercury are harsh after the songs of Apollo' – but not cruel. The lovers are all young and a holiday romance needs testing in the real world before it can be built upon. *Love's Labour's Lost* has a wistful ending – they must all wait a year. For their labours to be won would require more testing, more suffering, more learning. In the same way that we have *Twelfth Night* (*or What You Will*) might we not once have had *Loves Labour's Won* (or *As You Like It*)?

LS: Monsieur Marcadé brings with him the harsh realities of the outside world. Life and death happen and the seeming love (as each of the ladies points out in her own way) is, at the moment, of the two-fold variety – head and loins, but lacking the final ingredient of the heart. There has not been time for three-fold love to develop. The women are all too well aware of this from the start, but might have been swept away if not for Marcadé and his news. I think the darkness of the ending is intended. In our production, Marcadé was the last character to leave the stage, a looker-on of the characters and the audience. The lovers were not without hope for the future, but it was not a certainty either that they would be reunited after a year's time. When we listen to the song of the Owl and the Cuckoo that ends the play and recognize the necessity of the separation of the couples, we realize that this ending is not at all arbitrary or out of sync with the rest of the play. Reality is harsh after the illusions of the ideal so easily attained.

APPROACHING *LOVE'S LABOUR'S*: REFLECTIONS BY GREGORY DORAN

Gregory Doran, born in 1958, studied at Bristol University and the Bristol Old Vic theatre school. He began his career as an actor, before becoming Associate Director at the Nottingham Playhouse. He played some minor roles in the RSC ensemble before directing for the company, first as a freelance, then as Associate and subsequently Chief Associate Director. His productions, several of which have starred his partner Antony Sher, are characterized by extreme intelligence and lucidity. He has made a particular mark with several of Shakespeare's lesser-known plays and the revival of works by his Elizabethan and Jacobean contemporaries. He directed *Love's Labour's Lost* for the RSC in 2008, with David Tennant in the role of Berowne.

Sometimes the difficulty of directing Shakespeare on the stage is to match the thrill of reading him on the page. In a play like *Macbeth* it is hard to capture in production that hurtling pace, the intense sense of danger and darkness, the contaminating touch of evil. With a play like *Love's Labour's Lost* the challenge is precisely opposite.

The play on the page can seem almost impossibly impenetrable in places. You sometimes feel as if you are simply not being let in on the joke; as if there a number of real people being satirized, of whom you know nothing, and therefore don't understand the references. This may of course be the case. Scholars have suggested a great variety of specific individual people who may or may not be the butt of the humour in the play. I find the theories all fascinating. Is Armado really Walter Ralegh? Is Holofernes meant to be John Florio, the translator of Montaigne? Is the entry of the lovers dressed as Muscovites a satirical reference to the arrival of the Russian embassy in London to woo Lady Mary Hastings on behalf of the Czar, Ivan the

Terrible? The theories are all intriguing, but in the end don't really help the actors achieve their performances.

The play's big challenge is the language. These are young people who delight in oracy, the desire to express yourself through language. They prize verbal dexterity, they enjoy scintillating banter. Holofernes and Sir Nathaniel are absurdly impressed by their own pretentious cleverness, whereas Costard has a natural gift of the gab, and when he and Moth get together they burst into what seems to me to be the equivalent of Elizabethan rap, which leaves the poseur, Don Armado, with his deliciously mangled eloquence, speechless. Getting the actors to appreciate and relish the thrill of those verbal tennis matches is the most important work in rehearsal.

John Barton says it a great actors' play, and he's right. It's a great company play with lots of appetizing roles. If you have a good cast most of your work is done. It doesn't seem to me that the work of the director on this particular play is interpretative. It's really very straightforward. It doesn't want to be over-designed, or have too much concept applied to it (as Adrian Noble says, it doesn't need concept in the Teutonic sense with a capital K and an umlaut). And yet to pitch the playfulness of the piece, to allow it to rise with lightness and air, takes a lot of work. As any master chef will tell you, a soufflé is one of the hardest dishes to bake.

Like *Hamlet* and *Dream*, *Love's Labour's Lost* features a play within a play. As the professional actors arrive at Elsinore to present *The Mousetrap*, and the rude Mechanicals offer their amateur efforts with 'Pyramus and Thisbe' for the wedding celebrations of Duke Theseus and Hippolyta, so in this play the pretentious pageant of the Nine Worthies is provided for the royal party by the scholars. These reminders to the audience of the process of theatre-making, and the different levels of reality and artifice, can be fascinating to compare and contrast. Of course, the procession of the Nine Worthies gets very short shrift in this play and as the play collapses the action is interrupted by events.

There isn't a great deal of significant plot, so the audience needs to be content to sit back comfortably and bask in the sheer fun of being in the company of these leisurely people. I think the initial vow of chastity and then the endless love games need to be lightly but sincerely played, so that when the real world of responsibility and duty strides into the play with the black-clad Marcadé at the end, you have a genuine feeling of caring for these young folk. The silliness and the game-playing must stop and some real commitment must be engaged in order for lasting relationships to be earned and won.

And it seems to me that the play delivers to the audience at the end a benediction, similar to the arrival of the fairies to bless the house in the last moments of [*A Midsummer Night's*] *Dream*: as the scholars and Armado redeem themselves with the dialogue between Spring and Winter maintained by the Owl and the Cuckoo. It gives the action some sort of placing within the diurnal round of the seasons, and though autumn has come to this summer play, and winter will follow, spring will most surely come again.

Gregory Doran

SHAKESPEARE'S CAREER
IN THE THEATRE

BEGINNINGS

William Shakespeare was an extraordinarily intelligent man who was born and died in an ordinary market town in the English Midlands. He lived an uneventful life in an eventful age. Born in April 1564, he was the eldest son of John Shakespeare, a glove-maker who was prominent on the town council until he fell into financial difficulties. Young William was educated at the local grammar in Stratford-upon-Avon, Warwickshire, where he gained a thorough grounding in the Latin language, the art of rhetoric and classical poetry. He married Ann Hathaway and had three children (Susanna, then the twins Hamnet and Judith) before his twenty-first birthday: an exceptionally young age for the period. We do not know how he supported his family in the mid-1580s.

Like many clever country boys, he moved to the city in order to make his way in the world. Like many creative people, he found a career in the entertainment business. Public playhouses and professional full-time acting companies reliant on the market for their income were born in Shakespeare's childhood. When he arrived in London as a man, sometime in the late 1580s, a new phenomenon was in the making: the actor who is so successful that he becomes a 'star'. The word did not exist in its modern sense, but the pattern is recognizable: audiences went to the theatre not so much to see a particular show as to witness the comedian Richard Tarlton or the dramatic actor Edward Alleyn.

Shakespeare was an actor before he was a writer. It appears not to have been long before he realized that he was never going to grow into a great comedian like Tarlton or a great tragedian like Alleyn.

Instead, he found a role within his company as the man who patched up old plays, breathing new life, new dramatic twists, into tired repertory pieces. He paid close attention to the work of the university-educated dramatists who were writing history plays and tragedies for the public stage in a style more ambitious, sweeping and poetically grand than anything which had been seen before. But he may also have noted that what his friend and rival Ben Jonson would call 'Marlowe's mighty line' sometimes faltered in the mode of comedy. Going to university, as Christopher Marlowe did, was all well and good for honing the arts of rhetorical elaboration and classical allusion, but it could lead to a loss of the common touch. To stay close to a large segment of the potential audience for public theatre, it was necessary to write for clowns as well as kings and to intersperse the flights of poetry with the humour of the tavern, the privy and the brothel: Shakespeare was the first to establish himself early in his career as an equal master of tragedy, comedy and history. He realized that theatre could be the medium to make the national past available to a wider audience than the elite who could afford to read large history books: his signature early works include not only the classical tragedy *Titus Andronicus* but also the sequence of English historical plays on the Wars of the Roses.

He also invented a new role for himself, that of in-house company dramatist. Where his peers and predecessors had to sell their plays to the theatre managers on a poorly-paid piecework basis, Shakespeare took a percentage of the box-office income. The Lord Chamberlain's Men constituted themselves in 1594 as a joint stock company, with the profits being distributed among the core actors who had invested as sharers. Shakespeare acted himself – he appears in the cast lists of some of Ben Jonson's plays as well as the list of actors' names at the beginning of his own collected works – but his principal duty was to write two or three plays a year for the company. By holding shares, he was effectively earning himself a royalty on his work, something no author had ever done before in England. When the Lord Chamberlain's Men collected their fee for performance at court in the Christmas season of 1594, three of them went along to the Treasurer of the Chamber: not just Richard

Burbage the tragedian and Will Kempe the clown, but also Shakespeare the scriptwriter. That was something new.

The next four years were the golden period in Shakespeare's career, though overshadowed by the death of his only son Hamnet, aged eleven, in 1596. In his early thirties and in full command of both his poetic and his theatrical medium, he perfected his art of comedy, while also developing his tragic and historical writing in new ways. In 1598, Francis Meres, a Cambridge University graduate with his finger on the pulse of the London literary world, praised Shakespeare for his excellence across the genres:

> As Plautus and Seneca are accounted the best for comedy and tragedy among the Latins, so Shakespeare among the English is the most excellent in both kinds for the stage; for comedy, witness his *Gentlemen of Verona*, his *Errors*, his *Love Labours Lost*, his *Love Labours Won*, his *Midsummer Night Dream* and his *Merchant of Venice*: for tragedy his *Richard the 2*, *Richard the 3*, *Henry the 4*, *King John*, *Titus Andronicus* and his *Romeo and Juliet*.

For Meres, as for the many writers who praised the 'honey-flowing vein' of *Venus and Adonis* and *Lucrece*, narrative poems written when the theatres were closed due to plague in 1593–94, Shakespeare was marked above all by his linguistic skill, by the gift of turning elegant poetic phrases.

PLAYHOUSES

Elizabethan playhouses were 'thrust' or 'one-room' theatres. To understand Shakespeare's original theatrical life, we have to forget about the indoor theatre of later times, with its proscenium arch and curtain that would be opened at the beginning and closed at the end of each act. In the proscenium arch theatre, stage and auditorium are effectively two separate rooms: the audience looks from one world into another as if through the imaginary 'fourth wall' framed by the proscenium. The picture-frame stage, together with the elaborate scenic effects and backdrops beyond it, created the illusion of a self-contained world – especially once nineteenth-century developments in the control of artificial lighting meant that the auditorium could be darkened and the spectators made to focus on the lighted stage. Shakespeare, by contrast, wrote for a bare platform stage with a standing audience gathered around it in a courtyard in full daylight. The audience were always conscious of themselves and their fellow-spectators, and they shared the same 'room' as the actors. A sense of immediate presence and the creation of rapport with the audience were all-important. The actor could not afford to imagine he was in a closed world, with silent witnesses dutifully observing him from the darkness.

Shakespeare's theatrical career began at the Rose Theatre in Southwark. The stage was wide and shallow, trapezoid in shape, like a lozenge. This design had a great deal of potential for the theatrical equivalent of cinematic split-screen effects, whereby one group of characters would enter at the door at one end of the tiring-house wall at the back of the stage and another group through the door at the other end, thus creating two rival tableaux. Many of the battle-heavy and faction-filled plays that premiered at the Rose have scenes of just this sort.

At the rear of the Rose stage, there were three capacious exits, each over ten feet wide. Unfortunately, the very limited excavation of a fragmentary portion of the original Globe site, also in 1989, revealed nothing about the stage. The first Globe was built in 1599 with similar proportions to those of another theatre, the Fortune, albeit that the former was polygonal and looked circular, whereas the latter was rectangular. The building contract for the Fortune survives and allows us to infer that the stage of the Globe was probably substantially wider than it was deep (perhaps forty-three feet wide and twenty-seven feet deep). It may well have been tapered at the front, like that of the Rose.

The capacity of the Globe was said to have been enormous, perhaps in excess of three thousand. It has been conjectured that about eight hundred people may have stood in the yard, with two thousand or more in the three layers of covered galleries. The other 'public' playhouses were also of large capacity, whereas the indoor Blackfriars theatre that Shakespeare's company began using in

1608 – the former refectory of a monastery – had overall internal dimensions of a mere forty-six by sixty feet. It would have made for a much more intimate theatrical experience and had a much smaller capacity, probably of about six hundred people. Since they paid at least sixpence a head, the Blackfriars attracted a more select or 'private' audience. The atmosphere would have been closer to that of an indoor performance before the court in the Whitehall Palace or at Richmond. That Shakespeare always wrote for indoor production at court as well as outdoor performance in the public theatre should make us cautious about inferring, as some scholars have, that the opportunity provided by the intimacy of the Blackfriars led to a significant change towards a 'chamber' style in his last plays – which, besides, were performed at both the Globe and the Blackfriars. After the occupation of the Blackfriars a five-act structure seems to have become more important to Shakespeare. That was because of artificial lighting: there were musical interludes between the acts, while the candles were trimmed and replaced. Again, though, something similar must have been necessary for indoor court performances throughout his career.

Front of house there were the 'gatherers' who collected the money from audience members: a penny to stand in the open-air yard, another penny for a place in the covered galleries, sixpence for the prominent 'lord's rooms' to the side of the stage. In the indoor 'private' theatres, gallants from the audience who fancied making themselves part of the spectacle sat on stools on the edge of the stage itself. Scholars debate as to how widespread this practice was in the public theatres such as the Globe. Once the audience were in place and the money counted, the gatherers were available to be extras on stage. That is one reason why battles and crowd scenes often come later rather than early in Shakespeare's plays. There was no formal prohibition upon performance by women, and there certainly were women among the gatherers, so it is not beyond the bounds of possibility that female crowd members were played by females.

The play began at two o'clock in the afternoon and the theatre had to be cleared by five. After the main show, there would be a jig – which consisted not only of dancing, but also of knockabout comedy (it is the origin of the farcical 'afterpiece' in the eighteenth-century theatre). So the time available for a Shakespeare play was about two and a half hours, somewhere between the 'two hours' traffic' mentioned in the prologue to *Romeo and Juliet* and the 'three hours' spectacle' referred to in the preface to the 1647 Folio of Beaumont and Fletcher's plays. The prologue to a play by Thomas Middleton refers to a thousand lines as 'one hour's words', so the likelihood is that about two and a half thousand, or a maximum of three thousand lines made up the performed text. This is indeed the length of most of Shakespeare's comedies, whereas many of his tragedies and histories are much longer, raising the possibility that he wrote full scripts, possibly with eventual publication in mind, in the full knowledge that the stage version would be heavily cut. The short Quarto texts published in his lifetime – they used to be called 'Bad' Quartos – provide fascinating evidence as to the kind of cutting that probably took place. So, for instance, the First Quarto of *Hamlet* neatly merges two occasions when Hamlet is overheard, the 'Fishmonger' and the 'nunnery' scenes.

The social composition of the audience was mixed. The poet Sir John Davies wrote of 'A thousand townsmen, gentlemen and whores, / Porters and servingmen' who would 'together throng' at the public playhouses. Though moralists associated female play-going with adultery and the sex trade, many perfectly respectable citizens' wives were regular attendees. Some, no doubt, resembled the modern groupie: a story attested in two different sources has one citizen's wife making a post-show assignation with Richard Burbage and ending up in bed with Shakespeare – supposedly eliciting from the latter the quip that William the Conqueror was before Richard III. Defenders of theatre liked to say that by witnessing the comeuppance of villains on the stage, audience members would repent of their own wrongdoings, but the reality is that most people went to the theatre then, as they do now, for entertainment more than moral edification. Besides, it would be foolish to suppose that audiences behaved in a homogeneous way: a pamphlet of the 1630s tells of how two men went to see *Pericles* and one of them laughed while the other wept. Bishop John Hall complained that people went to church for the same reasons that they went to the theatre: 'for company, for custom, for recreation ... to feed his eyes or his ears ... or perhaps for sleep'.

Men-about-town and clever young lawyers went to be seen as much as to see. In the modern popular imagination, shaped not least by *Shakespeare in Love* and the opening sequence of Laurence Olivier's *Henry V* film, the penny-paying groundlings stand in the yard hurling abuse or encouragement and hazelnuts or orange peel at the actors, while the sophisticates in the covered galleries appreciate Shakespeare's soaring poetry. The reality was probably the other way round. A 'groundling' was a kind of fish, so the nickname suggests the penny audience standing below the level of the stage and gazing in silent open-mouthed wonder at the spectacle unfolding above them. The more difficult audience members, who kept up a running commentary of clever remarks on the performance and who occasionally got into quarrels with players, were the gallants. Like Hollywood movies in modern times, Elizabethan and Jacobean plays exercised a powerful influence on the fashion and behaviour of the young. John Marston mocks the lawyers who would open their lips, perhaps to court a girl, and out would 'flow / Naught but pure Juliet and Romeo'.

THE ENSEMBLE AT WORK

In the absence of typewriters and photocopying machines, reading aloud would have been the means by which the company got to know a new play. The tradition of the playwright reading his complete script to the assembled company endured for generations. A copy would then have been taken to the Master of the Revels for licensing. The theatre book-holder or prompter would then have copied the parts for distribution to the actors. A partbook consisted of the character's lines, with each speech preceded by the last three or four words of the speech before, the so-called 'cue'. These would have been taken away and studied or 'conned'. During this period of learning the parts, an actor might have had some one-to-one instruction, perhaps from the dramatist, perhaps from a senior actor who had played the same part before, and, in the case of an apprentice, from his master. A high percentage of Desdemona's lines occur in dialogue with Othello, of Lady Macbeth's with Macbeth, Cleopatra's with Antony and Volumnia's with Coriolanus. The roles would almost certainly have been taken by the apprentice of the lead actor, usually Burbage, who delivers the majority of the cues. Given that apprentices lodged with their masters, there would have been ample opportunity for personal instruction, which may be what made it possible for young men to play such demanding parts.

After the parts were learned, there may have been no more than a single rehearsal before the first performance. With six different plays to be put on every week, there was no time for more. Actors, then, would go into a show with a very limited sense of the whole. The notion of a collective rehearsal process that is itself a process of discovery for the actors is wholly modern and would have been incomprehensible to Shakespeare and his original ensemble. Given

9. Hypothetical reconstruction of the interior of an Elizabethan playhouse during a performance.

the number of parts an actor had to hold in his memory, the forgetting of lines was probably more frequent than in the modern theatre. The book-holder was on hand to prompt.

Backstage personnel included the property man, the tire-man who oversaw the costumes, call-boys, attendants and the musicians, who might play at various times from the main stage, the rooms above and within the tiring-house. Scriptwriters sometimes made a nuisance of themselves backstage. There was often tension between the acting companies and the freelance playwrights from whom they purchased scripts: it was a smart move on the part of Shakespeare and the Lord Chamberlain's Men to bring the writing process in-house.

Scenery was limited, though sometimes set-pieces were brought on (a bank of flowers, a bed, the mouth of hell). The trapdoor from below, the gallery stage above and the curtained discovery-space at the back allowed for an array of special effects: the rising of ghosts and apparitions, the descent of gods, dialogue between a character at a window and another at ground level, the revelation of a statue or a pair of lovers playing at chess. Ingenious use could be made of props, as with the ass's head in *A Midsummer Night's Dream*. In a theatre that does not clutter the stage with the material paraphernalia of everyday life, those objects that are deployed may take on powerful symbolic weight, as when Shylock bears his weighing scales in one hand and knife in the other, thus becoming a parody of the figure of Justice who traditionally bears a sword and a balance. Among the more significant items in the property cupboard of Shakespeare's company, there would have been a throne (the 'chair of state'), joint stools, books, bottles, coins, purses, letters (which are brought on stage, read or referred to on about eighty occasions in the complete works), maps, gloves, a set of stocks (in which Kent is put in *King Lear*), rings, rapiers, daggers, broadswords, staves, pistols, masks and vizards, heads and skulls, torches and tapers and lanterns which served to signal night scenes on the daylit stage, a buck's head, an ass's head, animal costumes. Live animals also put in appearances, most notably the dog Crab in *The*

Two Gentlemen of Verona and possibly a young polar bear in *The Winter's Tale*.

The costumes were the most important visual dimension of the play. Playwrights were paid between £2 and £6 per script, whereas Alleyn was not averse to paying £20 for 'a black velvet cloak with sleeves embroidered all with silver and gold'. No matter the period of the play, actors always wore contemporary costume. The excitement for the audience came not from any impression of historical accuracy, but from the richness of the attire and perhaps the transgressive thrill of the knowledge that here were commoners like themselves strutting in the costumes of courtiers in effective defiance of the strict sumptuary laws whereby in real life people had to wear the clothes that befitted their social station.

To an even greater degree than props, costumes could carry symbolic importance. Racial characteristics could be suggested: a breastplate and helmet for a Roman soldier, a turban for a Turk, long robes for exotic characters such as Moors, a gabardine for a Jew. The figure of Time, as in *The Winter's Tale*, would be equipped with hourglass, scythe and wings; Rumour, who speaks the prologue of *2 Henry IV*, wore a costume adorned with a thousand tongues. The wardrobe in the tiring-house of the Globe would have contained much of the same stock as that of rival manager Philip Henslowe at the Rose: green gowns for outlaws and foresters, black for melancholy men such as Jaques and people in mourning such as the Countess in *All's Well that Ends Well* (at the beginning of *Hamlet*, the prince is still in mourning black when everyone else is in festive garb for the wedding of the new king), a gown and hood for a friar (or a feigned friar like the duke in *Measure for Measure*), blue coats and tawny to distinguish the followers of rival factions, a leather apron and ruler for a carpenter (as in the opening scene of *Julius Caesar* – and in *A Midsummer Night's Dream*, where this is the only sign that Peter Quince is a carpenter), a cockle hat with staff and a pair of sandals for a pilgrim or palmer (the disguise assumed by Helen in *All's Well*), bodices and kirtles with farthingales beneath for the boys who are to be dressed as girls. A gender switch such as that of Rosalind or Jessica seems to have taken between fifty and eighty lines of dialogue – Viola does not resume her 'maiden weeds', but remains in her boy's costume to the end of *Twelfth Night* because a change would have slowed down the action at just the moment it was speeding to a climax. Henslowe's inventory also included 'a robe for to go invisible': Oberon, Puck and Ariel must have had something similar.

As the costumes appealed to the eyes, so there was music for the ears. Comedies included many songs. Desdemona's willow song, perhaps a late addition to the text, is a rare and thus exceptionally poignant example from tragedy. Trumpets and tuckets sounded for ceremonial entrances, drums denoted an army on the march. Background music could create atmosphere, as at the beginning of *Twelfth Night*, during the lovers' dialogue near the end of *The Merchant of Venice*, when the statue seemingly comes to life in *The Winter's Tale*, and for the revival of Pericles and of Lear (in the Quarto text, but not the Folio). The haunting sound of the hautboy suggested a realm beyond the human, as when the god Hercules is imagined deserting Mark Antony. Dances symbolized the harmony of the end of a comedy – though in Shakespeare's world of mingled joy and sorrow, someone is usually left out of the circle.

The most important resource was, of course, the actors themselves. They needed many skills: in the words of one contemporary commentator, 'dancing, activity, music, song, elocution, ability of body, memory, skill of weapon, pregnancy of wit'. Their bodies were as significant as their voices. Hamlet tells the player to 'suit the action to the word, the word to the action': moments of strong emotion, known as 'passions', relied on a repertoire of dramatic gestures as well as a modulation of the voice. When Titus Andronicus has had his hand chopped off, he asks 'How can I grace my talk, / Wanting a hand to give it action?' A pen portrait of 'The Character of an Excellent Actor' by the dramatist John Webster is almost certainly based on his impression of Shakespeare's leading man, Richard Burbage: 'By a full and significant action of body, he charms our attention: sit in a full theatre, and you will think you see so many lines drawn from the circumference of so many ears, whiles the actor is the centre . . . .'

Though Burbage was admired above all others, praise was also heaped upon the apprentice players whose alto voices fitted them for the parts of women. A spectator at Oxford in 1610 records how the audience were reduced to tears by the pathos of Desdemona's death. The puritans who fumed about the biblical prohibition upon cross-dressing and the encouragement to sodomy constituted by the sight of an adult male kissing a teenage boy on stage were a small minority. Little is known, however, about the characteristics of the leading apprentices in Shakespeare's company. It may perhaps be inferred that one was a lot taller than the other, since Shakespeare often wrote for a pair of female friends, one tall and fair, the other short and dark (Helena and Hermia, Rosalind and Celia, Beatrice and Hero).

We know little about Shakespeare's own acting roles – an early allusion indicates that he often took royal parts, and a venerable tradition gives him old Adam in *As You Like It* and the ghost of old King Hamlet. Save for Burbage's lead roles and the generic part of the clown, all such castings are mere speculation. We do not even know for sure whether the original Falstaff was Will Kempe or another actor who specialized in comic roles, Thomas Pope.

Kempe left the company in early 1599. Tradition has it that he fell out with Shakespeare over the matter of excessive improvisation. He was replaced by Robert Armin, who was less of a clown and more of a cerebral wit: this explains the difference between such parts as Lancelet Gobbo and Dogberry, which were written for Kempe, and the more verbally sophisticated Feste and Lear's Fool, which were written for Armin.

One thing that is clear from surviving 'plots' or story-boards of plays from the period is that a degree of doubling was necessary. *2 Henry VI* has over sixty speaking parts, but more than half of the characters only appear in a single scene and most scenes have only six to eight speakers. At a stretch, the play could be performed by thirteen actors. When Thomas Platter saw *Julius Caesar* at the Globe in 1599, he noted that there were about fifteen. Why doesn't Paris go to the Capulet ball in *Romeo and Juliet*? Perhaps because he was doubled with Mercutio, who does. In *The Winter's Tale*, Mamillius might have come back as Perdita and Antigonus been doubled by Camillo, making the partnership with Paulina at the end a very neat touch. Titania and Oberon are often played by the same pair as Hippolyta and Theseus, suggesting a symbolic matching of the rulers of the worlds of night and day, but it is questionable whether there would have been time for the necessary costume changes. As so often, one is left in a realm of tantalizing speculation.

THE KING'S MAN

The new king, James I, who had held the Scottish throne as James VI since he had been an infant, immediately took the Lord Chamberlain's Men under his direct patronage. Henceforth they would be the King's Men, and for the rest of Shakespeare's career they were favoured with far more court performances than any of their rivals. There even seem to have been rumours early in the reign that Shakespeare and Burbage were being considered for knighthoods, an unprecedented honour for mere actors – and one that in the event was not accorded to a member of the profession for nearly three hundred years, when the title was bestowed upon Henry Irving, the leading Shakespearean actor of Queen Victoria's reign.

Shakespeare's productivity rate slowed in the Jacobean years, not because of age or some personal trauma, but because there were frequent outbreaks of plague, causing the theatres to be closed for long periods. The King's Men were forced to spend many months on the road. Between November 1603 and 1608, they were to be found at various towns in the south and Midlands, though Shakespeare probably did not tour with them by this time. He had bought a large house back home in Stratford and was accumulating other property. He may indeed have stopped acting soon after the new king took the throne. With the London theatres closed so much of the time and a large repertoire on the stocks, Shakespeare seems to have focused his energies on writing a few long and complex tragedies that could have been played on demand at court: *Othello*, *King Lear*, *Antony and Cleopatra*, *Coriolanus* and *Cymbeline* are among his longest and poetically grandest plays. *Macbeth* only survives in a shorter text, which shows signs of adaptation after Shakespeare's death. The bitterly satirical *Timon of Athens*, apparently a collaboration with Thomas Middleton that may have failed on the stage, also belongs to this period. In comedy, too, he wrote longer and morally darker works than in the Elizabethan period, pushing at the very bounds of the form in *Measure for Measure* and *All's Well that Ends Well*.

From 1608 onwards, when the King's Men began occupying the indoor Blackfriars playhouse (as a winter house, meaning that they only used the outdoor Globe in summer?), Shakespeare turned to a more romantic style. His company had a great success with a revived and altered version of an old pastoral play called *Mucedorus*. It even featured a bear. The younger dramatist John Fletcher, meanwhile, sometimes working in collaboration with Francis Beaumont, was pioneering a new style of tragicomedy, a mix of romance and royalism laced with intrigue and pastoral excursions. Shakespeare experimented with this idiom in *Cymbeline* and it was presumably with his blessing that Fletcher eventually took over as the King's Men's company dramatist. The two writers apparently collaborated on three plays in the years 1612–14: a lost romance called *Cardenio* (based on the love-madness of a character in Cervantes' *Don Quixote*), *Henry VIII* (originally staged with the title 'All is True'), and *The Two Noble Kinsmen*, a dramatization of Chaucer's 'Knight's Tale' These were written after Shakespeare's two final solo-authored plays, *The Winter's Tale*, a self-consciously old-fashioned work dramatizing the pastoral romance of his old enemy Robert Greene, and *The Tempest*, which at one and the same time drew together multiple theatrical traditions, diverse reading and contemporary interest in the fate of a ship that had been wrecked on the way to the New World.

The collaborations with Fletcher suggest that Shakespeare's career ended with a slow fade rather than the sudden retirement supposed by the nineteenth-century Romantic critics who read Prospero's epilogue to *The Tempest* as Shakespeare's personal farewell to his art. In the last few years of his life Shakespeare certainly spent more of his time in Stratford-upon-Avon, where he became further involved in property dealing and litigation. But his London life also continued. In 1613 he made his first major London property purchase: a freehold house in the Blackfriars district, close to his company's indoor theatre. *The Two Noble Kinsmen* may have been written as late as 1614, and Shakespeare was in London on business a little over a year before he died of an unknown cause at home in Stratford-upon-Avon in 1616, probably on his fifty-second birthday.

About half the sum of his works were published in his lifetime, in texts of variable quality. A few years after his death, his fellow-actors began putting together an authorized edition of his complete *Comedies, Histories and Tragedies*. It appeared in 1623, in large 'Folio' format. This collection of thirty-six plays gave Shakespeare his immortality. In the words of his fellow-dramatist Ben Jonson, who contributed two poems of praise at the start of the Folio, the body of his work made him 'a monument without a tomb':

And art alive still while thy book doth live
And we have wits to read and praise to give ...
He was not of an age, but for all time!

SHAKESPEARE'S WORKS:
A CHRONOLOGY

1589–91	*? Arden of Faversham* (possible part authorship)
1589–92	*The Taming of the Shrew*
1589–92	*? Edward the Third* (possible part authorship)
1591	*The Second Part of Henry the Sixth*, originally called *The First Part of the Contention betwixt the Two Famous Houses of York and Lancaster* (element of co-authorship possible)
1591	*The Third Part of Henry the Sixth*, originally called *The True Tragedy of Richard Duke of York* (element of co-authorship probable)
1591–92	*The Two Gentlemen of Verona*
1591–92 perhaps revised 1594	*The Lamentable Tragedy of Titus Andronicus* (probably co-written with, or revising an earlier version by, George Peele)
1592	*The First Part of Henry the Sixth*, probably with Thomas Nashe and others
1592/94	*King Richard the Third*
1593	*Venus and Adonis* (poem)
1593–94	*The Rape of Lucrece* (poem)
1593–1608	*Sonnets* (154 poems, published 1609 with *A Lover's Complaint*, a poem of disputed authorship)
1592–94/ 1600–03	*Sir Thomas More* (a single scene for a play originally by Anthony Munday, with other revisions by Henry Chettle, Thomas Dekker and Thomas Heywood)
1594	*The Comedy of Errors*
1595	*Love's Labour's Lost*

1595–97	*Love's Labour's Won* (a lost play, unless the original title for another comedy)
1595–96	*A Midsummer Night's Dream*
1595–96	*The Tragedy of Romeo and Juliet*
1595–96	*King Richard the Second*
1595–97	*The Life and Death of King John* (possibly earlier)
1596–97	*The Merchant of Venice*
1596–97	*The First Part of Henry the Fourth*
1597–98	*The Second Part of Henry the Fourth*
1598	*Much Ado about Nothing*
1598–99	*The Passionate Pilgrim* (20 poems, some not by Shakespeare)
1599	*The Life of Henry the Fifth*
1599	'To the Queen' (epilogue for a court performance)
1599	*As You Like It*
1599	*The Tragedy of Julius Caesar*
1600–01	*The Tragedy of Hamlet, Prince of Denmark* (perhaps revising an earlier version)
1600–01	*The Merry Wives of Windsor* (perhaps revising version of 1597–99)
1601	'Let the Bird of Loudest Lay' (poem, known since 1807 as 'The Phoenix and Turtle' (turtle-dove))
1601	*Twelfth Night, or What You Will*
1601–02	*The Tragedy of Troilus and Cressida*
1604	*The Tragedy of Othello, the Moor of Venice*
1604	*Measure for Measure*
1605	*All's Well that Ends Well*
1605	*The Life of Timon of Athens*, with Thomas Middleton
1605–06	*The Tragedy of King Lear*
1605–08	? contribution to *The Four Plays in One* (lost, except for *A Yorkshire Tragedy*, mostly by Thomas Middleton)
1606	*The Tragedy of Macbeth* (surviving text has additional scenes by Thomas Middleton)
1606–07	*The Tragedy of Antony and Cleopatra*
1608	*The Tragedy of Coriolanus*

1608	*Pericles, Prince of Tyre*, with George Wilkins
1610	*The Tragedy of Cymbeline*
1611	*The Winter's Tale*
1611	*The Tempest*
1612–13	*Cardenio*, with John Fletcher (survives only in later adaptation called *Double Falsehood* by Lewis Theobald)
1613	*Henry VIII (All is True)*, with John Fletcher
1613–14	*The Two Noble Kinsmen*, with John Fletcher

FURTHER READING
AND VIEWING

CRITICAL APPROACHES

Barber, C. L., *Shakespeare's Festive Comedy: A Study of Dramatic Form and its Relation to Social Custom* (1959). Half a century after publication, still the best book on Shakespearean comedy.

Breitenberg, Mark, 'The Anatomy of Masculine Desire in *Love's Labour's Lost*', *Shakespeare Quarterly*, 43 (1992), pp. 430–49. Gender-aware reading.

Carroll, William C., *The Great Feast of Language in 'Love's Labour's Lost'* (1976). Excellent book devoted entirely to the play's wonderfully complex language.

Colie, Rosalie L., *Shakespeare's 'Living Art'* (1974). Unsurpassed account of Shakespeare's self-conscious artfulness.

Elam, Keir, *Shakespeare's Universe of Discourse: Language-Games in the Comedies* (1984). Sophisticated use of modern semiotics.

Lamb, Mary Ellen, 'The Nature of Topicality in *Love's Labour's Lost*', *Shakespeare Survey*, 38 (1985), pp. 49–59. The most sensible and balanced treatment of a vexed critical subject.

Londré, Felicia Hardison, ed., *Love's Labour's Lost: Critical Essays* (1997). Useful range of approaches.

Maslen, R. W., *Shakespeare and Comedy* (2005). Helpful setting of the full range of Shakespearean comedies in their context and traditions.

Nevo, Ruth, *Comic Transformations in Shakespeare* (1980). Good on psychology and structure.

Parker, Patricia, 'Preposterous Reversals: *Love's Labour's Lost*', *Modern Language Quarterly*, 54 (1993), pp. 435–82. Dazzling attention to rhetoric and wordplay.

Roesen, Bobbyann [Anne Barton], 'Love's Labour's Lost', *Shakespeare Quarterly*, 4 (1973), pp. 411–26. One of the first critical essays to take the play seriously.

Turner, John, 'Love's Labour's Lost: The Court at Play', in *Shakespeare: Out of Court: Dramatizations of Court Society*, ed. Graham Holderness, Nick Potter and John Turner (1990), pp. 19–48. Historical-sociological treatment.

THE PLAY IN PERFORMANCE

Branagh, Kenneth, 'Love's Labour's Lost', in *Shakespeare in Perspective Volume Two*, ed. Roger Sales (1985). Actor's perspective.

Brooke, Michael, 'Love's Labour's Lost on Screen', www.screenonline. org.uk/tv/id/564633/index.html. Pithy overview of 1965, 1975 and 1985 BBC television productions and 2000 Kenneth Branagh film.

Gilbert, Miriam, *Love's Labour's Lost*, Shakespeare in Performance (1993). Good overview.

Holland, Peter, *English Shakespeares: Shakespeare on the English Stage in the 1990s* (1997). Considers some key modern productions.

Luscombe, Christopher, 'Launcelot Gobbo and Moth', in *Players of Shakespeare 4*, ed. Robert Smallwood (1998). View from a small but key part.

Pendergast, John S., *Love's Labour's Lost: A Guide to the Play* (2002). Helpful insights.

Richardson, Ian, in *Shakespeare's Players*, ed. Judith Cook (1983). On playing Berowne.

RSC 'Exploring Shakespeare: Love's Labour's Lost'. Particular focus on Gregory Doran's 2008 production, starring David Tennant as Berowne.

For a more detailed Shakespeare bibliography and selections from a wide range of critical accounts of the play, with linking commentary, visit the edition website, www.rscshakespeare.co.uk.

AVAILABLE ON DVD

Love's Labour's Lost, directed by Elijah Moshinksy (BBC television Shakespeare, 1985). Very competent rendering in neo-classical, eighteenth-century setting.

Love's Labour's Lost, directed by Kenneth Branagh (2000). Not entirely successful updating into the style of a 1930s Cole Porter musical, with very heavily cut text.

REFERENCES

1 In each of his first two comedies, *The Blind Beggar of Alexandria* (1596) and *An Humorous Day's Mirth* (1597), the playwright George Chapman appears to allude to Shakespeare's play.
2 Quoted in E. K. Chambers, *William Shakespeare: A Study of Facts and Problems* (2 vols, 1930), Vol. 2, p. 332.
3 *Dr Johnson on Shakespeare*, ed. W. K. Wimsatt (1969), p. 108.
4 W. May Phelps and John Forbes-Robertson, *The Life and Life-Work of Samuel Phelps* (1886), p. 165, quoted in Miriam Gilbert, *Love's Labour's Lost*, Shakespeare in Performance (1993), p. 35.
5 *New York Times*, 29 March 1891.
6 Gordon Crosse, *Fifty Years of Shakespearean Playgoing* (1941), p. 94.
7 John Dover Wilson, *Shakespeare's Happy Comedies* (1962), pp. 64, 73.
8 *The Times*, 29 April 1946.
9 Sally Beauman, *The Royal Shakespeare Company: A History of Ten Decades* (1982), p. 166.
10 Lionel Hale, *The Old Vic: 1949–50* (1950), p. 32.
11 Helen Dawson, 'A Labour of Love?', *Plays and Players*, 16(5) (February 1969).
12 Irving Wardle, *The Times*, 20 December 1968.
13 Charles Marowitz, *New York Times*, 5 January 1969.
14 Gilbert, *Love's Labour's Lost*, pp. 78–9.
15 John S. Pendergast, *Love's Labour's Lost: A Guide to the Play* (2002), p. 156.
16 Robert Giroux, *New York Times*, 12 February 1989.
17 Sheridan Morley, *New Statesman*, 10 March 2003.
18 Stanley Kauffman, 'Well, Not Completely Lost', *New Republic*, 10–17 July 2000, pp. 32–3.
19 A. O. Scott, 'What Say You, My Lords? You'd Rather Charleston?', *New York Times*, 9 June 2000.
20 Andrew St George, *Financial Times*, 7 September 1990.
21 Harold Matthews, *Theatre World*, 61(484) (May 1965).
22 Irving Wardle, *The Times*, 8 August 1973.
23 Rhoda Koenig, *Independent*, 29 October 1993.
24 Peter Roberts, *Plays and Players*, 12(9) (June 1965).
25 B. A. Young, *Financial Times*, 8 April 1965.
26 Irving Wardle, *The Times*, 8 August 1973.
27 Roger Warren, *Shakespeare Survey*, 32 (1979).
28 Russell Jackson, *Cahiers Elisabéthains*, 28 (October 1985).
29 Christopher Edwards, *Spectator*, 27 October 1984.
30 Michael Coveney, *Observer*, 9 September 1990.
31 Peter Holland, *English Shakespeares*, (1997), p. 164.
32 Holland, *English Shakespeares*, p. 187.
33 Stanley Wells, *Times Literary Supplement*, 5 November 1993.
34 Wells, *Times Literary Supplement*, 5 November 1993.

35 Pendergast, *Love's Labour's Lost*, p. 106.
36 Robert Speaight, *Shakespeare Quarterly*, 16 (1965).
37 Christopher Luscombe, 'Launcelot Gobbo and Moth', in *Players of Shakespeare 4*, ed. Robert Smallwood (1998).
38 Kenneth Branagh, 'Love's Labour's Lost', in *Shakespeare in Perspective Volume Two*, ed. Roger Sales (1985).
39 Koenig, *Independent*, 29 October 1993.
40 Martin Dodsworth, *Times Literary Supplement*, 26 October 1984.
41 Jackson, *Cahiers Elisabéthains*.
42 Warren, *Shakespeare Survey*.
43 Gilbert, *Love's Labour's Lost*, p. 177.
44 Ian Richardson talking about playing Berowne (1975), in *Shakespeare's Players*, ed. Judith Cook (1983).
45 Michael Billington, *Guardian*, 10 May 1975.
46 John Barton, programme note for *Love's Labour's Lost*, RSC, 1965.
47 J. W. Lambert, *Drama*, 130 (Autumn 1978).
48 Gilbert, *Love's Labour Lost*, p. 173.
49 Warren, *Shakespeare Survey*.
50 Jackson, *Cahiers Elisabéthains*.
51 Michael Ratcliffe, *Observer*, 14 October 1984.
52 Gilbert, *Love's Labour's Lost*, p. 211.
53 Robert Smallwood, *Shakespeare Quarterly*, 42 (1991).
54 Holland, *English Shakespeares*, p. 191.
55 Janet Clare, 'Love's Labour's Lost', in *Shakespeare in Performance*, ed. Keith Parsons and Pamela Mason (1995).
56 Holland, *English Shakespeares*, p. 187.
57 Gilbert, *Love's Labour's Lost*, p. 212.
58 Holland, *English Shakespeares*, p. 197.
59 Samuel Schoenbaum, *Times Literary Supplement*, 27 October 1978.
60 Anne Barton, programme notes for *Love's Labour's Lost*, RSC, 1978.

ACKNOWLEDGEMENTS AND PICTURE CREDITS

Preparation of '*Love's Labour's Lost* in Performance' was assisted by a generous grant from the CAPITAL Centre (Creativity and Performance in Teaching and Learning) of the University of Warwick for research in the RSC archive at the Shakespeare Birthplace Trust. The Arts and Humanities Research Council (AHRC) funded a term's research leave that enabled Jonathan Bate to work on 'The Director's Cut'.

Picture research by Helen Robson and Jan Sewell. Grateful acknowledgement is made to the Shakespeare Birthplace Trust for assistance with picture research (special thanks to Helen Hargest) and reproduction fees.

Images of RSC productions are supplied by the Shakespeare Centre Library and Archive, Stratford-upon-Avon. This Library, maintained by the Shakespeare Birthplace Trust, holds the most important collection of Shakespeare material in the UK, including the Royal Shakespeare Company's official archives. It is open to the public free of charge.

For more information see www.shakespeare.org.uk.

1. Design for a knot-garden, private collection © Bardbiz Limited
2. Directed by Peter Brook (1946) Angus McBean © Royal Shakespeare Company
3. Old Vic (1949) © John Vickers Theatre Collection
4. Directed by Michael Kahn (2006) Malcolm Davies © Shakespeare Birthplace Trust
5. Directed by Barry Kyle (1984) © Stephen Macmillan

6. Directed by Ian Judge (1993) Malcolm Davies © Shakespeare Birthplace Trust
7. Directed by John Barton (1965) Tom Holte © Shakespeare Birthplace Trust
8. Directed by Terry Hands (1990) Joe Cocks Studio Collection © Shakespeare Birthplace Trust
9. Reconstructed Elizabethan playhouse © Charcoalblue

"Thanks to Bate and Rasmussen, we now have a rendering of the complete works that, in a rare publishing achievement, would also give complete satisfaction to the author himself."
- *Robert McCrum, The Observer*

Also Available:

A Midsummer Night's Dream	978-0-230-21789-8
Hamlet	978-0-230-21787-4
Love's Labour's Lost	978-0-230-21791-1
Richard III	978-0-230-22111-6
The Tempest	978-0-230-21785-0

The RSC Complete Works	
Hardback	978-0-230-00350-7
Paperback	978-0-230-20095-1
Leather-bound	978-0-230-00351-4

www.rscshakespeare.co.uk